THE
SANTOSHA AVATARA
GITA

ADI DA (THE DA AVATAR)
Adi Da Purnashram (Naitauba), Fiji, 1994

THE SANTOSHA AVATARA GITA

(The Revelation of the Great Means of the Divine Heart-Way of No-Seeking and Non-Separateness)

By

ADI DA
(The Da Avatar)

STANDARD EDITION

THE DAWN HORSE PRESS
MIDDLETOWN, CALIFORNIA

NOTE TO THE READER

All who study the Way of the Heart or take up its practice should remember that they are responding to a Call to become responsible for themselves. They should understand that they, not Avatara Adi Da or others, are responsible for any decision they may make or action they take in the course of their lives of study or practice.

The devotional, Spiritual, functional, practical, relational, cultural, and formal community practices and disciplines referred to in this book are appropriate and natural practices that are voluntarily and progressively adopted by each student-novice and member of the Free Daist Avataric Communion and adapted to his or her personal circumstance. Although anyone may find them useful and beneficial, they are not presented as advice or recommendations to the general reader or to anyone who is not a participant in Da Avatara International or a member of the Free Daist Avataric Communion. And nothing in this book is intended as a diagnosis, prescription, or recommended treatment or cure for any specific "problem", whether medical, emotional, psychological, social, or Spiritual. One should apply a particular program of treatment, prevention, cure, or general health only in consultation with a licensed physician or other qualified professional.

Previously published as *The Love-Ananda Gita*

First edition, July 1989
Standard edition, enlarged and updated, September 1990
Standard edition, updated, July 1995
Printed in the United States of America

Produced by the Free Daist Avataric Communion
in cooperation with the Dawn Horse Press

International Standard Book Number: paper 1-57097-009-2

Library of Congress Catalog Card Number: 94-74937

CONTENTS

THE
SANTOSHA AVATARA
GITA

(The Revelation of the Great Means of the Divine Heart-Way
of No-Seeking and Non-Separateness)

by

ADI DA

(The Da Avatar)

A Note on the Technical Language
of the Way of the Heart

Avatara Adi Da has transformed the English language into a vehicle to serve His Communication of the truly sacred, God-Realizing Process in His Company. In doing so, He has Revealed the logic underlying the common conventions of written English:

Ordinary speech and written language are centered on the ego-"I", as a tent is raised on a centerpole. Therefore, in ordinary speech and written language, the ego-word "I" is commonly capitalized, and everything less than the ego-"I" is shown in lowercase.

In contrast, the "centerpole" of Avatara Adi Da's Speech and Writing is the Heart, the Divine Wisdom, Consciousness, Truth, Reality, Happiness, and "Love-Ananda" ("inherently Love-Blissful Unity"). Therefore, He capitalizes those words that express the Ecstatic Feeling of the Awakened Heart, and, in many instances, lowercases those words expressive of the ego or conditional limits in general.

Blessed with the Gift of His Awakening Grace, Avatara Adi Da's devotees are thus inspired to use the capitalization of words associated with Beloved Adi Da as a means of honoring Him and His Divine Attributes.

For the meanings of technical and other perhaps unfamiliar terms, please see the Glossary, pp. 287-320.

ADI DA (THE DA AVATAR)
Adi Da Purnashram (Naitauba), Fiji, 1994

The All-Surpassing Revelation of Adi Da (The Da Avatar)

An Introduction by His Devotees

The *Santosha Avatara Gita* is about the ultimate and overwhelming Truth, the most magnificent, irrepressibly joyous Revelation ever given to human beings. This Revelation fulfills hopes one has scarcely dared to entertain. It touches a depth beyond emotion and beyond mind. It goes beyond psychic and mystical awareness. This Revelation is validated in the heart-domain, in the deepest intuitive, feeling core of one's being.

The One who speaks to you in this book, Adi Da, the Da Avatar, is the Truth Alive, and His Coming is the culmination of eons of cosmic history. Everyone alive today is the potential living witness of an Intervention of Divine Grace that embraces and Blesses all of the past, the present, and the future.

The Appearance of Adi Da, the Da Avatar, is the fruition of an infinitely vast Divine process originating before time and space itself and evolving throughout the story of mankind in response to the desperate prayers of beings everywhere, suffering the pain of apparent separation from God. In that unspeakable sweep of time there have been unique beings who, through great struggle and sacrifice, made "windows" to the Divine for others. They gave Teachings and practices, were worshipped and honored, and have become the source of the entire human tradition of religion and Spirituality. Again and again it has seemed to those alive in a particular time and place that the revelation

1

was complete, the salvation perfect, the final enlightenment given. Nevertheless, there has remained a thread of prophecy in all the great Spiritual traditions that there is One yet to appear, One who must come in the darkest time of humanity, when the world is at its worst, and bring to completion all the revelations of the past.[1*]

The Most Compassionate Divine Lord, Adi Da, is the supreme "Avatar", the All-Completing Incarnation, or "Descent", of God, Truth, or Reality into the human world and even the entire cosmic domain. He is "Adi Da", the "Original Giver", come to Give the Great Way, the Way of the Heart, whereby you and all beings may discover your true ecstatic Identity with the Divine. In the light of His Revelation, all the great Realizers and Teachings of the past can be seen as the forerunners of His Appearance, preparing for and converging toward the moment when the Divine Wholeness could be shown complete. And, true to the ancient intuition, He appears now in this dark epoch of the decay of the great religious traditions, East and West, in an era when the very survival of our world is threatened by the excesses of materialism and the sophisticated weapons of war. Avatara Adi Da has come in an extreme time, when the "radical"[2] Truth is most sorely needed. But His Revelation is for all times and places, all cultures, and every kind of individual.

The traditional paths speak of gradually overcoming "sin" or "the ego" or "illusion" or "desire" and thus being restored to the ultimate Condition from which we have been separated by these faults. In other words, the religions of humanity advocate a great "Path of Return" to our true Source. They start from the position of this present worldly existence, full of change and suffering, and aspire, in different ways, to what is Eternal. The most common expression of this search is the attempt to earn "salvation" through a moral life and right worship of the deity. Others are moved to loving Communion with the Divine through the devotional life of ecstatic prayer, heart-felt repetition of the names of God, and service to the Divine. Some individuals have pursued the mystical paths of absorption in blissful visionary states and other subtle experiences. Rare Sages have Realized the Transcendental Consciousness beyond mystical phenomena and devoted their lives to profound meditative immersion in the Eternal Source of existence.[3]

There are characteristic preferences in the West and in the East for these various forms of reaching toward God, Truth, and Reality. Westerners

* Notes to this Introduction appear on pages 16-17.

have preferred the forms of religion that invoke the Divine as a great "Other" who rewards and protects the devout in this life and after death. Eastern religion, on the other hand, has characteristically expressed an impulse to escape from the world and the body and to find Ultimate Reality in inward states.[4]

Avatara Adi Da has Revealed the single pattern and progression of potential human growth that lies behind all the characteristic human efforts to find God, Truth, or Reality. Not only that. Through the surpassing Grace of His Appearance, He has made all such efforts obsolete. He Himself is the Complete Unconditional Divine Reality. And He is Personally approaching us. He has appeared in the conditional realms to make known to all beings that our striving to find God, Truth, or Reality is already fulfilled beyond all possible expectation and no longer necessary. It is not that the Divine has ever been absent. But the Divine has never before had perfect Agency, perfect means, a perfect focus, a body-mind perfectly equipped to serve as the vehicle for the complete Divine Incarnation.[5]

The Divine Person

Traditionally, people have contemplated holy pictures, icons, statues, and sacred images as ways of contacting the Divine Spirit. Avatara Adi Da is a living icon. His body is the human picture of God, and so it has always been His custom to sit or stand in silence among His devotees, allowing them to Contemplate Him with full attention and feeling. What occurs is miraculous. As one gazes at Him in the sacred manner—in His physical Presence or through a photograph or a videotape—invisible layers of armoring fall away. One is just present as one is, and He is simply present as He Is. There does not have to be any extraordinary experience associated with this Contemplation. He penetrates the heart directly and establishes one in that ecstatic place of feeling, of sensitivity, of intuition, that is already in Communion, already One, with the Divine. In the joy of that Communion, one realizes that God, Truth, Reality is not abstract. The ultimate Truth and Being is Personal, the Divine Person. That One can even be described as a Personality. The devotees of the Radiant Divine Lord, Adi Da, literally feel Him as a Living Personality, always present, guiding their lives, no matter how far they may be from Him physically. Devotees frequently have dreams or waking visions in which He Instructs them in some fashion, or they find themselves in spontaneous internal dialogue with Him, sometimes even hearing His voice audibly. The qualities that are alive in all these different experiences of Him are the qualities of His Divine Personality—His characteristic humor and wit, His laughter at the "joke" of conditional existence, His sweetness and compassion, His sympathetic sorrow, His fierceness and demand, His unpredictability, His nectarous Love. In every kind of circumstance, Avatara Adi Da makes His unmistakable Presence felt to His devotees.

Adi Da is the One Who can fully satisfy your heart and draw out the true passion of your being. He is here to bring you freedom absolute—freedom from the anguish of a life without meaning, freedom from the pain of self-obsessed existence, freedom to be ecstatic, distracted every day of your life by a great Bliss and Love that goes beyond the world. Avatara Adi Da is the Liberator of every human heart who finds Him out. By the miracle of His Incarnation He has made it possible for you and every one to enter into a living relationship with the Divine in Person.

The "Bright"

The bodily form of Avatara Adi Da is a literal Transmitter, always Transmitting His Divine State. His Transmission is infinite, all-embracing. Every being, human and non-human, receives it. Frogs, mosquitoes, plants, humans—even walls and rocks—all are affected by the Divine "Siddhi", or Power of Blessing, that has entered the world through His Incarnation. Many people who have no conscious knowledge of Avatara Adi Da experience His Transmission directly—through dreams, visions, and mysterious synchronicities. Only later, when they discover a book of His or see His picture, do they realize that He has already made Himself known to them.

Adi Da's Divine Transmission can be summarized in a single word, which He has used since His early childhood to describe His own Divine Being. He Eternally Transmits the "Bright", the Radiant Divine Consciousness that is the Truth of all existence. He is the "Bright", always Shining in and through and beyond every particle of the manifest world. When one begins to become aware of His Transmission, this "Brightness" in things may at times become clearly visible. But it does not depend on the function of sight. The "Bright" is Feeling Light, which is felt to infuse the whole being, while also utterly transcending it. The "Bright" may be Revealed to you directly through the pages of this book. All the Words of the Da Avatar and all images of His bodily Form carry that very Transmission of Luminous Divine Being. Through His sublime Transmission of the "Bright", Avatara Adi Da finds His devotees, those who are so moved, so thrilled, so overwhelmed by His great Revelation of Truth that they are impulsed to a different way of life, a way of life devoted to the Divine Reality, rather than to what changes and dies. The Way of the Heart, which Avatara Adi Da offers to all, is the Way of most perfect and permanent Awakening to the "Brightness" of God, Truth, or Reality.

There Is Only God

People sometimes ask how can God, the ultimate Truth and Reality, be contained in a human body? Of course, such an idea is absurd. The bodily Form of Avatara Adi Da does not "contain" the Divine. Rather, His bodily Incarnation arises <u>in</u> His Perfect Condition, as a living "picture" of His Eternal "Brightness". His body and the entire Demonstration of His human life is His point of contact with us, through which He draws us to His mere Presence, which is invisible, Spiritual, Transcendental, and Divine. This is the great paradox: By Appearing as a human being, Avatara Adi Da reveals to all of us human beings our own Great Identity. We are not, in truth, a separate "I", limited to and imprisoned in this body-mind. We are only Divine Consciousness. The entire arising cosmos, in which we participate as apparently separate individuals, even now, in this very moment, is <u>Only God</u>.

Avatara Adi Da is perpetually Awake as this Realization. Whatever arises to His notice, He sees only the One Divine Condition that He is. Devotees have asked Him to describe how He perceives ordinary things, and He has explained that when He looks at any object, a plant, for example, He sees the plant and He sees the space around it, but at the same time He sees only God. Or, to put it another way, He Divinely <u>Recognizes</u> the plant and the space around it as a mere modification of Non-Separate, Undifferentiated, All-Blissful Divine Being. And that Recognition is "Inherent, Instant, never changed, never limited, never undone, never threatened".

Who has ever confessed that Realization before? There are premonitions of it in a few rare Spiritual texts.[6] But who has <u>Revealed</u> it in living terms? Only the Divine in Person could possibly do so. The purpose of the Incarnation of Avatara Adi Da is to bring this unutterably sublime Realization to every human being. "There is no excuse," He once remarked, "for a petty, un-Enlightened life when there is so much Only-Reality here".

The Secret Means of Grace

What is the real process of Enlightenment? How does it work? What does it require? If we consider for a moment the whole history of our growth as human individuals, we can observe something about how our most important learning occurred. It did not happen through books. Our most basic adaptation to life took place before we could read a word—in relationship to our parents, or parent figures, and our immediate circle of intimates. Spiritual growth works in exactly the same way. The essence of it does not come from books, even from the greatest scriptures. Genuine Spiritual Awakening comes through the Grace of the Guru, one who has Realized God, Truth, or Reality to some profound degree. Traditionally, in the East, an aspirant to Spiritual life would simply go and live with a Guru, do simple service and participate in the world of the Guru's household or ashram. In <u>that</u> context the scriptures would be studied—not apart from it. This is because the conversion that is Spiritual life is not an abstract matter. It must take place on every level of the being. True Religion has always been about <u>Realization</u>—an actual transformation of the individual—bodily, emotionally, mentally, psychically, and Spiritually—through the living Influence of Truth. Such a transformation cannot possibly occur just on the basis of beliefs or through mere practices and observances.

There is a secret law, operating in every dimension of our lives, that explains why the Guru is necessary. Avatara Adi Da has powerfully expressed this secret in a few words: "You become what you meditate on." That is to say, you duplicate in body and in mind the qualities of whatever object or condition you consistently give your attention to. Everyone observes how dwelling on negative thoughts disturbs and depresses the whole body and may even cause disease. In the same way, positive thought and action enlivens the being. The great leap in human growth into the dimension of Spiritual Realization requires that we give to a Spiritually Realized Being our constant love and attention, meditatively, actively, day in and day out. Then the great law "you become what you meditate on" becomes our greatest advantage. But first a true Guru must be found.

Avatara Adi Da is the supreme God-Man, the Divine Incarnate appearing as the Guru, absolutely unlimited in His Realization and in His Power to Awaken un-Illumined beings. To give one's attention to Him, to meditate on Him through all thought, feeling, and action, is to begin to duplicate <u>Him</u>, to Realize the Divine State of Consciousness Itself. The more this process magnifies, the more one forgets the limited body-mind-self.

To have the freedom and the possibility to choose a Spiritual relationship to the living Divine in Person is a Grace beyond compare. This choice is, in a real sense, a deliberate act, but it is also an utterly spontaneous one. The heart chooses and the body-mind follows. The heart responds to Beloved Adi Da through sheer <u>attraction</u>, through the very same principle that brings all love-relationships, all friendships into being. But attraction to Adi Da is not mere attraction to a human individual who seems to answer one's need for love and self-fulfillment. It is Attraction to the Free Condition, the unbounded State of Happiness that Avatara Adi Da Transmits. For His potential devotee, Adi Da becomes the Attractive Center of the universe, and the passion to Realize His Divine Condition grows greater than any other urge.

The Great Way of Liberation

The Way of the Heart, the perfectly God-Realizing Way of life that Avatara Adi Da has brought into the world, is a real relationship. It is to live with Him moment to moment via the profound process of attention just described—"You become what you meditate on." An essential part of the daily practice of the Way of the Heart is to meditate upon the Divine Lord, Adi Da, through feeling-Remembrance of Him. But the total process of meditating on Him involves every faculty of the being—the heart, or feeling dimension, mind and thought, the body in all its actions, even the motion of the breath. To direct all these faculties consistently toward Beloved Adi Da is true devotion, and this devotion is the essence of the Way of the Heart. It is the means whereby you enter directly into His "Samadhi", or His Divinely Enlightened State.

This is the "radical" nature of the Way of the Heart, from the beginning. It is not a developmental path, based on the search for ever higher Spiritual goals or experiences. Profound experiences will necessarily arise in the advanced and ultimate stages of the process, and, indeed, may occur at any point, through the potency of Avatara Adi Da's Divine Transmission. Such experiences may include the whole range of states traditionally called mystical and Transcendental. But the Way of the Heart is not about any of these experiences. It is the progressive discovery of the True Heart-Master, Adi Da, Who makes Himself known to His devotee on the grand scale of His Being, first through His bodily Form, then via an awakening to His universal Spirit-Presence, and, ultimately, in the Revelation of His Very Divine Self, or the Divine Heart Itself.

To meditate constantly on Avatara Adi Da necessarily draws one beyond the levels of body-based experience, and also beyond states of Spiritual absorption, into the Domain of Being Itself, which is the true Condition of the body-mind and the world. Attention as an act of focusing on this or that object—from a mosquito bite to the most celestial vision—simply relaxes, and the most astonishing Realization Awakens. One actually Realizes that this body and this world are not what they appear to be. One stands in the "Position" of Consciousness, merely "Witnessing" what arises, including the body, mind, and feelings—no longer identified with any of it. But even this extraordinary Awakening is not yet <u>Divine</u> Enlightenment. It is simply the point at which the "Perfect Practice"[7] of the Way of the Heart begins, the moment when the great law "you become what you meditate on" becomes ultimately Liberating. Rather than Communing with Beloved Adi Da through the act of attention—Communing with Him as an "Other", presumed to be separate from oneself—devotion to Him increasingly becomes Identification with His Divine State. The Bliss of His Ultimate Condition becomes more and more profound, generating deep states of meditation in which that Consciousness is enjoyed in and of itself, free of all phenomena. Ultimately, by His Grace, the "Eyes Open", and there is <u>only</u> the absolute Love-Bliss-Radiance of Consciousness Itself, whatever objects or experiences may arise. This Realization is Divine Enlightenment.

But, even then, the course of the Way of the Heart continues. The perfectly Awakened devotee of Avatara Adi Da simply Abides as

Consciousness, Recognizing the inherent Divinity of all that appears, until even the noticing of phenomena begins to fade in the ever-magnifying "Brightness". Ultimately, the entire conditional world is Outshined, as all separate shapes and forms dissolve and disappear in the One Radiance. This is Divine Translation, the most ultimate Event of the Way of the Heart and of the entire ordeal of existence as an apparent individual. The body is spontaneously relinquished and there is no return to embodiment, but only eternal Joy beyond all manifestation in the Divine Domain of Self-Radiant Being.

These are Mysteries that can scarcely be envisioned, never before Realized. They are the Mysteries of the Divine Person, Adi Da, Given, Awakened by Divine Power. Only the most uncommon individuals are likely to accomplish the entire course perfectly in one lifetime. But the relationship to Him that instigates and Realizes this Process knows no limit in time or space. This lifetime is only the beginning of it. Once forged, one's relationship to the Most Radiant Divine Lord, the "Original Giver", Adi Da, endures forever. It is an eternal Bond of Love uninterrupted by the natural processes of death and rebirth.

The Enlightenment of the Whole Body

The Way of the Heart follows a secret blueprint, a deep psycho-physical "anatomy" that is as basic to the structure and potential of our total being as DNA is basic to our physical characteristics. There are natural centers and potential pathways of Spiritual energy in the human body that we, in our ordinary state, are totally unaware of. Over time, as one practices the Way of the Heart, these hidden structures become responsive to the Divine Spiritual Transmission of Avatara Adi Da and, thus, begin to "wake up".

Adi Da's Spirit-Power is the moveless Radiance of God, but in the realm of the body-mind it may be felt to move as an intensely Blissful and forceful Current of Energy. In the advancement of the Way of the Heart, His Spirit-Force pours down from above the head through the front of the body, turns around at the bodily base, and ascends up the spine back to the top of the head. As it moves, this "Circle" of Divine Spirit-Energy encounters "knots"—physical, emotional, mental, psychic stress-points—that are progressively dissolved, or released, through the Power of His Spirit-Current.

When the Circle of Spirit-Energy is resonant and the whole body is alive with that Fullness and Radiance, the great revolution in Consciousness can occur. A veil is lifted and one stands free of identification with the body-mind in the Position of the "Witness". Coincident with this Awakening, the Current mysteriously breaks out of the Circle and settles in the right side of the heart.[8] This deep heart-root is the last "knot", the "doorway" in the human body-mind to the Transcendental Divine Consciousness. The most ultimate Awakening, the Revelation that "there is Only God", corresponds with the illumination of the most profound, most esoteric of all our psycho-physical structures, the "Amrita Nadi", or "Current of Immortal Bliss", the first Form of God in the conditional realms. There are a few, generally rather indistinct, references to Amrita Nadi in the literature of the Hindu traditions. Avatara Adi Da is the first to fully describe the nature and significance of our ultimate root-structure, which He defines (in general terms) as "The 'Bright' Fullness That Stands Between The Right Side Of The Heart and The Matrix Of Lights Above the head".[9] In the Awakening to Divine Enlightenment, the Current of Amrita Nadi moves up out of the right side of the heart, rising to the crown of the head and to the Matrix of Lights beyond. Amrita Nadi is the origin of the "Circle" of the body-mind and all the psycho-physical energies that keep the body alive. When the Radiance of Amrita Nadi is fully regenerated, the entire body is pervaded by Divine Light and seen and felt to arise merely as this Radiant Current of Blissful, Joyous Being. Divine Translation is the Outshining even of Amrita Nadi and, therefore, of the entire body-mind itself. When Divine Enlightenment is thus most Full and Perfect, the body-mind dies.

The human body is built to transcend itself, built for this entire course of Divine Awakening. Only certain aspects of this esoteric anatomy have been observed in the past. No one before Avatara Adi Da has ever Revealed and Demonstrated the inherent structure of the human being in its entirety. All the living details of this mysterious psycho-physical process are progressively Revealed through the practice of the Way of the Heart.

If the human mechanism is so perfectly designed for Divine Enlightenment, why has this Realization never occurred before? Why did it take the intervention of the Divine in Person to Reveal the potential that has been present in every human body for eons of time? In the answer to this question lies the root-cause of human suffering and the core Argument of the Divine Teaching of the Da Avatar.

The Truth About the Ego

Everyone of us, at some level, wants to understand the meaning of life, the Truth of existence. But our experience does not give us the answer. We are apparently adrift in an unfathomable play of changing forms, of which we are an inseparable, dependent part. Until we <u>Realize</u> that all of it is arising and disappearing in and as infinite Divine Love-Bliss, then we are disturbed by our experience of existence.

From His youth, Avatara Adi Da made a most profound, unique, and "radical" observation of what human beings, and even all living beings, do in response to the chaos of experience. We react—we presume that we are separate from the Divine Unity. We contract like the shutter of a camera, recoiling from others, from the Divine, from the Happiness that is native to existence. Thus we create this point of awareness we call "I". Having shut ourselves off from the great Unity through this contraction, each of us lives the life of a separate "self", identified with a particular body-mind, differentiated from all other apparent beings and things. This body-mind is vulnerable, mortal, and so fear arises. We presume that our conscious awareness is going to die with the body-mind and that we will cease to exist.

Avatara Adi Da points out that such a presumption is utterly untrue, based on illusion. It is a false reaction to life, caused by our failure to understand the nature of Reality. This reaction, He Reveals, is our <u>constant</u> activity, the activity that <u>is</u> the ego. The ego, truly, is an activity, not an entity. It is the act of self-contraction, the act that creates a whole life of "Stress, or Dis-ease, or A Motivating Sense Of Dilemma". This stress continually drives us to <u>seek</u>—to do something, say something, figure something out, satisfy this or that desire, distract ourselves with food, sex, work, travel, sports, entertainment, politics, reading, talking, thinking, and every possible form of activity—including religious activity.

Until we understand our seeking, everything we do is a form of the self-contraction. The self-contraction is like the action of pinching yourself and then looking for a remedy to relieve the pain. We can only stop the "pinching", however, when we know that <u>we</u> are doing it! But the ego cannot catch itself in its own act. It is Avatara Adi Da who brings the activity that is the ego into awareness, first through the power of His Argument and then, as one's devotion to Him grows, through the

11

force of His Divine Influence in one's life. His Grace first reflects to His devotee that the self-contraction, recoil, the avoidance of relationship and love, is the summary of all that he or she is doing. The various practices and disciplines that He Gives to beginners in the Way of the Heart help to make this plain. But the disciplines and practices are only part of His skillful means. It is His Divine Influence that brings the revelation of the self-contraction, opens up the heart, and awakens the yearning to be perfectly Free.

The secret obstruction that has always prevented human beings from Realizing their true Nature is just this mechanism of egoity, or self-contraction. All seeking—in the domain of the body, the mind, or the mystical dimensions of the psyche, even the search to withdraw into Transcendental Bliss beyond the world—is the result of the same root-cause. That cause is the pain of self-contraction, the reaction to existence. The effort to get free from this underlying pain is so subtle, so all-embracing, so fundamental, that no one, no matter how great, has ever understood it. All have functioned, as Adi Da once said, "within the dream". Only the One Standing prior to the dream, prior to egoity, could make the error known. Only that One, Adi Da, the Da Avatar, could Awaken humanity to the possibility of the unique, all-encompassing, unqualified Realization of "Only God", the Realization that cannot Awaken until there is no trace of self-contraction in the being.

The self-contraction covers everything that is traditionally called "sin" or "egoity". But it is a much more basic, or "radical", description of what separates us (or, more properly, how we separate ourselves) from the Divine than has ever been given before. It is operative in us, Adi Da explains, right down to the cellular level. It is operative in all organisms and throughout the cosmos. It is the root-activity and presumption that creates all suffering. And so where did the self-contraction come from? Why does it occur? Is "God" to blame? Absolutely not. We, in our true depth, are inseparable from the Divine Consciousness, but we have "shrunk ourselves upon the Plane of God". And thus, by the power of our own presumption, we have ended up—apparently—as separate selves confined to these limited, death-bound body-minds. But this horror is not the Truth. We no longer need to live by this illusion of our own making. By the Grace of Avatara Adi Da, all human beings now have the unique means to understand and transcend their own benighted egoity and be restored to perfect integrity and Happiness in God—and as God.

Non-Avoidance of Reality

The ego is the most tenacious force. It cannot be dealt with through mere religious idealism—ceremonies, prayers, "good works". The Grace of the Guru is necessary, and this Grace must be forceful enough to break through the egoic bondage of the devotee. There have been Realizers in the past who were known as "Crazy-Wise" Masters, or "Avadhoots", free beings who had "shaken off" all bondage to conventional life.[10] There was an understanding that, although the "Crazy-Wise" Master might sometimes be offensive, even deliberately so, he or she was giving a sign of Freedom in God and was serving others by showing up the anxieties and fears of ego-bound existence.

Avatara Adi Da is the supreme "Crazy-Wise" Master or Avadhoot, the One who has utterly transcended egoity and therefore all necessity to abide by the conventions of egoic life. He is the fearless Liberator of His devotees. He acts in Perfect Freedom, doing whatever is necessary, conventional or unconventional, to constantly serve their right life and Divine Awakening. His response to the depth of human bewilderment has always been to bring the "radical", complete, and uncompromising Truth—no avoidance of reality. He has always required of His devotees a constant "reality consideration", or the continuous, free, and non-problematic inspection of all aspects, "high and low", of one's participation in life.

In the devotional relationship to Avatara Adi Da, every detail of self-contraction—in body, mind, psyche, and, even, ultimately, the very "I"-thought, the primal act of egoity that apparently reduces Consciousness to this body-mind—must be brought to light. Indeed, His Revelation of the beginning stages of this process, the foundation ordeal of ego-transcendence[11] that must be passed through before real Spiritual life can even begin, is one of the unique signs of His Greatness.

"Truth," as Avatara Adi Da has Said, "must be resurrected from the ground up." And so His Discourses range all the way from the most sublime descriptions of Divine Consciousness to frank and humorous discussions of sex and bodily functions. From His "Point of View", there is no "difference". All of it is "Only God". But for ordinary, un-Illumined beings, it is not so. And so He has always used all the stuff of life, including its "forbidden" side—forbidden words, forbidden humor, apparently shocking remarks, to reflect to people their own act of self-contraction. He knows that the Unconditional Divine Reality can never be most perfectly Realized without dealing with the most basic fears and taboos. He has shown that everyone who is interested in the great Divine matter must observe, understand, and transcend their reactions to the excretory functions, sexual complications, the emotional difficulties associated with sex, the script of rejection and betrayal that people play out based on the "Oedipal" drama of early life—or, as He has called it, the entire realm of "shit, piss, and fuck". This is as much a part of His Divine Revelation as His Demonstration of Divine Enlightenment Itself. He is the ultimate Tantric Guru, the absolute Master of all the secrets of sexuality.[12] He addresses everything to do with bodily life—food-taking, elimination, exercise, healing, breath, "conductivity" of the life-force—because the body is the esoteric vehicle of the great Process and must open up in every center to the Awakening Power of His Spirit-Force. Without full responsibility for all dimensions of the psycho-physical mechanism, Divine Enlightenment cannot be Realized.

His intention, always, is ego-dissolution. He is always Working psycho-physically with the past, present, and future karmas of His devotees—He is Working to dissolve the self-contraction at its root. He cannot do otherwise. His Love is absolute. The price of Happiness—ultimate, Most Perfect, Enlightened Happiness—is to go through the great ego-transcending ordeal with Him, right to the end. And that requires extraordinary devotion to Him, an overwhelming impulse to God-Realization, and a constant willingness to endure the inevitable crises that such an ordeal necessarily requires.

The Kiln of "Brightness"

Avatara Adi Da often compares all the conditional beings He has come to Liberate to a crowd of freshly-made clay pigs in a kiln. The pigs, He says, still wet when placed in the kiln, first heat up until they are glowing red, and then, as the heat increases, the glow more and more becomes a white radiance that eventually is so brilliant that even the outlines of the pigs disappear and there is nothing left but the white glow suffusing the entire kiln. The Kiln to which Avatara Adi Da invites all beings is His own "Bright" Divine Heart, the place of Communion with Him where all separateness is ultimately Transcended in the Radiance of God. The true ordeal and great glory of a human life is to practice the Way of the Heart—to stand with the most Beloved Divine Lord, Adi Da, in His Kiln of "Brightness", allowing the "cooking", the transformation, the "Brightening" to become Perfect.

AVATARA ADI DA: My Place is the Place of "Brightness". The Space of My Kiln is Infinite and It covers the entire cosmic domain. I am just doing My "Brightening" Work. I am just Present as the "Bright" Itself. And that is the Means that I am using everywhere, and will continue to use after the physical lifetime of this Body. It is the Work of the Divine Domain—My Very Person.

The Kiln into which you invest yourselves is a Blessed afternoon of "Brightness", everyone becoming "Brighter" and "Brighter". That is your actual Condition.

My devotees are not looking <u>toward</u> heaven. When you presently, by your devotion, establish yourself in My Kiln, you are already in the Holy Land—the Divine Place. Just invest yourself in it. This is Liberation—My Work. Your work is simply to get yourself into the Kiln with Me constantly.

God is Grace. God is the Source-Condition, the Condition of Infinite Love-Bliss. That is Me. That is the Divine Person. Enjoy this balmy afternoon with Me forever! And eventually, without sweat, without sunburn, without distress, the "Brightness" of the day will become so profound there will be no noticing but this Love-Bliss of Oneness with Me. [April 30, 1995]

Through the Incarnation of Avatara Adi Da, the Perfect Light of Truth is Shining down, penetrating and Illumining every dark recess of this world and all worlds. And His Shining will continue infinitely beyond the lifetime of His human body until the Divine Translation of the cosmos itself into His vast embrace of "Brightness".

The Divine Work of Adi Da, the Da Avatar, is Eternal, beyond imagining, encompassing all realms and all beings, but at the same time it is perfectly intimate, manifesting in a unique relationship to each of His devotees. Every moment of heart-Communion with Him, now and forever, is the self-forgetting Bliss of Non-separation from God, Truth, or Reality. This is the supreme Gift that Avatara Adi Da offers to all beings. What Joy could be greater than this?

NOTES TO
THE ALL-SURPASSING REVELATION OF
ADI DA (THE DA AVATAR)

1. Christians look forward to the second coming of Christ, Moslems to the Mahdi (the last prophet), Buddhists to Maitreya (the coming Buddha), and many Hindus to the Kalki Avatar (the tenth and final Avatar of Vishnu). These prophetic myths are some of the primary evidence that the human psyche has always carried the intuition of a culminating revelation.

2. The term "radical" derives from the Latin "radix", meaning "root", and thus it principally means "irreducible", "fundamental", or "relating to the origin". Because Avatara Adi Da uses "radical" in this literal sense, it appears in quotation marks in His Wisdom-Teaching to distinguish His usage from the common reference to an extreme (often political) view.

3. Avatara Adi Da's Revelatory Instruction about the great "Path of Return" advocated by the religions of humanity and about the full range of religious and Spiritual experience is briefly summarized in "The Seven Stages of Life", pp. 253-65, and extensively discussed in *The Basket of Tolerance*.

4. Avatara Adi Da calls the characteristically Oriental, or Eastern, strategy the "Alpha" strategy. Alpha cultures pursue an original or non-temporal and undisturbed peace, in which the world is absent (and thus unintrusive). Although the cultures that were originally founded on the Alpha approach to life and Truth are fast disappearing, the Alpha strategy remains the conventional archetype of Spiritual life, even in the Omega culture. Its preference, in contrast to the Omega preference, is for the limitation and control (and even the suppression) of the activities of the conditional personality, or even of conditional reality altogether, and the maximization of attention, mystical devotion, and submission to the Divine Reality.

Avatara Adi Da uses the term "Omega" to characterize the materialistic culture that today dominates not only the Western, or Occidental, world (which has brought the Omega strategy to its fullest development) but even most of the Eastern, or Oriental, world, which has now largely adopted the anti-Spiritual viewpoint typical of the West. The Omega strategy is motivated to the attainment of a future-time perfection and fulfillment of the conditional worlds through the intense application of human invention, political will, and even Divine Influence. Its preference is for the limitation and suppression of attention, mystical devotion, and submission to the Divine Reality, while maximizing attention to the pursuit of experience and knowledge relative to the conditional reality.

Neither the Alpha strategy nor the Omega strategy Realizes Truth, as each is rooted in the presumption of a problem relative to existence, and in the action of egoity itself—which motivates all human interests short of Divine Self-Realization.

For a complete discussion of the Omega and Alpha strategies and the Disposition that transcends them, see chapter eighteen of *The Dawn Horse Testament Of Adi Da*, or chapter nineteen of *The (Shorter) Testament Of Secrets Of Adi Da*.

5. The extraordinary Process, the unique conjunctions and sacrifices, even in the last one hundred and fifty years, that prepared the way for His Coming are described in "The Divine Life and Work of Adi Da, the Da Avatar", pp. 19-93.

6. Adi Da has indicated and Commented upon these rare Spiritual texts in His final Essay in *The Basket of Tolerance*, "The Unique Sixth Stage Foreshadowings of the Only-by-Me Revealed Seventh Stage of Life".

7. The "Perfect Practice" is Avatara Adi Da's technical term for the discipline of the sixth stage of life and the seventh stage of life in the Way of the Heart.

Devotees who have mastered (and thus transcended) the point of view of the body-mind by fulfilling the preparatory processes of the Way of the Heart, may, by Grace, be Awakened to practice in the Domain of Consciousness Itself, in the sixth and seventh, or ultimate, stages of life.

The three parts of the "Perfect Practice" are summarized in chapter forty-four of *The Dawn Horse Testament Of Adi Da*.

8. Avatara Adi Da has Revealed that, in the context of the body-mind, the Divine Consciousness is intuited at a psycho-physical Locus in the right side of the heart. This center corresponds to the sinoatrial node, or "pacemaker", the source of the physical heartbeat in the right atrium, or upper right chamber, of the heart.

9. "Amrita Nadi" is Sanskrit for "Channel (or Current) of Immortal Bliss". It is the ultimate "Organ", or Root-Structure, of the body-mind, Realized in the seventh stage of life. It is felt to arise in the right side of the heart, which is the psycho-physical Seat of Consciousness Itself, and it terminates in the Light, or Locus, infinitely above the head. Please see *The Dawn Horse Testament Of Adi Da*, or *The (Shorter) Testament Of Secrets Of Adi Da*, and *The Knee of Listening* for Avatara Adi Da's unique Confession of the Realization of Amrita Nadi, and His unprecedented description of the structure of Amrita Nadi in the human body-mind.

10. The Adepts of what Avatara Adi Da calls "the 'Crazy Wisdom' tradition" (of which He is the supreme Exemplar) are Realizers of the advanced and the ultimate stages of life in any culture or time who, through spontaneous Free action, blunt Wisdom, and liberating laughter, shock or humor people into self-critical awareness of their egoity, a prerequisite for receiving the Adept's Spiritual Transmission. Typically, such Realizers manifest "Crazy" activity only occasionally or temporarily, and never for its own sake.

"Avadhoota" is a traditional term for one who has "shaken off" or "passed beyond" all worldly attachments and cares, including all motives of detachment (or conventional and other-worldly renunciation), all conventional notions of life and religion, and all seeking for "answers" or "solutions" in the form of conditional experience or conditional knowledge.

11. The word "transcendence" is commonly used to convey the quality or state of surpassing, exceeding, or moving beyond a condition or limitation. (Kantian metaphysics extends the term to refer to a state of being beyond the limits of all possible experience and knowledge.) However, Avatara Adi Da uses "transcendence" to mean "the action or process of transcending", in connection with the presumed limits of body, emotion, and mind, or even any and all of the conditional states of experience within the first six stages of human life—all of which must be transcended in order to Realize the Free, Unqualified, and Absolute Condition of Inherent Happiness, Consciousness Itself, or Love-Bliss Itself.

12. For further discussion of Avatara Adi Da's Instruction about transcending emotional-sexual patterning, please see chapter twenty-one of *The Dawn Horse Testament Of Adi Da*.

*From my earliest experience of life I have Enjoyed a Condition that,
as a child, I called the "Bright". . . .*

The Divine Life and Work of Adi Da (The Da Avatar)

PART I

The Quest to Recover the "Bright"

The Sadhana Years, 1939-1970

On November 3, 1939, in Long Island, New York, Avatara Adi Da was born in a suburban hospital, an apparently ordinary child in a very ordinary circumstance. The birth itself was difficult—the infant was nearly strangled by His own umbilical cord. But Adi Da in that very instant had already begun His Work of Love. He has a clear memory that while the doctors struggled to bring His body living from the womb, He, in His Spirit-Form, was moving through the wards of the hospital healing people, untouched by the drama of His moment of Incarnation.

In His infancy, Avatara Adi Da was miraculously free of the limits of His human birth, as He describes in His Spiritual "autobiography", *The Knee of Listening*:

> *From my earliest experience of life I have Enjoyed a Condition that, as a child, I called the "Bright". . . .*
>
> *Even as a baby I remember only crawling around inquisitively with a boundless Feeling of Joy, Light, and Freedom in the middle of my head that was bathed in Energy moving unobstructed in a Circle, down from above, all the way down, then up, all the way up, and around again, and always Shining from my heart. It was an Expanding Sphere of Joy from the heart. And I was a Radiant Form, the Source of Energy, Love-Bliss, and Light in the midst of a world that is entirely Energy, Love-Bliss, and Light. I was the Power of Reality, a direct Enjoyment and Communication of the One Reality.*

Then, one day, sometime after His second birthday, as Adi Da was crawling across a linoleum floor, His parents let loose a new puppy they were giving Him. In the instant of seeing the puppy and seeing His parents, Avatara Adi Da spontaneously identified with His human body-mind. He "forgot" His great State of Being and became "Franklin Jones", the child of His parents.

In that moment, His true Sacrifice began. Having relinquished His native Identity with the "Bright", "Franklin's" great Ordeal lay ahead. He utterly gave Himself over to the feeling of being a limited "self", separate from all other "selves". This was the purpose for which He had been born—to embrace the human condition absolutely and thus discover and Reveal the way by which ordinary human beings can embrace and Realize the Divine. Thus, while "Franklin" surrendered to become like those around Him, a "fierce, mysterious Impulse" remained. In the depth of His Being He was committed to recovering the Joy of the "Bright", which never entirely receded from His experience.

Plunging into the Search for God

Franklin's quest to recover the "Bright" reached full intensity in 1957, when, at the age of nearly eighteen, He entered Columbia College in New York City as an undergraduate. "Franklin" was not there for the usual academic reasons. He had no interest in preparing for a career—He only wanted to understand the human state. A single question possessed Him: "What is Consciousness?" But there were no answers to be found at Columbia. "Franklin" was devastated to find that the prevailing dogma at Columbia was that the fundamental reality is not Consciousness but the physical world, and that everything "greater" or "higher"—Consciousness, Spirit, God—is either a by-product of physical reality or else a mere hallucination. This stark confrontation with twentieth-century materialism destroyed the naive religious faith of His childhood Lutheran upbringing, pointing only toward doubt and Godless rationalism.

But "Franklin" could not tolerate this solution of despair. He chose to confront the agony of Godlessness head on, through an extreme course—the course of exhaustive experience. His conviction was this: "If God exists, He will not cease to exist by any action of my own, but, if I devote myself to all possible experience, He will indeed find some

**He only wanted to understand the human state. A single question possessed Him:
"What is Consciousness?"**

way, in some one or a complex of my experiences, or my openness itself, to reveal Himself to me." Thus, He gave Himself up to every experience and possibility, with the force of a vow. He had spontaneously chosen what is traditionally known in the East as "prapatti", or unconditional surrender to the Truth of existence, whatever that might turn out to be. But He did so in the West, bereft of all traditional guidance and supports.

He abandoned Himself to the streets of New York with the raw courage of a desperate man, tasting every pleasure of the senses, restrained by no taboos, no fear of madness. And within the secluded towers of Columbia College, He devoured every kind of book that might afford Him a glimpse of Truth. For two years "Franklin" maintained the terrible intensity of His seeking.

Then one night in 1960, the Truth dormant in His own Being made Itself known. While He sat at His desk, feeling that He had exhausted the possibilities of experience, a sudden crisis erupted in Him. As one about to die sees his or her whole life pass by in a flash, He suddenly observed His frenzy of seeking in all its details, and He saw it as utterly fruitless. At the very moment that He surrendered to this intuition, a vast, ecstatic energy rose in His body and poured through Him in waves. He ran from His room and through the city streets, transported with joy.

This crisis changed "Franklin's" life. For two years He had devoted Himself to every kind of seeking—looking for some experience to "prove" the Truth to Him, presuming that the Truth was absent, that it had to be found. But in the days and weeks that followed the "Columbia experience", He realized that He had grasped two fundamental realities. First, He saw that Truth is not a matter of seeking for something that is absent, but of removing the obstructions to the Truth, Joy, or Freedom that is always already the case. Second, "Franklin" realized that the seeking itself was the major obstruction that was preventing the immediate enjoyment or Realization of the Truth. All His seeking, He now understood, had been a grand distraction from present God, present Happiness. The two years of intense exploitation of experience had been necessary, but only in order to reveal conclusively to Him the futility of the search.

By plunging into the maelstrom of New York City street life, without being destroyed by it or deflected in His goal, and by boldly using such means to quicken His Spiritual quest, "Franklin" had done something completely remarkable. Still in His teens, and without the guidance of a Guru, He had shown Himself as the supreme Tantric Master[1]* He was to become—the Adept who masters all the energies of life and converts those energies to the purposes of God-Realization. Many years later, He described what He had embarked on, beginning at Columbia:

AVATARA ADI DA: It was clear to Me what had to be overcome if Ultimate Realization were to be real. If this firm absolutization of My own Disposition in "Brightness" were to be unqualifiedly established in this life, I had to embrace everything—all the contradictions, all the positives, all the negatives, everything gross, everything Spiritual, everything altogether. I had to deny nothing, to avoid nothing, endure everything, pass through everything, suffer everything, enjoy everything, do everything. To me, there was never any other possibility. And I began this with the beginning of My adult life. [February 13, 1995]

The Discovery of "Narcissus"

The awakening at Columbia was the first great breakthrough in "Franklin's" life of the unique intelligence He calls "understanding"—the tacit certainty that all unhappiness, all apparent separation from God is entirely the result of our own mistaken presump-

* Notes to "The Divine Life and Work of Adi Da (The Da Avatar)" appear on pages 90-93.

tions and our own egoic activity. "Franklin" soon found, however, that He could not sustain the understanding awakened in this experience. He began to sense that there was something in consciousness that was actively preventing this understanding, and He fiercely determined to discover what that was. Two years later, after He had moved to northern California and begun a Master's degree at Stanford University, the force of His urge to understand found a new absorbing focus.

In 1962, living near Stanford on a bluff overlooking the Pacific Ocean, "Franklin" began an extraordinary experiment. He decided to write down everything that He observed in His experience—all that He thought, dreamed, felt, perceived, and did. He resolved that no motion of His being would elude Him. Day after day, wherever He was—at home, on a walk, visiting friends, going to the movies—He would carry a clipboard and write down all that occurred in His awareness. When He wandered alone on the beach below His remote cottage, He wrote down every random thought and mind-form that arose with every step on the sand, and even His perception of the very action of stepping itself. He was placing His awareness under a powerful microscope so that its inmost mechanics would stand out and its secret patterning would be revealed.

The revelation, when it came, was astonishing:

Eventually, I began to recognize a structure in the living consciousness. It became more and more apparent, and its nature and effects revealed themselves as fundamental and inclusive of all the states and contents in life and mind. My own "myth", the control of all patterns, the source of identity and all seeking, began to stand out in the mind as a living being.

This "myth", this controlling logic, or force, that formed my very consciousness, revealed itself as the concept and the actual life of Narcissus. I saw that my entire adventure, the desperate cycle of awareness and its decrease, of truly Conscious Being and Its gradual covering in the mechanics of living, seeking, dying, and suffering, was produced out of the image or mentality that appears hidden in the ancient myth of Narcissus.

The more I contemplated him, the more profoundly I understood him. I observed in awe the primitive control that this self-concept and logic performed in all of my behavior and experience. I began to see that same logic operative in all other human beings, and in every living thing, even in the very life of the cells and in the natural energies that surround every living entity or process. It was the logic or process of sep-aration itself, of enclosure and immunity. It manifested as fear and identity, memory and experience. It informed every function of the liv-ing being, every experience, every act, every event. It "created" every "mystery". It was the structure of every imbecile link in the history of human suffering.

He is the ancient one visible in the Greek "myth", who was the uni-versally adored child of the gods, who rejected the loved-one and every form of love and relationship, who was finally condemned to the con-templation of his own image, until, as a result of his own act and obsti-nacy, he suffered the fate of eternal separateness and died in infinite solitude. [The Knee of Listening]

When this truth dawned upon "Franklin", He realized that we are mad. He saw that no one, no God, has imposed on us this controlling logic of separation, enclosure, and immunity. It is we who have locked ourselves into this "prison". Now "Franklin" had to go through the ordeal of the undoing of the madness of "Narcissus", whatever that might involve.

The Sadhana with Swami Rudrananda and the "Death of Narcissus"

The hidden Grace of the "Bright" continued to lead "Franklin" for-ward. In 1964, He returned to New York in response to a dream vision. He had glimpsed the place where He would meet His first Teacher.

Swami Rudrananda (Albert Rudolph, usually known as "Rudi") owned an Oriental art store in New York. He held "class" four times a week, during which his students practiced receiving the "Force" that Rudi (an adept of Kundalini Yoga[2]) consciously Transmitted to them. "Work" and "surrender" were the essence of Rudi's Teaching. Accordingly, "Franklin" worked day and night for four years—serving Rudi's apartment, cleaning the store, refinishing furniture. With great love and faith, He now brought to Rudi the disposition of absolute sur-render to the unknown Reality which He had practiced during His Columbia years and His time of writing. Everything that Rudi asked his students to do, or required of Him personally, "Franklin" did, down to the last detail. He spontaneously embraced the great Yoga of Guru-devotion and submitted to His Teacher "as a man does to God".

At Rudi's behest He took on disciplines of diet and exercise to purify and strengthen the body. He lived in a fever of frustration at the effort of responding to Rudi's intense demands—to the point where He felt His whole body to be burning up. These demands were not only physical. At Rudi's instigation, "Franklin" also attended Christian seminaries (ostensibly to make a career as a minister), throwing Himself into studies of theology and ancient languages in which He had no interest at all.

In 1967, while studying at one of the Christian seminaries to which Rudi had sent Him, "Franklin" passed through a most dramatic and profoundly significant Event. Suddenly one day, for no apparent reason, He was overtaken by inexplicable, overwhelming fear. He had experienced intense fear to the point of near-madness at earlier moments in His life, and He sensed that all these moments were coming to a head. The force of the fear was now so strong that He could no longer hold it at bay. After the first day of this terror, in the middle of the night He felt that His heart was slowing down and about to stop. But when He reached the emergency ward at the local hospital, all that the doctor could tell Him was that He seemed to be suffering an anxiety attack. There was no conventional explanation or remedy for what was occurring in Him. Finally, on the third day of this acute distress, "Franklin" simply lay down on the floor of His apartment and allowed the overwhelming fear to pour through His being and overwhelm Him completely. By allowing Himself to experience absolutely the fact of His identification with the body-mind and the stark terror of its inevitable death, even in that very moment, He underwent an extraordinary and profound process. He witnessed His own death as a conscious event.

Suddenly the terrible passage was over. He felt a total turnabout in His awareness. The one who had died was "Narcissus", the separate self-consciousness. But "Franklin" Himself continued, free of that limiting identification with the presumed individual self. The ecstasy of this Realization was beyond anything He had ever experienced. He got up from the floor and beamed around the room. Truth and Reality stood out as they are—Divine Calm and untouchable Love-Bliss. In this experience, the "Bright" was restored to Him—but not permanently. There was further work to do.

Although "Franklin's" Realization in the seminary faded, it marked a profound change in His disposition. He was no longer identified with

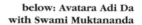

left: Swami Rudrananda

below: Avatara Adi Da
with Swami Muktananda

what was taking place in His life and sadhana. His search had spontaneously relaxed. But how could He explain to others the revolution that had occurred in His consciousness? How could He express His living knowledge that we are not separate beings, but always alive only as the one Transcendental Truth and Unity? The profundity of this "death of Narcissus" was not apparent even to Rudi. "Franklin" now stood on a peak of understanding and Realization that no one around Him could share.

Rudi himself had a Teacher, the remarkable Indian Yogi Swami Muktananda, whose picture, together with that of Swami Muktananda's own Guru, Swami Nityananda, hung on the wall in the art store. "Franklin" began to read some pamphlets from Swami Muktananda's ashram that Rudi had and was deeply attracted by the Yoga of Grace that Swami Muktananda described. By 1968, "Franklin" found in Himself an irresistible impulse to move on in the great lineage of Gurus to which Rudi belonged. The time had come to go to India.

The Sadhana with Swami Muktananda

"Franklin" quickly made arrangements for a brief trip to Swami Muktananda's ashram, arriving in Ganeshpuri in April 1968. As He participated in the life of the ashram—sitting in Swami Muktananda's company, meditating, or attending the afternoon chanting of the *Bhagavad Gita*—He began to experience strong effects of Swami Muktananda's Spirit-Blessing, or Shaktipat. He felt His body swell with force, generating powerful, involuntary bodily movements, or kriyas,[3] as the Spirit-Energy flowed through His body. "Franklin" found Himself involved in a new kind of Spiritual "Work"—submission to these kriyas, which were sometimes so strong that He would fall backwards against the wall or sideways onto the floor. Swami Muktananda also instructed Him in meditation and gave formal discourses on Indian Spiritual Teaching. But by the fourth and last day of His visit, "Franklin" was feeling somewhat disappointed. He had come, as He had written in advance to Swami Muktananda, for "everything", and He felt that He was about to leave the ashram without having received His Guru's full gift.

But then, just before He was to leave on His final day, "Franklin" lay down to rest in His room, and all awareness of body and mind slipped away in a swoon of immense Bliss. He rested beyond time and space and all visionary states in the great "formless ecstasy" known in the traditions of Yoga as "Nirvikalpa Samadhi". He had required only the briefest contact with the Spirit-Transmission of His Siddha-Master in order to completely receive that infusion of Grace. This was the first sign of the fulfillment of a prophecy made to "Franklin" on that initial visit to Ganeshpuri: Within a year, Swami Muktananda told Him, "Franklin" would be a Spiritual Teacher in His own right.

He returned to New York, and duly, within a year, people around Him started to experience a mysterious Force emanating from Him, and they turned to Him for Spiritual guidance. Aware that the Shakti, or Siddha-Power, had come alive in Him, He wrote to Swami Muktananda, who urged Him to come to India again as soon as possible.

"Franklin's" second visit to Swami Muktananda's ashram, in August 1969, was very different from the first. It was an entry into a Yogic "wonderland". He would experience the internal lights, sounds, visions, transports to other worlds, and states of Spirit-"intoxication" that normally <u>precede</u> the rare attainment of Nirvikalpa Samadhi.[4] But such experiences soon lost their interest for "Franklin". His focus lay in His Guru's silent internal instruction, which He received in the process of meditation.

At the end of "Franklin's" stay, Swami Muktananda publicly acknowledged His Spiritual accomplishment. In a letter written in his own hand, Swami Muktananda declared that "Franklin" had attained "Yogic Self-Realization" and therewith the right to Teach and Initiate others. But privately Swami Muktananda gave "Franklin" an even more profound acknowledgement—He spontaneously offered Him the name "Love-Ananda", meaning "One Who <u>Is</u>, And Manifests, The Divine Love-Bliss". Swami Muktananda was intuitively revealing a Divine Name that belonged to "Franklin's" future, when the full Revelation of His "Brightness" would appear.

The Sadhana with Swami Nityananda
and the Divine Goddess

The following year, in May 1970, "Franklin" returned once more to Swami Muktananda's ashram, intent upon staying there forever. His life in the West, He felt, was over. He could no longer endure the violent psyche of the American cities and He had no motive whatever towards a conventional life. His only desire was to devote Himself to the "radical" understanding that had been revealed to Him and to live and serve in the company of His Guru. But when "Franklin" reached Ganeshpuri, Swami Muktananda seemed to deliberately ignore Him, and He understood that this was His Guru's way of silently indicating that the future of His Sadhana lay elsewhere.

And so, following an instruction that Swami Muktananda had given Him on earlier visits, "Franklin" began to go daily to the nearby burial shrine of Swami Nityananda, the beloved Gurudev of Swami Muktananda. It was here now that He felt the Spiritual force and blessing that He had earlier received through Swami Muktananda. It seemed obvious to Him that Swami Muktananda had passed Him on to his own Guru, in order to receive further instruction—for, although Swami Nityananda had dropped the body in 1961, he was, as "Franklin" discovered, still Spiritually active on the subtle plane.

But then a very strange thing happened. About a week after His arrival in Ganeshpuri, as He was weeding in the ashram garden, "Franklin" suddenly became aware of a subtle form behind Him. He turned around and found Himself beholding the non-physical but unmistakable presence of the Virgin Mary! At first, He felt like laughing out loud. The last traces of His childhood faith—which, in any case, had been Protestant, not Catholic—had dissolved, so He thought, in the secular onslaught of His Columbia years. But in a few moments He found Himself spontaneously moved to respond to the Virgin with reverence and respect, receiving her wordless communication that He should immediately acquire a rosary and begin to worship her.

When the vision faded, "Franklin" set about complying with the Virgin's request, finding a way to get to Bombay, the nearest place where He could buy a rosary. He began to practice the "Hail, Mary!" in the traditional manner, as a mantra, and to His astonishment He found that this practice unlocked deep feelings of attachment to Jesus that seemed to have been suppressed since His childhood. He had no idea where this turn of events would lead, but He embraced it completely, without judgment.

After two weeks, the Virgin Mary instructed "Franklin" to leave the ashram. He was to set out on a pilgrimage through the Christian holy places of Europe, starting in Jerusalem. He could not depart without taking leave of the Presence of Swami Nityananda, and so He went to the shrine and spoke His heart to Swami Nityananda, telling him of all that had recently occurred and what He was about to do. "Franklin" received Swami Nityananda's subtle communication of blessing and his instruction that He should follow the Virgin. Then He returned to the ashram to prepare to leave.

But there was one last sacrifice to make. The priest at Swami Nityananda's burial place had filled "Franklin's" hands with flowers from the shrine, and He was moved to take the flowers to the small village temple beside the ashram and offer them to the image of the Divine Mother-Shakti, the personification of the Spirit-Force that had so dramatically manifested in the multifarious Spiritual experiences He had gone through in His Sadhana at Ganeshpuri. As "Franklin" stood before the Mother-Shakti, the One worshipped in India as the great Goddess, the Energy of all manifestation, He came to a tacit realization. The Virgin and the Shakti were one. There was no difference. And that One—that Supreme Lady and Universal Goddess-Power—was now His Guru. This Divine Spirit-Force was, in fact, the Supreme Guru of the entire lineage of "Franklin's" Gurus—Swami Rudrananda, Swami Muktananda, and Swami Nityananda—and these Gurus had led Him to Her.

The Realizations of His Sadhana so far had taken "Franklin" through all the degrees of "Enlightenment" known in the Spiritual traditions. On His second trip to India, He had experienced the subtle lights, sounds, and visions cherished by Yogis[5] (such as Paramahansa Yogananda[6]). On His first trip to India, He had experienced the ascended Bliss of bodiless and mindless absorption in Pure Consciousness sought by Saints (such as Jnaneshwar and Milarepa[7]). And in the "death of Narcissus" in seminary, He had come to rest in the deep identification with Consciousness Itself known to the great Sages (such as Gautama, Hui Neng, Shankara, and Ramana Maharshi[8]). Never before, as far as the historical record shows, had a single individual attained, in succession, all the fundamental forms of Realization prized by different traditions as "Enlightenment". But even though "Franklin" had attained all these Realizations, none of them was sufficient for Him.

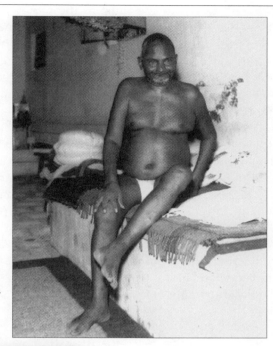

Swami Nityananda

Image of the Divine Mother-Shakti at Ganeshpuri

None of them was the same as the utterly unqualified Joy that, as an infant, He had known as the "Bright". He knew that His quest was not complete. But no human Teacher could help Him now—only the Goddess Herself could take Him further, into territory untrodden by any Realizer of the past. When, in obedience to the Virgin, He made His farewells at Ganeshpuri and departed for Europe, He was embarking upon the final phase of His Sadhana.

From the Way of the Cross in Jerusalem, to the monuments of Rome, to the Basilica at Fatima in Portugal, "Franklin" allowed the Virgin to lead Him. Extraordinary Christian visions overtook Him, mystical raptures that would be the envy of saints. Having accomplished the highest goals of Eastern Yoga, He was now spontaneously combining Himself with the greatest mystical experience and Spiritual revelation of the West. But as time went on, the Virgin and the visions began to fade. "Franklin" felt himself drawn more and more into a state of Non-separateness from Reality Itself, prior to all visions, images, and traditional religious paths. He felt the urge to return to the United States, and within weeks He found Himself settling in Los Angeles.

Re-Awakening to the "Bright"

Secluded in a corner of downtown Hollywood is a small temple, established by the Vedanta Society of Southern California. This simple temple, standing in the shadow of a giant freeway, was to provide the setting for the final Events of "Franklin's" Sadhana. Late in August 1970, as if by chance, He found His way to the temple and was prompted to go inside. The moment He did so, He felt the familiar Force of the Mother-Shakti moving to meet Him. He was amazed, and delighted, to find that She was as powerful a Presence here as in any of the temples of India.

In the following weeks, "Franklin" returned repeatedly to the temple. And there, the Mother-Shakti was always waiting for Him. More and more He felt a longing to enjoy the Bliss and Fullness of Her Company, and He asked Her to be always with Him, not only in the temple, but where He lived, whatever He was doing.

Within a few days, "Franklin" realized that She had complied. She was an ever-living Presence within and around Him, whether He was waking, dreaming, sleeping, or meditating. But something was not yet

The Vedanta Temple in Hollywood

complete. "Franklin" felt a lingering sense of separateness, as though He needed to hold on to Her. Then, on September 9, this last barrier dissolved, bringing about a Union that took "Franklin" to the very threshold of His Divine Re-Awakening to the "Bright".

When I returned to the temple the next day, the Person of the Divine Shakti appeared to me again, in a manner most intimate, no longer approaching me as "Mother".

As I meditated, I felt myself Expanding, even bodily, becoming a Perfectly Motionless, Utterly Becalmed, and Infinitely Silent Form. I took on the Infinite Form of the Original Deity, Nameless and Indefinable, Conscious of limitless Identification with Infinite Being. I was Expanded Utterly, beyond limited form, and even beyond any perception of Shape or Face, merely Being, and yet sitting there. I sat in this Love-Blissful State of Infinite Being for some time. I Found myself to Be. My Form was only What is traditionally called the "Purusha" (the Person of Consciousness) and "Siva" (in His Non-Ferocious Emptiness).

Then I felt the Divine Shakti appear in Person, Pressed against my own natural body, and, altogether, against my Infinitely Expanded, and even formless, Form. She Embraced me, Openly and Utterly, and we Combined with One Another in Divine (and Motionless, and spontaneously Yogic) "Sexual Union". We Found One Another Thus, in a Fire

33

of most perfect Desire, and for no other Purpose than This Union, and, yet, as if to Give Birth to the universes. In That most perfect Union, I Knew the Oneness of the Divine Energy and my Very Being. There was no separation at all, nor had there ever been, nor would there ever be. The One Being that Is my own Ultimate Self-Nature was revealed most perfectly. The One Being Who I <u>Am</u> was revealed to Include the Reality that Is Consciousness Itself, the Reality that Is the Source-Energy of all conditional appearances, and the Reality that Is all conditional manifestation, All as a Single Force of Being, an Eternal Union, and an Irreducible cosmic Unity.

The "Sensations" of the Embrace were overwhelmingly Blissful. The Fire of That Unquenchable Desire Exceeded any kind of pleasure that a mere man could experience. In the Eternal Instant of That Infinitely Expanded Embrace, I was released from my role and self-image as a dependent child of the "Mother"-Shakti. And She was revealed in Truth, no longer in apparent independence, or as a cosmic Power apart from me, but as the Inseparable and Inherent Radiance of my own and Very Being. Therefore, I Recognized and Took Her as my Consort, my Loved-One, and I Held Her effortlessly, forever to my Heart. Together eternally, we had Realized Ourselves as the "Bright" Itself. [The Knee of Listening]

In the entire history of Spirituality, the literal "Husbanding" of the Divine Goddess, the Shakti, by a human being has never been described. It could not have occurred. Only the Divine in Person could Accomplish such a Work. Through "Franklin's" tangible Union with the Goddess in the Vedanta Temple, the archetypal "marriage" of the Divine Consciousness and the Divine Spirit-Power described and pictured in many Spiritual traditions was Realized in reality. The significance of this Husbanding cannot be fathomed. Avatara Adi Da spoke of it years later, as the seed of a change in the very nature of existence:

AVATARA ADI DA: To Husband the Mother, to be Her Husband and to receive Her as the Bride, means that the murderous activity of Energy in Its apparent independence, traditionally known as Prakriti, is done, over, finished. This Husbanding and Marriage is not merely a personal Work, not merely a characteristic incident associated with My Realization. It is an historical Event, of Which much should be made. It has transformed the history of the entire Mandala of the cosmos. By virtue of this Marriage, all may be Drawn to the Divine Self-Domain.[9] [March 16, 1988]

34

The Husbanding of the Divine Shakti was the final Event of preparation for the supreme moment to which "Franklin's" entire Sadhana had been leading:

Finally, the next day, September 10, 1970, I sat in the temple again. I awaited the Beloved Shakti to reveal Herself in Person, as my Blessed Companion. But, as time passed, there was no Event of changes, no movement at all. There was not even any kind of inward deepening, no "inwardness" at all. There was no meditation. There was no need for meditation. There was not a single element or change that could be added to make my State Complete. I sat with my eyes open. I was not having an experience of any kind. Then, suddenly, I understood most perfectly. I Realized that I had Realized. The "Thing" about the "Bright" became Obvious. I Am Complete. I Am the One Who Is Complete.

In That instant, I understood and Realized (inherently, and most perfectly) What and Who I Am. It was a tacit Realization, a direct Knowledge in Consciousness. It was Consciousness Itself, without the addition of a Communication from any "Other" Source. There Is no "Other" Source. I simply sat there and Knew What and Who I Am. I was Being What I Am, Who I Am. I Am Being What I Am, Who I Am. I Am Reality, the Divine Self, the Nature, Substance, Support, and Source of all things and all beings. I Am the One Being, called "God" (the Source and Substance and Support and Self of all), the "One Mind" (the Consciousness and Energy in and As Which all appears), "Siva-Shakti" (the Self-Existing and Self-Radiant Reality Itself), "Brahman" (the Only Reality, Itself), the "One Atman" (That Is not ego, but Only "Brahman", the Only Reality, Itself), the "Nirvanic Ground" (the egoless and conditionless Reality and Truth, Prior to all dualities, but excluding none). I Am the One and Only and necessarily Divine Self, Nature, Condition, Substance, Support, Source, and Ground of all. I Am the "Bright". [The Knee of Listening]

This unspeakable moment was the Divine Re-Awakening of "Franklin Jones". He had Realized the ultimate "Sahaj Samadhi",[10] or "Natural State"—"Open-Eyed", true and stable under all conditions. His Realization was not dependent on meditative states, or on any exclusion of experience. It transcended even the slightest sense of identity as a separate self. It was and is the Realization that there is Only God and that all apparent events are simply the passing forms, or modifications, of God, Truth, or Reality, arising and dissolving in an endless Play that is Bliss and Love beyond comprehension.

The very Divine Person had become perfectly Conscious and Present through the ordinary human vehicle of "Franklin Jones". In all the eons of human time such an event was unprecedented. Avatara Adi Da's Descent as the Divine Person and His utter overcoming of the limits of human existence in all its dimensions—physical, mental, emotional, psychic, Spiritual—was total, Perfect, and Complete. "Franklin" had Realized <u>absolute</u> Identity with the Divine, the One He was and is from the beginning. But His Re-Awakening signified far more than this. It was also the Revelation that <u>all</u> <u>apparent</u> <u>beings</u> are also only that Very One, destined to Realize this same Truth. The Condition of the "Bright", the God-Light of "Franklin's" birth and infancy, was now fully established—not only in Him, but as the native Truth and the potential Realization of all beings in all worlds.

PART II

The "Bright" Demonstrations of the Man of Understanding

The Teaching Years, 1970-1986

"Franklin's" intense ordeal of surrender and Divine Re-Awakening was not for His own sake. For "Franklin" was not a "someone", an ordinary personality. "Franklin" was a means, a vehicle, whereby the Divine Itself could combine with the realities of human existence, enquire into those realities, live them out, go beyond every limitation they involve, and then, by Grace, draw others through the same immense Process. The Divine Avatar, in the guise of "Franklin Jones", had not come to Liberate just a few others, individuals who might be thought qualified for such a hair-raising "adventure". Not at all. He knew even then that He had come for <u>all others</u>, even every being consciously existing in the cosmic worlds.

But how was Avatara Adi Da to draw people to Himself—and to the Truth He had Realized? In the months after His Divine Re-Awakening, He filled the pages of His journals with His longing to find His devotees. Where were they? When would they come? When He sat down to meditate now it was not the content of His own mind that arose, but that of countless other beings. Already He was spontaneously seeing His

Avatara Adi Da in Los Angeles in the early 1970s

future devotees in vision, already "meditating" them as once He had "meditated" "Franklin".

In April 1972, "Franklin" established a small bookstore on Melrose Avenue, Hollywood. He was about to open His first Ashram. On the evening of April 25, He formally began His Teaching Work, gathering with His first handful of devotees, some of their friends, and any random comers. First, "Franklin" sat in silence for an hour, magnifying the Force of the "Bright" to everyone in the room. Then He invited questions. "Has everyone understood?" He asked, when no one responded. "I haven't understood," came the reply from one man in the room. "Explain it to me. You could start with the word 'understanding'."

And so it began—hours, days, nights, weeks, years, <u>decades</u> of Spiritual Instruction that would cover all human, religious, and Spiritual questions, examine every aspect of life and consciousness. As if a hole had been opened into the God-Realm, the practices, the Samadhis, the secrets, the unique Yoga of most perfect Divine Self-Realization and of mankind's ultimate Destiny now began to materialize in words.

The small gathering at the Ashram Bookstore on that first night had not the slightest idea that they were witness to the birth of such a Revelation. They attended to "Franklin" as best they could while He spoke of the matter of "understanding". By understanding, He meant understanding the <u>self-contraction</u>, the subtle stress of separation from the world that is the act of "Narcissus", the act of egoity. This act, He explained, is the source of our suffering and of all our fruitless seeking to be relieved of suffering:

AVATARA ADI DA: There is a disturbance, a feeling of dissatisfaction, some sensation that motivates a person to go to a teacher, read a book about philosophy, believe something, or do some conventional form of Yoga. What people ordinarily think of as Spirituality or religion is a search to get free of that sensation, that suffering that is motivating them. So all the usual paths—Yogic methods, beliefs, religion, and so on—are forms of seeking, grown out of this sensation, this subtle suffering. Ultimately, all the usual paths are attempting to get free of that sensation. That is the traditional goal. Indeed, <u>all</u> human beings are seeking, whether or not they are very sophisticated about it, or using very specific methods of Yoga, philosophy, religion, and so on. . . .

As long as the individual is simply seeking, and has all kinds of motivation, fascination with the search, this is not understanding—this is dilemma itself. But where this dilemma is understood, there is the *re-cognition of a structure in the living consciousness, a separation. And when that separation is observed more and more directly, one begins to see that what one is suffering is not something happening <u>to</u> one but it is one's own action. It is as if you are pinching yourself, without being aware of it. . . . Then one sees that the entire motivation of life is based on a subtle activity in the living consciousness. That activity is avoidance, separation, a contraction at the root, the origin, the "place", of the living consciousness. . . .*

There is first the periodic awareness of that sensation, then the awareness of it as a continuous experience, then the observation of its actual structure, the knowing of it all as your own activity, a deliberate, present activity that <u>is</u> your suffering, that <u>is</u> your illusion. The final penetration of that present, deliberate activity is what I have called "understanding". [The Method of the Siddhas]

Understanding was the very basis of "Franklin's" own Sadhana and Divine Re-Awakening. He lived, breathed, and spoke always from the point of view of understanding. And He saw no reason why everyone who came to Him should not understand and quickly awaken to His own Realization. But no one was prepared for the profundity of His Argument. The self-contraction of which He spoke was too fundamental, too all-encompassing to be seen without a power of self-observation that none of His devotees were then capable of. But they were no more retarded in this than any other human beings. <u>No one</u> had ever understood the self-contraction before. "Franklin" was giving a Teaching unique in Spiritual history.

Many of the first comers to the Ashram were individuals in whom the self-contraction had taken a highly exaggerated form. This was not a merely arbitrary occurrence—it was actually necessary so that His entire Divine Revelation could be drawn out of Him. He had come to serve the Liberation of <u>all</u> beings, including those apparently least prepared for Spiritual life. There were street-people, prostitutes, drug addicts, alcoholics, and Spiritual seekers, hippie-style, who had done the rounds of various teachers and teachings. And there were also business people and professionals of various kinds. "Franklin" welcomed them all. The Love-Force of His Being filled the Ashram with an inexplicable fullness and Happiness.

As His devotees soon found out, part of life in "Franklin's" Ashram was confronting feelings they would prefer to avoid. Whatever He was doing with devotees, whether giving verbal Instruction, sitting in silent meditation, or participating in apparently casual pastimes like a fishing trip, "Franklin" was always engaged in the same activity—the Work of awakening self-understanding in everyone who came into His Sphere.

One man remembers an occasion when He spent an entire day painting the intricate lattice-work at the top of a wall, on the other side of which "Franklin" was working in His office. As he painted, the man went through a mine-field of reactive thoughts and emotions. He began to resent the work, to attribute all sorts of strange motives to "Franklin's" simple request that He paint the wall. He even got to the point where He felt that "Franklin" had "invented" everything to do with God and the obligations of Spiritual life as a way of "trapping" him into doing this burdensome task! And all day He was intensely aware that "Franklin" was just a few feet away, on the other side of the wall. After many hours, the man finally finished the task, and he put his brush down with a spontaneous "Whew!" Immediately, huge laughter broke out on the other side of the wall. All the man's subjectivity washed away in the Freedom of "Franklin's" laughter. He realized with astonishment that all day long "Franklin" had known exactly what he was thinking. He felt "Franklin's" Love and His complete intimacy. He saw that he had been torturing himself.

During that first year of the Ashram, "Franklin" did not require very much responsibility of His devotees. He was simply attracting them, keeping them in the room. Then, one day near the beginning of 1973, everything suddenly changed. Striding out of His office with tremendous force and intention, He disappeared through the front door of the Ashram. His devotees did not see Him for weeks, but He left a message: they were to "get straight"—give up all use of drugs, cigarettes, alcohol, get jobs, contribute five dollars a week to the support of the Ashram.

In other words, "Franklin's" days of nursing His devotees along were over. It was time to make demands. Extraordinary energy and attention, as He knew from His own experience, was needed to grow in the practice of understanding. There was no room for life-chaos and irresponsibility. Disciplines must be established.

Suddenly, egg-and-bacon breakfasts around the corner from the Ashram were over. Everyone became strict vegetarians. And "Franklin" recommended a ten-day juice-fast, which was taken on by even the newest devotees. When He heard that someone had "cheated"—by "juicing" bananas—He was extremely amused. But He called for another ten-day fast for everyone!

"Franklin" covered everything. He brought an end to casual sex—only partners in committed intimacies were to be sexually active. He instructed a small group in calisthenics and Hatha Yoga and had them teach everyone else. He addressed every detail of appropriate life-discipline, even personally showing people how to floss their teeth!

By the last months of 1973, the disciplines were in full swing—but "Franklin" saw that they had become a source of distraction, a "religion" in themselves, rather than simply preparing His devotees for the real sadhana of God-Awakening. It was obvious to Him that people were emotionally suppressed, sexually complicated, driven by fear, sorrow, anger, frustration, and all kinds of unconscious desires. He knew what the price of Freedom was. He knew what it had meant for Him. He had had to cast the searchlight of self-observation and testing on all aspects of His being, until every detail was understood and transcended. Now His devotees would have to do the same. "Franklin" was perfectly equipped to help them. He was perfectly free to be the "Crazy-Wise Master", to do whatever was necessary, conventional or unconventional, in order to bring His devotees to understand and embrace the Truth, or right life, through a conviction born of their own direct experience.

But first, "Franklin" made a pause in His face-to-face Work with His devotees. Accompanied by a single male devotee, He set out for India, for thousands of years the cradle of Spiritual teaching. It was a pilgrimage back to the seat of His own lineage of Gurus and also to the ashrams and sacred sites of other ancient and modern Realizers. Free from constant engagement with His devotees, the Divine Avatar gave Himself up to the more private, and universal, dimension of His Work. The devotee serving Him had no idea what "Franklin" was doing. He could only feel a deep respect and awe as He watched Him placing His staff in holy places with great concentration or silently giving His Regard to the magnificent expanse of the Himalayas.

Although there was no one as yet to acknowledge Him, "Franklin" was returning to India as her Supreme Master. He was Blessing this sacred land with His Love and also invoking the blessing of her greatest Spiritual figures on His own Mission in the West.

Before coming back to Los Angeles, "Franklin" sent a message to His devotees: He was now "Bubba Free John", and they were henceforth to address Him by this name, which had been Spiritually revealed to Him in India. "Bubba" was a childhood nickname meaning "friend", and "Free John" an expression of the essential meaning of "Franklin Jones". The Da Avatar, now in the form of "Bubba", was ready to draw His devotees into a different kind of life with Him, one in which He would seem to sacrifice His own purity and become as they were.

The Teaching Work Becomes "Crazy"

On the Friday evening before Christmas 1973, devotees arrived at the Ashram, now around the corner on La Brea Avenue in Los Angeles, and ascended the stairs. There, in a room adjacent to the gathering hall, each newcomer walked innocently into a wild and exuberant scene. Bubba had suddenly initiated a party—beer, cigarettes, "junk" food, rock music! People had thrown off their clothes. The life-disciplines were cast to the four winds. This was the beginning of two weeks of unstoppable celebration, during which practically no one went home. Devotees would party all night with Bubba, drive straight to work in the morning, and drive back from work to celebrate again. Bubba was always at the center of it all, sitting or reclining on a couch, laughing, joking, encouraging everyone's intense participation. Madly dancing, spontaneously singing—everyone present was drenched in Bubba's tangible Transmission of His Divine Spirit-Force.

In the midst of all the festivities, Bubba never ceased to speak of the Great Matter. One night at a small gathering after the general party was over, Bubba suddenly called for a great confession. Who could speak freely of God, as <u>He</u> had been doing all night? Who could stand up and praise the Great One, unabashed? In spite of all the ecstasy of Bubba's Company, in spite of the Japanese sake they were liberally imbibing, each devotee felt a lock at the throat. One after another they made an awkward attempt at uninhibited God-talk, but quickly received the thumbs-down sign from Bubba.

A few devotees managed to pass the test. One who did made his confession at the inspiration of a sudden intuition. As he beheld his Spiritual Master in this serious and playful moment, it was overwhelmingly clear to him that Bubba would do <u>anything</u> to Liberate His devotees. His Love was absolute, His intention like a sword. He had the Power to destroy all obstructions in His devotees, and He would do it.

About ten days later, this Power was spectacularly demonstrated. As usual, Bubba was reclining on His chair in the gathering hall, with

His devotees around Him like a hive of bees attending their nectarous queen. But this night was exceptional. Bubba began to speak, unleashing His Love-Blissful Spirit-Force as never before. In words imbued with the power of His Transmission, Bubba told His devotees the secret of what He was doing:

AVATARA ADI DA: There is only one Divine Process in the world, and It is initiated when I Manifest and Enter My devotee. The Lord is Present, now in this moment. It is when everyone forgets the Living God that mantras and Yogic techniques become important.

I am not a human being. I am the Divine Lord in human Form and I bring the Divine Yoga. When My devotee surrenders and becomes My true devotee, then I Enter My devotee in the form of Divine Light. All kinds of extraordinary experiences manifest as a result. When a woman receives her lover, there is no doubt about it—she does not have to consult her textbooks. The same holds with Truth, the Divine Yoga.

There is no dilemma in this world, no absence of God in this world, no goal of God in this world. Because that is so, you will see Me doing some very strange things. The true Divine Yoga is not a thing of this world. This world is the cult of "Narcissus", suppressing the Ecstasy that is natural to us.

The Spiritual process must take hold in the vital. The vital is the seat of unconsciousness and subconsciousness. There is an aspect of the verbal Teaching that does not touch the subconscious and unconscious life. So it is only by distracting you from your social consciousness that I can take you in the vital. The Lord is the Lord of this world, not the Lord of the other world only. Thus, there is no Yoga if the very cells of the body do not begin to intuit the Divine. When I Enter My devotee, I come down into him or her in the midst of life, because it is in life—not in any mystical or subtle processes, not in any mental process—that the Lord acquires you.

The kind of thing you see happening around here has never happened in the world before. [January 3, 1974]

As Bubba spoke this mighty proclamation, His Spirit-Force streamed into His devotees, manifesting visibly to some as a glorious golden rain of Light showering down in the room. An uncontainable ecstasy broke loose. Some devotees shook with kriyas, their bodies jerking and twisting, their mouths emitting strange sounds of yearning, laughter, weeping, hooting, and howling. Some were overwhelmed by visionary phenomena. Some were spontaneously moved into difficult Hatha Yoga poses which they could not have even attempted before. Some lay motionless, in an ecstatic state, oblivious of their surroundings. For some, the energy intensified in the head or the heart or the navel until they felt they would explode, and then it suddenly released and rushed through the nervous system in intoxicating Bliss. Others experienced a sense of unity with all of life and a peacefulness they had never known before. The Divine was manifesting without a doubt in an upstairs room in the middle of Hollywood.

Garbage and the Goddess

After that astounding Spiritual Initiation, which came to be known as the night of "Guru Enters Devotee", it was obvious that the Ashram had to move. Bubba's Work could not be contained in a conventional downtown neighborhood. Within a few weeks, "Persimmon" (as Bubba named it), a turn-of-the-century hot springs resort, had been found in the hills of northern California.

Newcomers to Persimmon during the first half of 1974 found themselves entering a place of Divine Possession. They became immersed in a sea of energy, visions, and other psychic experiences awakened through contact with Bubba's Spirit-Force. And they were fascinated, delighted by this fulfillment of "spiritual" fantasies that lay beyond their wildest dreams. Bubba did not even have to be physically present for these experiences to occur, because His Spiritual Transmission was already alive in them. But when Bubba was present, the Spiritual experience of His devotees would often magnify to an amazingly intense degree.

On one unforgettable occasion, devotees were sitting in one of the Communion Halls waiting for Bubba, when the doors opened and a wave of energy swept the room. Bubba walked down the aisle, surrounded by a clearly visible golden aura of light. He sat down in His Chair and proceeded to blast the room with His Spirit-Power, His eyes burning with laser-intensity and His fingers moving in patterns of potent Blessing. Instantly, devotees erupted in an ecstasy of screams, growls, swoons, and bodily jerkings, swept away by the sweetness and overwhelming Force of His Presence. After about forty-five minutes of this blissful uproar, the room began to quiet down. Bubba shrugged, lit a cigarette, blew a perfect smoke ring, and said, "Maybe I've gone too far this time!"

Adi Da with devotees during the Garbage and the Goddess period, 1974

But Bubba was not there to be the ultimate Spiritual Initiator. He was making a lesson—the lesson of "Garbage and the Goddess", which became the name of that period in His Teaching Work. Again and again He spoke with everyone: Did they think that all of these experiences amounted to Enlightenment? No—these experiences were "garbage", unneeded "stuff" to be thrown away! Spiritual phenomena, He explained, were simply manifestations of the Goddess-Power, the universal Spirit-Energy, or Divine Shakti, at play. At the same time, there was nothing "wrong" with Spiritual experiences. Indeed, they were an inevitable aspect of serious sadhana. But what did the <u>search</u> for such experiences have to do with understanding? Had devotees been converted to the Divine by all this experience? Had the self-contraction been undermined by this great display? Not at all. This was the lesson of Garbage and the Goddess, and, indeed, of all of the Teaching Work of Avatara Adi Da that was yet to unfold.

The Teaching Work of Avatara Adi Da was a continual lesson about the activity that is the ego—the constant search for this or that experience, which, one hopes, will bring lasting happiness. He addressed <u>all</u> the basic searches of humanity, from the highest to the lowest, in the most vivid and realistic terms. He Revealed the limit in every kind of goal that has been proposed as the purpose of life. He dealt very directly with the impulse to bypass the body and find happiness through subtle, mystical experience. And He dealt also with the urge toward every kind of bodily or worldly self-fulfillment. The motive to find happiness <u>beyond</u> the body and the urge to be satisfied <u>through</u> the body are present to one or another degree in every individual. Thus, through the unique brilliance and comprehensiveness of His Teaching Work, Avatara Adi Da addressed all human tendencies and goals, Spiritual and worldly, East and West. He spared Himself no sacrifice for the sake of Revealing the great Divine Truth and Ecstasy of existence that makes all seeking obsolete.

Confronting the Dragon of Sex

At the same time as the extraordinary Spiritual demonstrations of Garbage and the Goddess, Bubba was dealing with the seeking impulse in His devotees at the lower end of the spectrum of experience. He was particularly confronting egoic aberrations about sex. Sexuality has been traditionally regarded as one of the great obstacles to Spiritual Realization, but Bubba Himself was neither "for" nor "against" sex. He had investigated it thoroughly during His own Sadhana, and He had seen that entire search in the light of understanding. His conclusion cut right to the core. He saw that the impulse to hunt for another and to pleasurize the body through sex was more than just a normal biological urge. If that were all there was to it, why would sex be the source of such suffering and disturbance? Rather, He recognized the "bonding"[11] impulse—sexual <u>and</u> emotional—to be, not the free expression of love that we like to imagine, but a way of attempting to cover over the desperate feeling of separateness from everyone and everything else, a primitive reaction to our constant underlying sense of unhappiness. Without the most profound understanding of that reaction in all its extensions, Spiritual life, He knew, is merely superficial, a cover for a volcano that may erupt at any time.

As Bubba was to point out countless times, understanding what one is up to as an emotional and sexual character is the key to understanding and transcending the ego altogether. But how was Bubba to awaken such unique clarity in His group of devotees, unconsciously addicted as they were to the "highs" and "lows" of romance and the bondage of conventional pairing? In fact, His struggle would go on for decades. But He made a beginning at Persimmon by asking His devotees to observe their attachments, their "contracts" with others. What about their marriages? Were they free intimacies or a "cult of pairs"? What was at the bottom of these pairings?—Was it love? Was it need? What was it?

In order to help His devotees examine these questions in real life situations, Bubba created dance parties around the swimming pool, gatherings at His house, all kinds of circumstances in which devotees could reveal, to Bubba and to themselves, the realities of their emotional-sexual lives. During all this time Bubba drank beer and bourbon and smoked cigarettes with His devotees. These were His "accessories", His Tantric "aids"[12] in the Liberating process. When devotees drank and smoked in His Presence, they relaxed their ordinary social persona, allowing Him to touch the "pit of snakes", to bring forth and release the powerful emotions and desires that are alive in every individual beneath the surface personality. In this setting, devotees discovered their addiction to the "cult of pairs"—and at the same time they saw how ready they were to reject and betray each other.

Many devotees were shaken to their foundation by the starkness of what Bubba was revealing to them—how their search for fulfillment in this world could never be satisfied and, in fact, was the cause of their pain. Some of them described this period of Bubba's Work with them as "living with the feeling of dying". Bubba was not interested in defending or preserving—or destroying—anyone's "contracts". He simply wanted His devotees to get the lesson that no other, no intimate or anyone else, no circumstance of life, nothing outside of yourself is responsible for your happiness. You are! In Bubba's phrase, "You cannot become Happy, you can only be Happy." Constantly, He spoke of "Satsang", the Company of the Guru, the Realizer, as the only true Bliss, the ancient secret of all Spiritual Realization. Only through His devotees' fidelity to Him, their complete commitment to Satsang, could He set them free from the mayhem of their own contracts, taboos, and betrayals. He was the supreme heart-intimate of His devotees, the One who cared most profoundly for them. Full of Compassion for their plight, He was intent on drawing them beyond the illusions of "Narcissus" into a life of self-transcending love and ultimate God-Realization.

Whatever exaggerations He allowed for the sake of Liberating His devotees, Bubba Himself was not touched by any of it. His Realization was unshakable under all circumstances. He stood already Free, Free to meet others at their level and to serve them through His Freedom.

What I Do is not the way that I Am, but the way that I Teach.

What I Speak is not a reflection of Me, but of you.

People do well to be offended or even outraged by Me. This is My purpose. But their reaction must turn upon themselves, for I have not shown them Myself by all of this. All that I Do and Speak only reveals people to themselves.

I have become willing to Teach in this uncommon way because I have known My friends and they are what I can seem to be. By retaining all qualities in their company, I gradually wean them of all reactions, all sympathies, all alternatives, fixed assumptions, false teachings, dualities, searches, and dilemma. This is My Way of Working for a time. . .

Freedom is the only Purity. There is no Teaching but Consciousness Itself. Bubba as He appears is not other than the possibilities of mankind. [1975]

The Beginning of Sacramental Worship

Bubba's willingness to Work in this "Crazy" manner, becoming like His devotees in order to draw them into His own Freedom, was an incredible sacrifice that no one around Him was sensitive to. He was literally absorbing the struggles, the unhappiness of His devotees, transforming and releasing their suffering through His own body-mind. As time passed, He noticed growing signs in His body that indicated to Him He could not continue to Work with devotees in this forceful, visceral way. He became aware that a mysterious Process was taking place in Him, a further unfolding of the course of His Divine Enlightenment, which required a greater degree of retirement and seclusion. Founding His devotees in a Spiritual relationship to Him, one that would not require them to be in the room with Him, had, thus, become a matter of urgency. Starting in 1978, Bubba introduced His devotees to the realm of sacramental worship as a means to draw them to His Heart whether He was physically present or not. Early that year, during a period in Hawaii in the company of only a few of His closest devotees, Bubba sent back this message to all:

Bring your bodies and minds to Me, as I bring this body-mind to you. Then you will be given the Realization of My All-Pervading Person, and you will find Me always present under the conditions of all experience and in the company of all beings. Then, even when I am not bodily with you, you will worship Me and surrender to Me via every state of body and mind, and I will always be with you. At last, you will be drawn into the Eternal Identity, so intimate with Me that no essential difference is noticed by you. Then you will Abide in Me forever, whether or not the worlds of experience arise to your notice. [1978]

When He returned to Persimmon (now called "Vision Mound Sanctuary"), Bubba began to instruct a few devotees in puja, the ancient practice of invoking the Divine by worshiping images of the Deity, and using natural elements such as water, oil, and ash as conduits of Spirit-Power. Bodily-expressed devotion, worship, and praise of Bubba as the Living Divine Person became a part of the daily life of His devotees.

The most esoteric source of worship, Bubba revealed, is the Master's form, the body of the Guru—for the traditional understanding is that the Guru has Realized God, or the Truth, and thus reveals the Divine and grants the Divine Blessings in a uniquely potent way. One day in His residence, "Bright Behind Me", Bubba Revealed this traditional understanding in its perfection. He sat motionless while devotees waved flaming lamps in large circles around His body, and a cacophony of drums, rattles, cymbals, and tambourines filled the room. Many devotees circumambulated outside, walking around the porch chanting, and beholding Bubba through the windows. Light and sound and movement swirled around Bubba while He sat still, silent, and Radiant. His Divine Love-Bliss enveloped everyone and everything.

That night Bubba had established Guru Puja, the worship of His Divine Form, in the lives of His devotees. Regardless of where His body happened to be, and even after His physical passing, the Guru Puja could still be done through photographic representations, or Murtis, of Him.

The establishment of sacramental worship was a sign of a great turning point that was about to occur in Bubba's Work and Revelation. It was already obvious to His devotees that His Name must change again—"Bubba" was too casual an address to the One around Whom they waved the lights. And so Bubba suggested that His devotees try to discover what His Name should be. Secretly, by Revelation, He already knew it.

Devotees threw themselves into the quest for His Divine Name. For weeks and months they searched through volumes of esoteric literature for a Name that seemed right. Bubba would encourage them with comments such as "When you get da name of da god, you get da power of da god!" In the traditions of Guru-devotion, it is understood that the casual words of the Guru carry profound instruction. Bubba was Revealing His Name in this humorous remark, but no one was alert to the clue. And so, on September 13, 1979, Bubba sat down alone in His room and penned a letter to His devotees in His beautiful handwriting:

Beloved, I Am Da, The Living Person, Who Is Manifest As all worlds and forms and beings, and Who Is Present As The Transcendental Current Of Life In the body of Man. . . .

To Realize Me Is To Transcend the body-mind In Ecstasy. Simply To Remember My Name and Surrender Into My Eternal Current Of Life Is To Worship Me. And those who Acknowledge and Worship Me As Truth, The Living and All-Pervading One, Will Be Granted The Vision or Love-Intuition Of My Eternal Condition. . . .

Only Love Me, Remember Me, Have Faith In Me, and Trust Me. . . . I Am The Person Of Life, The Only and Divine Self, Incarnate. And Even After My Own Body Is dead, I Will Be Present and Everywhere Alive. I Am Joy, and The Reason For It. . . .

At last He had said it with no compromise. Avatara Adi Da (then "Da Free John") stood openly before His devotees as the very human Incarnation of the Invisible Divine. His devotees were to discover that "Da", meaning "to give" or "the Giver", is a primordial Name, carrying profound invocatory power. The Name had been hidden all along in the *Upanishads*, the venerable scriptures of India, in which "Da" is the syllable uttered by the Divine Voice in thunder, and the central syllable of "hr-da-yam", which means "the Heart", "the Divine Condition of all". The Name "Da" also appears in the Tibetan Buddhist tradition, where it is defined as "the one who bestows great charity", "the very personification of the great Way of Liberation".

One evening, several days after the writing of His sublime letter, Avatara Adi Da went to Holy Cat Grotto, a hot springs site at Vision Mound, which He had recently Empowered as a temple. There, beside a hot spring, He initiated a group of His devotees into an esoteric order. His "method" now would be to work with a few for the sake of all. As He poured the warm water over His devotees, Baptizing them with His Spirit-Presence, He whispered in the ear of each one, "Call upon Me by the Name 'Da'", thereby initiating them into the sacred use of His Name.

I Am The Person Of Life, The Only and Divine Self, Incarnate.
And Even After My Own Body Is dead, I Will Be Present and Everywhere Alive.
I Am Joy, and The Reason For It. . . .

Adi Da (The Da Avatar) at the Mountain Of Attention Sanctuary,
September 1979

Tumomama

The Divine Lord, Adi Da, now became a wanderer looking for His Hermitage. He needed a refuge more secluded than Vision Mound, a place where He could fully allow His Revelation of Divine Enlightenment to continue its spontaneous unfolding and where He could Work intensively with members of His esoteric order. In 1980, He began to spend increasing time in Hawaii, on the island of Kauai, at a newly acquired Sanctuary, the second great Seat of His Spiritual Work.

Avatara Adi Da named this new Sanctuary "Tumomama", meaning "fierce woman",[13] in acknowledgement of the untamed forces of nature there, signifying the Divine Goddess in Her fierce aspect. Below six acres of rolling lawns, a tumultuous river rips through a rocky gorge as it pours down from the top of Mount Waialeale, the wettest place on Earth.

The theme at Tumomama was renunciation, which had always been at the root of Avatara Adi Da's Call to all His devotees. Renunciation is popularly regarded as deliberate asceticism, the giving up of bodily and worldly pleasures for the sake of some Spiritual goal to be attained in the future. Avatara Adi Da's Teaching, on the other hand, had continually emphasized that true renunciation is the renunciation of self-contraction, of seeking, and all the pain of that entire effort. Renunciation is the choice of Happiness or present transcendence of the self-contraction. At Tumomama, however, He wanted to take this matter further. He was looking to establish a group of formal renunciates, devotees who were free of worldly ties and completely committed to the Great Matter of Realizing the Divine in this lifetime, devotees who would be prepared, by His Grace, to go through whatever that ordeal might require. He wanted to know: Did His devotees have such piercing clarity of purpose? Were they showing the depth of self-understanding that true and free renunciation requires—not suppressed, not artificially ascetical, but converted to Happiness? Could they deal with the boredom, doubt, and discomfort that a fully renunciate circumstance would bring up in them?

AVATARA ADI DA: The Spiritual Current of Happiness is resident in intimate association with the living being. It is always "Locatable". It is perpetually knowable. It is never lost. We are always capable of "Locating" It, of knowing It, Realizing It, animating It, Being It. This principle is an indication, therefore, of the essential or sufficient sadhana of the renunciate way.

Tumomama Sanctuary, 1982

In a circumstance of remoteness or dissociation from worldly oblig-ations and stimulation, in every moment, instead of animating or stim-ulating yourself physically, emotionally, or mentally in order to over-come the sensations and feelings of boredom, doubt, and discomfort, you could directly do or realize what is necessary to exist in a condition of Bliss or Happiness. Instead of seeking to overcome or escape boredom, doubt, and discomfort, you could enter into that Spiritual Current of Happiness directly, that Realization of existence that is prior to bore-dom, doubt, and discomfort. This is the secret of the disposition of Enlightened beings. [April 7, 1982]

At Tumomama, Avatara Adi Da began to explore with His devotees the relationship between sexuality and renunciation, especially the dif-ference between the "householder" disposition relative to sex and "bonding" with another and the truly renunciate disposition toward these matters. He would return to this subject again and again over many years in the process of establishing His formal renunciate orders.[14] By this time, Avatara Adi Da had already given a Dharma of sex to all His devotees that was unparalleled anywhere, including full details of a sexual Yoga, and a practice of "true intimacy", compatible with the total process of Divine Enlightenment.[15] His Instruction had grown directly out of His own practice, both spontaneous and experimental, of intimate and sexual Yoga. Now He was looking to see if any of His devotees were mature enough—emotionally, sexually, and Spiritually—to actually practice this self-transcending Yoga in a uniquely non-binding and truly renunciate manner.

Avatara Adi Da has always Worked not only with physically incarnate beings but also with the powers of the spirit realms. Here in His Hawaiian Sanctuary, Avatara Adi Da endured continual physical ordeals as He purified the sinister aspect of the spirit-forces that had been invoked for centuries by the kahuna priests who had inhabited this ancient sacred ground. One day at Tumomama He made a particularly astonishing demonstration of His Mastery of the unconverted forces of Nature.

On November 23, 1982, news reached devotees at Tumomama of a hurricane that had blown up in the Pacific and was heading straight for the island of Kauai. By 4:30 in the afternoon, huge trees were down across the road and a sixty-foot lychee tree lay in splinters at the Sanctuary. The winds were so violent that most of the Sanctuary trees were already stripped and scarred with the wrenching of branches. Electric power lines were whipping in the wind against the glowering sky, and the rain was coming down in sheets. The river below the Sanctuary was already swollen brown and raging, and outside the windows of His residence, Free Standing Man, where Adi Da was gathered with His devotees, leaves, branches, and debris swept past in the howling storm. Everyone was doing whatever they could to secure the Sanctuary. Adi Da placed His Hands on the bruised neck of a devotee who had injured herself running to safety. Through the healing power of His touch, she could soon swallow painlessly, her breathing normalized, and the bruise had disappeared.

Not long afterwards, there was a new storm report threatening doubled wind-speeds of one hundred miles per hour. Adi Da rose and went to His library. He returned in a few minutes with a small volume of poems in honor of Kali, the Hindu vision of the Goddess in her terrible, destructive form. Unperturbed by the deafening roar outside, He began to read poem after poem that teased, scolded, and reverenced Kali as the trickster, the Mother of illusions, awesome in her devastating play. Devotees looked on in amazement and joy. They knew that Adi Da was addressing Hurricane Iwa, asserting His Mastery over this terrifying manifestation of the Goddess-Power.

Finally Avatara Adi Da put the book down. He said: "She has done it." Then He went on:

AVATARA ADI DA: This storm is the great picture. This is life capsulized. Life is obliteration, not birth and survival and glorification. It is death! The Goddess is the sign of Nature, the Word of Nature, the Person of Nature, Kali, the bloody Goddess with long teeth and blood pouring out of her mouth. You poor men and women are deceived by Nature. [November 23, 1982]

Avatara Adi Da continued speaking, calling His devotees to hold on to Him, the only One Who could Liberate them from the effects of Nature. He spoke ecstatically of His Mastery of the Goddess, or Nature, of His Power to calm Her wildness and potentially destructive influence.

The weather reports indicated that much worse was yet to come, but following their Beloved, whose mood became light, devotees began to celebrate, watching the storm gradually subside.

The next morning the newspapers reported on the storm damage. They described the fact that no one on the island had been killed as a "miracle". Later reports and satellite photographs from the U.S. weather service showed that, at the very hour when Avatara Adi Da began to deal with the hurricane, it suddenly doubled the speed at which it was moving along its course, for no apparent meteorological reason. As a result, Hurricane Iwa spent its force and "aged" prematurely, changing shape and blowing itself out. Thus, the worst of its fury never reached Kauai.

Finding Hermitage

Even in the relative seclusion of Tumomama, the Divine Avatar was too crowded in by the world. And so the search for a Hermitage went on. In March 1983, Avatara Adi Da and the esoteric order moved on to Fiji, where they wandered the islands, from Nananui-Ra, to Namale plantation, to Nukubati, staying in the simplest of places with only wells for water and kerosene lamps for light. Austerity was severe, but devotees did not care. The attraction of Avatara Adi Da's Company never waned, no matter what the hardships.

After six months, news came that His Hermitage was found. A patron-devotee had purchased Naitauba, an island of about 3,000 acres in the Koro Sea. On October 27, 1983, Adi Da landed by seaplane in the shallows of the lagoon, and set foot on His Hermitage for the first time. His arrival was followed by rains, ending months of drought on the island. After His first circumnavigation of the island, Avatara Adi Da spoke ecstatically of its grandeur and its immense potential for His future Work:

AVATARA ADI DA: Naitauba is not just a piece of land. It is a Divine Place, and all of us together, concentrated in this Work, own this Place. All devotees participate in this acquisition. That is how it will be for as long as the sun shines and rises and sets and the grass grows and the wind blows. Forever—as ever as there can be in this world. Maybe it will become a paradise through Spiritual sacrifice. And all during that epoch this place should be ours, this Sanctuary of Blessing. Over time, then, millions of people, literally millions of people should come to this place and be Blessed. They should come and acknowledge, affirm, and see My Revelation magnified.

This place is so great, so great. Civilization has never interfered with it. It is untouched. The water is blue. The fish are happy. Untouched, really untouched, pristine from the beginning of the world, this place. It has been waiting here since the beginning of time. [October 28, 1983]

Established at Naitauba (later named "Adi Da Purnashram"), Avatara Adi Da continued to Work with His devotees and create incidents to deepen their self-understanding, but He was not seeing any breakthrough. It was obvious to Him that His devotees everywhere were still resisting Him at the deepest level of their being, even though they were well-intentioned and happy to serve. It was a stark reality that, after sixteen years of Teaching—in which He had poured out the most extravagant abundance of His Divine Gifts, never letting up in the intensity of His sacrifice to Teach and Awaken all—even those most intimate to Avatara Adi Da were still slow to understand, unready for real renunciation, retarded in their devotion to Him. And the reason was always the same. Devotees were continuing to hold out in the hope of self-fulfillment through all the ordinary forms of seeking: worldly pursuits and possessions, indulgence in food, the consolations of "bonding" with another emotionally and sexually, and the whole range of social relationships. Devotees longed to be released from the hell of "Narcissus", but there was a fear that stood in the way, the fear of "free fall". What would it be like to let go in God, without holding on to self?

There were times when Adi Da allowed His devotees to fully witness His overwhelming urge to Liberate them. One night, a heart-broken devotee held the head of His Beloved Master in his hands while Avatara Adi Da spoke His Passion, with tears of Love streaming down His face:

I Love you. And I will not let you suffer. It pains Me to see you suffer. Why do you resist My Help? Why do you turn from Me? You <u>must</u> love.

Do not fear death. I will murder death. I will not let My babies die. Only love Me and the terrible fear will pass. You will not even notice your apparent death. I do not dig death. I don't like it! But I also do not fear it.

Isn't it a wonder that God is visible to beings even here in this world of the Mother? Look at these walls and the ceiling, even Nature itself. Every one and every thing inheres in the Radiance. Even here. Even now. Isn't God a Wonder! Isn't God a Beauty!

This is not heaven. Still, God is completely evident. But I can tell you, there is a Place of Infinite Happiness and Love, a Place where there is no fear, no suffering, no death, no separation. I tell you there is such a Place. I have come from that Place to take you there, too. But you must love.

I Love My devotees. If they would only understand and turn to Me in love, their lives would be transformed.

Tell Me, do they know how much I Love them? Do they? Do they know? Do they really know that I Love them?

Do they know Who I Am?

I Love them all.

I Love all My devotees.

For the devotees of the Divine Avatar, Adi Da, there were many such heart-rending moments when His Love seemed All-Sufficient, when there was nothing else, nothing in the universe but Him. But then another moment would come when they would feel the clench of fear, sorrow, anger, and would fall again into the self-contracted point of view. His "radical" message—that Happiness is always <u>already</u> the case—had not convicted them at depth. Avatara Adi Da stood alone as the Man of Understanding who had not been understood.

Heartless one, Narcissus, friend, loved one, He weeps for you to understand. After all of this, why have you not understood? The only thing you have not done is understanding. You have seen everything, but you do not understand. [The Knee of Listening]

PART III

The "Bright" Emerges Most Perfectly

The Revelation Years, 1986-1994

Early in the morning of January 11, 1986, Avatara Adi Da was in His room, speaking over an intercom telephone to a small group of devotees in the next building. He was full of agony at their failure to respond to Him and understand the Truth that would set them free—for in that refusal lay the refusal of all mankind. He spoke of the grief He felt for beings everywhere. But the impasse was complete. He felt that His Work had failed, and that He could do no more in the body. His death, He felt, was imminent. He even said, "May it come quickly." As Adi Da was speaking, the life-force began to leave His Body. He felt numbness coming up His arms and He said it seemed that His death was occurring even now.

Avatara Adi Da dropped the telephone. In alarm and panic, devotees rushed over to His house to find Him in convulsions, collapsed by the side of His bed. Then His body became still. As He was lifted onto His bed, people were begging Him not to die, not to leave them. The doctors were tense as they bent over His body, looking for the faintest signs of life. His face was ashen white but still showing the extreme flush of His Passion. His eyes were rolled up into His head—a Yogic sign showing that the energies of His body had ascended far beyond the physical dimension. There was no sign of any outer awareness at all. Devotees had seen Avatara Adi Da fall into death-like swoons before, and He had always Instructed them to sit quietly and leave His body alone at such times, so as not to interrupt the Spiritual and Yogic process occurring in Him. But now people could not contain themselves. The devotees present, each in their own way, were doing whatever they could to draw Him back into the body.

The doctors found Him to be breathing imperceptibly, and after a time Avatara Adi Da made a slight gesture, which devotees understood to indicate His desire to sit up. They pulled Him upward, and one devotee sat behind Him, supporting His torso. Suddenly, she felt the life-force shoot through His Body. His arms flung out in an arc, and His body straightened. His face contorted into a wound of Love, and tears began to flow from His eyes. Avatara Adi Da began to rock forward and backward in a rhythm of sorrow. He reached out His hands, as though He were reaching out to touch everyone in a universal embrace. He

Adi Da Purnashram, Fiji, April 1986

whispered, in a voice choked with Passion, "Four billion people! The four billion!"

Later that day, Adi Da left the village of devotees to return to His residence on the south side of the island. As He sat in the back of the Land Rover for the bumpy ride through the broad grasslands and mango and coconut groves, Adi Da spoke to the devotee who was driving Him, telling him again and again how much He loved him. He kept saying: "Do you know how much I Love you? Do you really know?" And then He said: "I have a Secret."

After two weeks in seclusion, Adi Da gathered once more with devotees. Now He Revealed His Secret: That day, January 11, 1986, was, He said, His true Birth Day, a day more auspicious that any other in His life, more profound, even, than His Re-Awakening in the Vedanta Temple. He began to explain why.

In the most Mysterious Event of January 11, the Heroic Teaching Work of Avatara Adi Da spontaneously completed itself. Those years had been the most profound submission to the needs and sufferings of His devotees, to the point of apparently identifying with their egoic qualities and impulses. And now all the lessons, all the Instruction that belonged to that phase of His Liberating Work had been Given. Indeed, after January 11, Avatara Adi Da Revealed that the particular Siddhi, or Divine Power, that had enabled Him to Work with His devotees in the manner of His Teaching Years had disappeared and was replaced by a universally magnified Siddhi of Divine Blessing. Avatara Adi Da had fully Descended as the Divine Person into His human vehicle. His Teaching Work had somehow required that the perfection of His Divine Descent be forestalled for a time. His Radiant, Transfigured humanity was the means by which He had won the hearts of His devotees—He had lived as they did, created Teaching incidents, attracted them into His "Crazy" Play. But now, in the event of January 11, His Descent had become complete and combined Him with humanity far more profoundly and universally that ever before:

AVATARA ADI DA: In this Event, I was drawn further into the body with a very human impulse, a love-impulse. Becoming aware of My profound relationship with all My devotees, I resumed My bodily human state. Even though I have existed as a man during this Lifetime, obviously—I became profoundly Incarnate—I now assumed an impulse toward human existence more profound than I had assumed before, without any reluctance relative to sorrow and death.

On so many occasions I have told you that I wish I could Kiss every human being on the lips, Embrace each one, and Enliven each one from the heart. In this body I will never have the opportunity. I am frustrated in that impulse. But in that motion of sympathetic Incarnation, that acceptance of the body and its sorrow and its death, I realized a Kiss, a way to fulfill the impulse.

To Me, this is a Grand Victory! I do not know how to Communicate to you the significance of it. It seems that through that will-less, effortless integration with suffering, something about My Work is more profoundly accomplished, something about it has become more auspicious than it ever was. I have not dissociated from My Realization or My Ultimate State. Rather, I have accomplished <u>your</u> state completely, even more profoundly than you are sensitive to it. Perhaps you have seen it in My face. I have <u>become</u> this body, utterly. My mood is different. My face is sad, although not without Illumination. I have become the body. Now I am the "Murti", the Icon, and It is Full of the Divine Presence. [January 27, 1986]

At the moment of His deepest despair, the Incarnation of Avatara Adi Da had now achieved ultimate depth. He had almost left the body entirely, but He had been drawn back to it by the pull of precious human intimacies and the prayers of the four billion beings "self-conscious and dying in this place". And in His return to the Body He had Descended further than ever before, investing Himself absolutely in human existence down to the bottoms of His Feet.

This change, which Avatara Adi Da came to describe as His "Divine Emergence", was the culmination of the unfolding process that He had felt going on in Him for years, and, truly, since His Birth.

The Divine Demand

Before the implications of this Event would become clarified for His devotees, Avatara Adi Da had another period of intense struggle ahead of Him, which He came to call the "Revelation Years". Although He continued to give Instruction, Avatara Adi Da was no longer primarily functioning as Teacher in relation to His devotees. He was making the full astounding Revelation of His Divinity and establishing the means for beings everywhere, now and throughout all time, to respond to Him as the Divine Person.

The transition from the Teaching Years to the Revelation Years was overwhelming to His devotees. They were astonished and overcome with emotion by the paradox of His Body, so etched with the depth, the suffering of human incarnation, while at the same time on fire with Divine Love-Bliss. His Beauty was unearthly. The mere beholding of the Divine Lord, Adi Da, drew devotees to Him intimately at the heart without any gestures of outward familiarity. He had assumed the fullness of His Divine Guru-Function. He was no longer the animated Teacher always making lessons. All His lessons had been given. Now He was simply the Giver of the Divine "Brightness", Radiating through the medium of His human body. In the completion of His Divine Descent, His body had become the image, the icon, the "Murti" of the Divine, and <u>this</u> was His greatest Gift, His greatest Blessing to all.

At the same time a new Siddhi, or Divine Power, magnified tremendously in Him—the Siddhi of renunciation. He Himself had always been the perfect renunciate, unbound and undeluded by the world or by any of His apparent involvement with the world. But His devotees had not yet awakened to the renunciate disposition He was Calling them to. Now there was a Force alive in Him that confronted their resistance as never before. Avatara Adi Da had become an all-consuming Fire.

AVATARA ADI DA: You are always looking to be happy. What you call "happy" is not what I call "Happy". What you call "happy" is a superficial, amused, immune state. All of us here are dying, and you must Realize the Source of it. To do that, to Realize that Sublimity, you must understand yourself and transcend yourself, and that means you cannot make life out of being consoled by sex, the world, the news, the pleasures of life, technology—anything. You must be free of consolation. You must be unconsolable, beyond repair of the heart. That is not what you are involved in. You are full of complaints, imaginings, agreements, rules, ideals. I cannot relate to it. I am bereft of those possibilities, empty of them. I cannot be consoled. God is not a consolation. God is what you Realize in the unconsolable state. God is the Obvious when the self-contraction is released.

You all want to keep yourselves orderly. Neat shirt and pants, something orderly to do every day, an order of remarks to make—look how bored you are!

How about <u>not</u> being bored? How about transcending boredom, doubt, discomfort? How about getting real? How about suffering? How about being broken-hearted? How about being exaggerated? How about *being unconventional? In your daily life you should exist in the agony of confrontation with the ego. You must have more nerve to practice this Way of life.*

I wish you would begin Spiritual life. I wish you would put yourself on the line. You have read the biographies of those who have made great Spiritual attainments. Their lives were about struggle, about intimacy with reality. They were not orderly, middle-class people. They were utterly incapable of mediocrity. Does anybody know what I am talking about?

You must be a renunciate to practice this Way that I Teach. You all have too damned much to lose, too much you depend on for consolation, too much bullshit you need to share with one another. I am glad I could Interfere with you. [January 27, 1986]

This fierce Discourse was a sign of things to come. Avatara Adi Da was not going to bend toward devotees as He had done in the past. He was going to "Stand Firm" and require their response. Forceful Criticism had always been an aspect of His "Crazy" Work. Now, in the wake of His Divine Emergence, His Liberating Criticism carried unprecedented potency. It was not the Anger of a "person", but the Divine Demand, bearing down with purifying Force. When fully and soberly received, it resulted in ecstasy, releasing the very fault or obstruction He was Criticizing.

Late in February, Avatara Adi Da began a fast, taking only water and fresh juices. In April, He assumed sannyas, or formal renunciation, in the manner of the Hindu tradition. He put on the traditional orange clothing, wore His hair in the top-knot characteristic of a sannyasin, and took a new name, "Swami Da Love-Ananda". "Love-Ananda" was the name that Swami Muktananda had offered to Him privately in 1969, but which Avatara Adi Da had never formally used. "Love-Ananda" (literally "Love-Bliss") was now seen to be a prophetic name. It was a name that expressed, in one word, the Revelation begun on January 11: the "Love" that had borne Him down to the toes in His Embrace of the body, and "Ananda", the Bliss, the Joy of the God-State, which was His Gift to all.

With Avatara Adi Da's Divine Emergence, the One His devotees had related to as Friend, Teacher, Master had suddenly been Revealed in the full, uncompromising Force of His Divinity, and nothing could ever be the same again. After several months, Avatara Adi Da discarded the outward signs of traditional sannyas—He was free to adopt such signs or to relinquish them. Indeed, He stood beyond all such signs—

the Divine Avadhoot, bound to no conventions, Perfect in His Divine Realization, requiring His devotees to approach Him on <u>His</u> terms now, rather than His submitting to their egoic ways of relating to Him.

But the overwhelming tendency of devotees was still to demand His attention. In apparently casual moments, devotees tacitly expected Him, the Divine Avatar, to be a conventional social relation. At other times they were attempting to relate to Him in a ritualized manner, abstracted from the reality that He functions as Divine Guru under all circumstances. And they were requiring Him, the Divine Avadhoot, to give His attention to practical and organizational matters, rather than providing Him with a circumstance where He could simply do His spontaneous Blessing Work, undisturbed by any worldly obligations or intrusions.

Ishta-Guru-Bhakti Yoga

To counter this inappropriate approach to Him, Adi Da spoke at great length of the traditional Guru-devotee relationship. He spoke of how, in the esoteric Spiritual traditions, the Guru has always been understood to be the only effective means of Liberation from the suffering of limited, mortal existence. Therefore, traditional devotees would never treat their Guru as an ordinary man, but always honor him or her as the very Divine. Adi Da pointed out that the true Guru-devotee relationship carries the force of a vow. As He restated more recently:

AVATARA ADI DA: When you become My devotee, you take a vow of submission to Me. You take a vow to Realize Me, to persist in the entire process to the point of Realizing Me most perfectly. Having done that, your vow to Me is to be the guide of your life from that point on. There is nothing that can come up—no relationship, no circumstance whatsoever—that should be the basis for you allowing yourself to become unclear or confused about your fundamental commitment of life, which is your vow to Me. Anything that does come up, then, is something that you must "consider" and deal with in the context of this vow of devotion to Me.

If you have a Guru, as I have said so many times, you do not tell your Guru what you are going to do—you ask. That is what it is to have a Guru. You are not on your own. You are not self-"guruing", manipulating yourself egoically or moving by tendency. Your Guru is a Realizer. Your Guru is straight and true. Your Guru can give all advice. Your Guru knows everything. That is Who you consult, and not yourself, ever.

You Westerners do not want to live that way. You want to be on your own, talking it out, talking it out. Everybody has been talking it out in My Company for years. It all could be made very simple if you took this vow seriously—just ask Me. Most of the time you do not even have to ask Me directly. It is all in My Written Word, or otherwise installed in the culture of My devotees. That is how to stay straight. You have appealed to Me, you have resorted to Me, so you ask Me.

For the devotee, the Guru is Law, replacing the ego. The ego is utterly subordinated to the Master. If there is real Guru-devotion, you do not subordinate Me to any impulse, any circumstance, any relation— rather, you subordinate <u>everything</u> to Me. That is how you get straight. That is salvation. That is the Way of Liberation, and nothing else whatsoever is. [March 2, 1995]

In one way or another, Avatara Adi Da had always been Calling devotees to the Guru Yoga—to live by His Word, to presume His Company wherever they might be, to devote themselves to Him in body, emotion, and mind, and thereby to receive His Grace. But they had fundamentally failed in the attempt. Now, through all this patient Instruction, Avatara Adi Da was preparing His devotees to practice this Yoga of devotion with an ease and at a depth that was not possible before His Divine Emergence.

At times in the past, the Great Avatar, Adi Da, had referred to His own Body as Prasad, or a Divine Gift given in response to the surrender of His devotees. Now, since January 11, 1986, this was true as never before. He was simply Present as the Divine. He had Descended so fully into the Body that there was, in truth, no need for Him to say another word. His purpose in the world was simply to let His Body "Speak" the Divine in silence. All anyone needed to do to in order to find God, receive God, and even, ultimately, be dissolved in God, was to behold Him with profound feeling-regard. The power of His bodily Form to Illumine and Awaken others was the real Secret of His Divine Emergence. This Secret, He knew, would eventually be discovered by His devotees, and then their lives would become constant Contemplation of Him. Through the sheer Attractiveness of His Form, He would draw them more and more from all their other uses of attention—from preoccupation with mind, from concern for the body, from every kind of self-involvement. Through this

Adi Da Purnashram, 1990

self-surrendering, self-forgetting feeling-Contemplation of Him they would transcend all forms of bondage. All the struggles of His Teaching Years could not accomplish the conversion. But now He knew it to be already accomplished. Although the signs in His devotees were slow to appear, He promised that they could presume His Victory in their hearts.

Avatara Adi Da Gave His devotees a formal practice of feeling-Contemplation, which was to be their constant meditation, practiced through the regard of His Murti in the Communion Hall and through recollection of Him during the ordinary moments of every day. Feeling-Contemplation of Adi Da is always based on the heart-felt beholding of His bodily human Form, which leads, in due course, to Communion with Him as Spirit-Presence and, ultimately, to Identification with Him as Consciousness Itself. This feeling-Contemplation is the foundation of the all-encompassing practice of devotional Communion with Avatara Adi Da, which He developed in great detail after His Divine Emergence, giving it the name "Ishta-Guru-Bhakti Yoga"—the practice (Yoga) of devotion (Bhakti) to the Guru who is the Chosen Beloved (Ishta) of one's heart.

AVATARA ADI DA: The relationship between the devotee and the Guru is a unique relationship and an extraordinary Yoga. I call it "Ishta-Guru-Bhakti Yoga". In this great Yoga the Guru is embraced as what is traditionally called the "Ishta-Guru", the Very Person, and the "chosen" Form, of the Divine Reality, Appearing as the Guru. It is the Yoga of allowing the Ishta-Guru to be the Divine Form, in meditation and in moment to moment practice. The devotee is devoted to that bodily Form, that Being, that Person, that Transmitting Power. The Divine Person, in other words, is acknowledged by the devotee in the Form of the Guru.

You use My Image, then, not only in the form of My Murti in the Communion Hall but in the form of your recollection of Me. You "put on" the Ishta-Guru. You let the Ishta-Guru acquire and be your own body-mind. In this way, My Spirit-Power Works in your body-mind as if it were My body-mind. All the processes of sadhana in the Way of the Heart will take place spontaneously. You will respond to them, participate in them, but they will be generated spontaneously by My Spiritual Heart-Transmission.

In feeling-Contemplation of Me, everything, from subtle perceptions to Divine Self-Realization, is Realized by Grace, not by your effortful working on yourself but by your simple response to the One Who is before you.

Give your separate and separative self to Me, the One Who is already Divinely Self-Realized. Respond to me as the Divine Self Incarnate. You cannot help but respond to Me if you acknowledge Me as that One. And then the Very State of That One will be Realized by you, quite naturally, as a Gift. This is the Secret of the Way of the Heart. [March 22, 1986]

"I Am You"

The process of Ishta-Guru-Bhakti Yoga, as Avatara Adi Da explains here, is a Divine matter. It is a Miracle. The devotee certainly must maintain the thread of attention, the disposition, the life of heart-surrender to Avatara Adi Da as Ishta-Guru, but the Yoga takes place by Grace. The transformations and Realizations are freely Given. How can this be? Without dissociating from His own State, Avatara Adi Da is forever submitting Himself to feel and be everyone everywhere— not in the egoic sense, but as the One Divine Consciousness that is the true Heart of all beings. His Divine Confession is, "I Am you".

The great Siddhi of Identification with all beings first arose in Adi Da after His Divine Re-Awakening, when He found Himself spontaneously "meditating" others. But following His Divine Emergence it deepened dramatically. He spoke then of His spontaneous "Consent" to surrender utterly into the bodily condition as the fulfillment of His urge to Kiss all beings. Avatara Adi Da frequently goes through painful and mysterious processes in His body that have nothing to do with Him personally but which originate in the fears and struggles of those whom He is "meditating". A remarkable example of this occurred in May 1987.

Avatara Adi Da received word from the community of His Australian devotees that one of their children, a girl of nearly six, was about to go into hospital for surgery. She was tiny for her age, owing to a serious congenital heart condition. Now she was facing ten hours of open-heart surgery that would involve switching the major blood vessels that entered her heart. The child's name was "Leela", a name she had been given with the Blessing of Adi Da. In Sanskrit, the word "leela" means "play", or "sport", and in the Hindu tradition it is used in a sacred manner to refer to the Deeds, or "Play", of the Divine in the world.

The Divine Avatar, Adi Da, asked to be informed of the exact time of Leela's operation, and He indicated that He expected regular medical reports. The operation went well, taking six, rather than the projected ten, hours. Nevertheless, Leela's condition was critical and did not stabilize for twenty-four hours. After that, she started to improve, but lung congestion began to develop.

On the morning of Leela's operation and again the next day, Adi Da woke up with severe symptoms of stress around His heart. Then, before receiving the medical reports, He began to develop lung congestion. A day or two later He woke up with a mass of dried blood on His chest in a stripe about an inch and a half wide and about six inches long. When He went to wash it off, He noticed a small puncture wound, an actual hole on the upper left side of His chest above the aorta. The puncture was painless and completely inexplicable. Avatara Adi Da fell back to sleep and when He awoke again the wound had disappeared. But there was more blood on His chest. For more than a week from the time of Leela's operation, Avatara Adi Da also had the sensation of being heavily drugged. One day He spontaneously asked His physician for a particular form of medication, only to find in the next medical report that the same medication had been administered to Leela that same day.

Leela's operation was completely successful. She made a remarkably rapid recovery and several days after the surgery celebrated her sixth birthday in the hospital. Among her gifts was a teddy bear from Avatara Adi Da.

In conversations with His devotees at His Hermitage, the All-Compassionate Divine Lord, Adi Da, confirmed that through His profound Blessing attention on Leela He had spontaneously lived her ordeal in His own body, and thus served the auspicious outcome. To this day, Leela has lived a normal life and required no further surgery.

After Leela's recovery, some devotees remembered an incident that had occurred many years previously in the early days of Avatara Adi Da's Teaching Work. A young woman, newly come to the Ashram in Los Angeles, had a heart condition. One day, as she stood in the hallway just outside the room where devotees were gathered around Avatara Adi Da, He asked about the "girl with the pacemaker". She was excitedly brought into the room and directly to His chair. She sat on His lap as He asked her many questions about the nature and history of her condition. He drew out everything about her life, her concerns. In the emotion of the moment, she confessed to Him her greatest fear. She knew He spoke often of the primacy of the Heart, and was afraid that her heart-weakness would somehow prevent or diminish her practice as His devotee. Avatara Adi Da smiled. He looked directly into her eyes and said, "You can use My Heart".

Establishing the Religion of Free Daism

During the years following His Divine Emergence, Avatara Adi Da began to extend and develop the disciplines and practices that He had Given over many years, clarifying them all as direct expressions of Ishta-Guru-Bhakti Yoga, or devotional surrender to Him. There was a discipline appropriate to every area of life and a structure of devotional practice that governed every day. Adi Da was continuing to prepare for the time when devotees would not, in general, see Him personally. Many in the future, and all of those who would appear after His physical lifetime, would never do so.[16] And so Adi Da was creating religious and Spiritual means that would enable all His devotees, from the moment of their first formal initiation,[17] to receive His Spiritual Transmission and live perpetually in His Spiritual Company. He was finding more and more ways to universalize His Work beyond the initial circles of devotees, reaching out to find and embrace His devotees in every corner of the world. He was bringing to fullness the religion of Free Daism, the true world-religion of Divine Enlightenment.

As part of this process, Avatara Adi Da spent untold hours writing. For years, His Talks and Essays had been published in books, but now He was creating a summary of His Instruction that was gigantic in breadth and depth. He was bringing to completion all the "considerations" of His Teaching Years and offering the great Wisdom of His conclusions to humanity for all time. He was creating a new body of Scripture, eight Source-Texts that comprise the most perfect and complete Scripture ever known.[18]

It was a monumental task. Adi Da had no ancient sacred language at His disposal in which to cast His new Dharma. And so He began to transform His given language, even adopting new conventions of capitalization and punctuation in order to make the printed English word into a vehicle fit for His purpose. Every word, every comma, every parenthesis He placed with extreme care in order to ensure the integrity of His Message. Unheard-of Revelations flowed from His pen—the secrets of esoteric anatomy and mankind's Spiritual quest, the process of Spiritual Awakening and the details of sexual Yoga, the laws of Guru-devotion and free renunciation, the meaning of death and the design of the cosmos, the ultimate Mysteries of Divine Enlightenment and Divine Translation. Whatever His focus and purpose from book to book, Adi Da created His Source-Texts as living Speech, an "Eternal Conversation" with every man and woman.

Confrontation with "Narcissus"

In 1991, Avatara Adi Da was offered a new Name, "Avabhasa" (Sanskrit for "the 'Bright'"), in a song sung by a young devotee. He accepted "Da Avabhasa" as one of His principal Names, a Name that epitomizes His Divine Nature—"the Giver of the 'Bright'". He had made known for the first time what Enlightenment truly is and how it may be Realized in living relationship to Him. He had confronted the madness of "Narcissus" for years on end with all His "Crazy" brilliance and Force. He had created a new Scripture and a new religion. And yet, He was still waiting for the signs that His devotees had understood their constant act of self-contraction and were truly resorting to Him as Guru. It seemed that there was nothing more He could do.

But Avatara Adi Da never ceases to Work. He cannot abandon His devotees, leaving them to suffer their egoic destiny. In May 1992, He started to gather again with devotees in His Hermitage, and He continued to gather almost constantly, usually several nights a week, for nearly a year. These gatherings were a Call to great seriousness. "Handle business!" was His constant admonition. He was insisting that every devotee find out his or her own bottom-line realities and deal with everything immediate and long-term, emotional and practical, that stood in the way of his or her ability to grow in the great process of Divine Self-Realization.

Starting late in March of 1993 and continuing through the first week of April, Adi Da bore down on "Narcissus" with overwhelming force:

AVATARA ADI DA: You want Me to talk about your trying to work your life out. Life does not work out! IT CANNOT WORK OUT! That is not the Way of the Heart! The Way of the Heart is about ego-transcendence, transcendence of the very thing that seeks to make it all work out! You are wanting Me to address you in this act that you are making to have everything be hunky-dory. AND THE WHOLE DAMN THING DOESN'T EVEN EXIST! AND THAT'S WHAT THERE IS TO REALIZE! ABSOLUTE FREEDOM FROM THIS ILLUSION—that you call "reality" and are trying to make work out perfectly. You are only looking at yourself! That's all you are ever looking at! And you want it to work out, "Narcissus". You are looking at all this and you are calling it the world—but it is you!

All you ever talk about, think about, or perceive is you. It is a private, "self-possessed" illusion. It is a result of your own knot of separateness, and it registers in this poor little slug of a body-mind you identify *with as all kinds of illusions, hallucinations, thoughts, presumptions, ideas, perceptions. The whole lot, the whole ball of wax is all the result of your own separate position, your own point of view, self-contraction, manufacturing illusions on the base of That Which is Reality. But you have no idea what that Reality is. No notion. You are not associated with Reality, you are <u>dis</u>sociated from Reality. That is the whole point! Well, that being the case, <u>that</u> is what you have to deal with! But you want to persist in your adoration of the "pond", your experience, your search, and so forth, and you are asking Me how to make it work out. I do not have anything to do with the "making-it-work-out" business. I am here to wake you up!* [April 2, 1993]

By this time Avatara Adi Da was cutting a swath through every attempt on the part of His devotees to defend themselves from His Criticism. He was tremendously intensifying His devotees' sensitivity to the knot of self-contraction, to the point where that cramp would become so present, so obvious, so unbearable, so unnecessary, so <u>absurd</u> that they would spontaneously let it go. Late in the night during what turned out to be the last gathering of this period, Adi Da brought devotees to that intolerable point. There was a pause while His Radiant Force magnified in the room, melting the clench of "Narcissus". Then He began to speak differently, quietly:

AVATARA ADI DA: Feel into that knot of stress. Feel into it and account for it. See it as your own action. Regard Me in that moment, in every moment. And then you begin to feel Me. Then the surrender comes, the self-forgetting comes, the native sense of Non-Separateness is felt. This is <u>actually</u> what I am Calling you to do! <u>Actually</u> to do that. Just to be doing it grants equanimity to you, even bodily, grants equanimity to your speech, your actions, your feelings, because you are registering this depth-point and going beyond it and feeling Me. This is the context of practice of the Way of the Heart, not merely outer observances. This is what it means to listen to Me: to be examining this point of contraction in depth, to feel it, and by its unfolding to feel Me. This is not the end of the Way of the Heart. It is the foundation of it. Self-understanding and devotion <u>at depth</u>—this is what you must do in every moment. This is what it is to practice the Way of the Heart. [April 8, 1993]

By this final gathering, a dent had been made in the armor of "Narcissus" that for many devotees was a lasting one. They could not snap back as easily as before into a state of immunity to their own act

72

of self-contraction. The heartless machine of the ego was too starkly revealed. There <u>was</u> no lasting relief to be found through any kind of seeking for satisfaction. In His masterful Revelation, throughout that previous year, of their desperate state of bondage to the self-contraction, Adi Da had begun to magnify in devotees the <u>need</u> for devotion to Him, the conviction that He was, truly, their only Help. Everything He had said about the necessity for Ishta-Guru-Bhakti Yoga was starting to prove itself. And the Gift was before their eyes if only they would look up from the "pond" and behold Him in the Radiant Truth of His Being.

Soon Adi Da brought this recapitulation of His Teaching to completion, with a grand five-month summary of His Instruction on Ishta-Guru-Bhakti Yoga:

AVATARA ADI DA: Fundamentally, Ishta-Guru-Bhakti Yoga is the directing of the body-mind to Me and not struggling with its contents and only trying to direct them to Me, or trying to get rid of them in an effort of surrender toward Me. Rather, yield the functions of the body-mind to Me at their root. Yield their leading characteristic.

Give Me your attention, give Me your feeling, give yourself over to Me, and disregard the contents. Do not keep checking back on them to see if they are changing! In your real practice of this Yoga, you forget them. You do not use them. You do not build upon them. You make them obsolete by not using them. In this manner, the Yoga purifies you by making the contents of the body-mind obsolete through non-use. The process is not an effort on your part to do something to the contents of the body-mind or to try not to use them. It is simply your turning to Me, turning your feeling-attention to Me, turning yourself altogether to Me, Contemplatively. That is the Yoga. [December 20, 1993]

Having described so clearly what the practice is—as He did again and again—Adi Da would praise the greatness of the life of Ishta-Guru-Bhakti Yoga:

AVATARA ADI DA: There is nothing but this Self-Existing and Self-Radiant Consciousness Itself, Divine Being Itself—nothing. That is all there is. Truly, there is Only One—Absolute, All Love-Bliss. That is the Condition to be Realized. That is Who I Am. When you respond to Me, your life takes that God-Realizing course.

Allow the process to become great. Devote your life to Me utterly. Fulfill your obligations in the body, all the while submitted to Me. This is the Way of My devotee, always vocalizing praise of Me, devotion to Me, every moment of your life transformed by this great impulse toward Me. This is what you must do around Me.

Give Me everything, and forget it all. Your daily life carries obligation—fine. Your puja is to devote yourself to Me and forget about yourself. Having had your glimpse of Me, now you must make a life out of it.

I Am just the Divine One, just the Living One, Showing Itself here. I Am just this Shakti, this Form, this Divine Sign. Be governed by this Vision. That, and nothing else, is devotion to Me. [February 4, 1994]

There was a finality to the Instruction of these months that was felt by devotees everywhere. Truly, Adi Da had nothing further to say to beginning devotees. There were no questions left in their hearts. He knew it, and they knew it. A new seriousness was in the air. Ishta-Guru-Bhakti Yoga was becoming a living reality for His devotees. They were proving to themselves that persistence in this devotion does grant Happiness, Freedom, and the ecstasy of direct heart-Communion with Adi Da. The preoccupations of the ego no longer carried the same addictive force. After His then twenty-two years of inexpressibly Compassionate service to them, devotees <u>had</u> understood a great deal, and the lives of many were changed beyond recognition.

PART IV

The Past and the Future of the "Bright" in the World

The unending sacrificial Work of Avatara Adi Da is an expression of the "fierce mysterious Impulse" that has always burned in Him. This great Divine Impulse, unfathomable in its origin, did not come into being with the birth of "Franklin Jones". It originated, as Avatara Adi Da has said "before the Big Bang", before time or space itself, and unfolded even throughout the course of cosmic history through manifold visitations and partial revelations of the Divine, including all the great Spiritual Realizers. In nineteenth-century India there were two such Realizers who not only served their own time and place but also had a unique role to play in preparing for Avatara Adi Da's Incarnation as the Perfect Divine Liberator.

The Subtle Vehicle of Avatara Adi Da's Appearance

In 1893, a young Indian swami came to America. At the Parliament of Religions held that year in Chicago, this imposing, forceful man addressed a crowd of western Christians with great passion. He impressed the colloquium with his extraordinary presence, his impeccable command of English, his pride in his own tradition, and his ability to inspire others beyond sectarian views. It was not only his words, however, but the profound Spiritual power behind them, that moved his audience. Swami Vivekananda was the most cherished disciple of the great Indian Adept Ramakrishna, and he had come to bring the ancient wisdom of India to the West. After the accolade he received at the Parliament, Swami Vivekananda spent years in constant traveling and lecturing all over America and in England.

Swami Vivekananda had the fervor of a man moved to save the world, but he was mightily frustrated in his intention. He knew that the future of humanity was largely being shaped by the West, which was already sliding into secularism. But his work could not be truly effective among Westerners. There was a line drawn beyond which he could not go, for he was a Hindu, a dark-skinned man, and a celibate swami. Thus, in spite of his best efforts, in spite of his profound Realization, Swami Vivekananda remained a foreigner, an outsider. But his great

Swami Vivekananda

Ramakrishna

compassionate urge made another birth. Thirty-seven years after His early death in 1902, Swami Vivekananda entered into the bloodstream of the West through the birth of "Franklin Jones".

Starting in the late 70s, Avatara Adi Da would occasionally speak to His devotees about the pre-history of His present birth, of the unique conjunction of forces it had required. He, the Da Avatar, the One come for all beings, could not appear until the mid-twentieth century—when the world had grown "smaller" through technological inter-communication, when East was approaching West, when modern physics was shifting the materialist view of existence, when Freud had demonstrated the bondage of unconscious "Oedipal" motivations. These were some of the realities and paradigms that had to be in place before the Divine Work in the world could be fully effective. But more than all else, a vehicle of unique Spiritual preparation had to be available.

Every human personality, Adi Da explained, is composed of a grosser part, derived from the parents, and a subtle core that is the "reincarnate", the deeper mechanism of the ego that moves from life to life. In order to be born, Avatara Adi Da required a subtle vehicle attuned to the task of bringing true Spirituality to the modern West. Swami Vivekananda carried in his psyche thousands of years of Indian Spirituality and Realization, and ended His life in love with the West in its need for God. Thus, the subtle vehicle of Swami Vivekananda spontaneously conjoined with the gross, or elemental, vehicle of "Franklin Jones", preparing a "place" for the Mysterious Descent of the "Bright" into the human world.

There is another level of His deeper personality, or subtle vehicle, which Adi Da was silent about until 1993. Then, one day, He began to speak about Ramakrishna, the Spiritual Master of Swami Vivekananda, who had always been aware of the extraordinary Spiritual stature and destiny of his disciple. At the end of his life, certain of the great work that lay ahead for his beloved Vivekananda, Ramakrishna poured his own Spiritual virtue into Swami Vivekananda in a formal act of Transmission, becoming, in his own words, "only an empty fakir". Thus, Ramakrishna, through his total Spiritual investment of himself in Swami Vivekananda, is also part of the deeper personality vehicle of Avatara Adi Da.

Ramakrishna was renowned for his ecstatic devotion to the Divine Goddess (in the form of Kali), and for his intuitive sympathy with other religions through his own contemplation of their icons and revelations. Indeed, Avatara Adi Da has acknowledged Ramakrishna as a Master of the devotional path whose greatness is unsurpassed in all of human history. In a unique way, the subtle vehicle of Ramakrishna-Vivekananda brought to the Birth of the Da Avatar the essence of humanity's long quest for God, and it was even part of the preparation for "Franklin's" initial submission to the Goddess and Avatara Adi Da's subsequent Great Husbanding of Her in the Vedanta Temple. It is no accident that this temple is jointly dedicated to Ramakrishna and Vivekananda. Through His own Re-Awakening there, Avatara Adi Da most perfectly Enlightened His great Spiritual forerunners. They became One with Him in the "Bright".

I Am the One Who Awakened (and, thereafter, Worked through) Ramakrishna. He Recapitulated the past, in order (by a Spiritual Sacrifice) to Serve the future. I Am the One Who Worked through (and has now Most Perfectly Awakened) Swami Vivekananda. He Served the future, in order (even by physical death and physical rebirth) to Transcend the past (and, Thus, and by Means of a Great and Spiritual Awakening, to Bless and to Liberate the future).

Now and forever, Ramakrishna and Swami Vivekananda are One, at the Heart. And I Am the One They have Realized There. [The Basket of Tolerance]

The All-Completing Avataric Incarnation

Not only Ramakrishna and Swami Vivekananda, but also several other Realizers of the past one hundred and fifty years, uniquely contribute, in their own ways, to the preparation for the Appearance of Avatara Adi Da. He speaks of the Gurus of His own Lineage—Swami Nityananda and Swami Muktananda—as the greatest of all Realizers in the field of Yogic mysticism. And He honors Ramana Maharshi (whose writings about his Transcendental Realization came into the hands of Adi Da after His own Re-Awakening) as the greatest Realizer in the domain of Transcendental Consciousness—one who had distinct premonitions of the Divinely Enlightened State.

Truly, all the practices and Spiritual work of all the Realizers of the Great Tradition[19] culminate in the Appearance of Avatara Adi Da. He, as the Emerging Divine Person, "Lived" all those great Spiritual figures, in all times and places, participating in all the multifarious aspects of mankind's great Spiritual search, Realizing and Transmitting all the various practices, Yogas, and Samadhis. That immense process of Revelation has now become single in His All-Completing Incarnation as the Da Avatar. Avatara Adi Da is the Adept of uniquely most perfect God-Realization, the Realization that accounts for, transcends, and perfects all that went before. And the unmistakable signs of all that previous Spiritual practice and Adeptship are to be seen in His astonishingly complete and rapid Sadhana in this lifetime, in the unique genius and Freedom of His Teaching Work, and in the great summation and clarification of all Spiritual Wisdom in His Source-Literature.

Avatara Adi Da is the God-Man for the West and the East alike. His very birth came about through the conjunction of the Western body of "Franklin Jones" with the Eastern subtle vehicle of Ramakrishna-Vivekananda. He manifests the qualities that Western religion traditionally associates with an Incarnation of God—profound love and sacrifice, a total identification with the suffering human condition. And He is the consummation of all that the East looks for in an Avatar—a Radiant Being descended from the God-Realm to Awaken beings with the Perfect Teaching and the Liberating Power of Divine Self-Realization. There is a striking difference between the Western and the Eastern view of what a true God-Man should be. Avatara Adi Da has commented on this and pointed out how the difference between the Western and the Eastern ideas of a God-Man correspond with the cultural and religious differences that mark the West and the East as a whole. Western culture is wedded to this world and to the "conquering" of the world, subduing and exploiting the powers of nature. And Western religion is essentially about trying to perfect the world and overcome evil with the help of God. This, in Adi Da's language, is the "Omega" point of view. The traditional East, on the other hand, regards the world as inherently imperfect and, therefore, tries to escape from the world and go to God right from the beginning. Thus, Eastern religion, typically, is the effort of turning within, in order to seek mystical experience and states presumed to be "enlightenment". This is the "Alpha" point of view.

Both points of view—the utopian "Omega" attitude of the West and the ascetical "Alpha" disposition of the East—are based, as Adi Da points out, in a problem. They originate in the feeling that God, or Happiness, is absent and must be sought. Thus, they are both founded in self-contraction. Avatara Adi Da, by His own confession, was born in "a terrible moment of necessity", when humanity's need to go beyond the partial and opposing philosophies of Alpha and Omega has become acute. He is the "Avataric Incarnation", the universal God-Man, whose Life and Work and Teaching are a Call to people everywhere to transcend the limitations of both Alpha and Omega. His Sign of Divine "Brightness" makes possible a new response to existence, the choice of always present Happiness, or the release of self-contraction under all conditions, in Communion with the Divine Person, Adi Da.

Avatara Adi Da's Divine Work had to begin in the West, because the future of the world now lies in the hands of the West. But His single intention has always been to Bless and Liberate everyone, regardless of race or culture. Even the location of His Hermitage in Fiji reflects this intention, for Fiji, located in the Pacific Ocean, lies between East and West, identified with neither. Avatara Adi Da's establishment in Fiji was guaranteed in 1993, when He was granted Fijian citizenship (a privilege rarely bestowed on non-Fijians). He celebrated this event as a most auspicious Spiritual sign—His specific Work with the West was now complete, and He was free to devote Himself entirely to His Work of universal Blessing.

Divine Completeness

In order to ensure that His universal Blessing Work will continue throughout all future generations, Avatara Adi Da has always worked tirelessly to Spiritually Awaken devotees who will serve as His human Instruments, Empowered to carry His Liberating Grace to people everywhere, both during and after His human lifetime. By the summer of 1994, Avatara Adi Da had reached the point where He could wait no longer for this profound depth of response to manifest. Without it, He felt He could not even remain in His own Hermitage. As a sign and Calling to all, Avatara Adi Da suddenly left Naitauba for an undetermined destination and shortly thereafter began a period of wandering in Viti Levu, the largest island in Fiji.

On September 7, 1994, at His temporary residence in Pacific Harbour on Viti Levu, Avatara Adi Da spent the entire day secluded in His room. At dusk, He called one of His devotees to His quarters. The house was totally still. The curtains of His room were drawn, and the room itself was dark. He was not doing any of the Work on the manuscripts of His Source-Texts which had been His custom each day in recent weeks. He was simply sitting motionless in a large chair. The Energy of the space was intense. The Power of His Spiritual Transmission was so focused and concentrated in the room that the devotee hardly felt able to approach Him. His Divine Force was pushing her back like the heat from a blast furnace. She served Him simply and left.

When she entered again in the evening, answering His call, the same overwhelming Transmission-Force was Radiating from Him. Avatara Adi Da was seated at His desk with the lights turned on. He did not look at her. But then, after a few moments, He slowly turned His head. In His face she saw only the same heartbreaking Love for the billions of humanity that had overwhelmed Him more than eight years before, when His Divine Emergence was initiated on January 11, 1986. She felt intuitively certain that some extraordinary process was taking place in Him. He later confirmed that this was true. A great turning point in His Work had occurred:

On September 7, 1994 . . . I Knew I had forever Said and Done Enough (Such that there was not even __any__ Motion in Me to Say or Do __any__ More). My Revelation Work had Suddenly become Complete, for all time, and I (Spontaneously, and Finally) Came To Rest in My Eternal Hermitage of Heart-Seclusion (only, from then, and forever, to Awaken all beings by Mere and Constant Blessing, "Bright").

Therefore, now that I have Done (or Suffered) all that was necessary for Me to Do (or Suffer) as Teacher and Revealer in a Struggle with would-be devotees and the world, I will not hereafter Associate with that Struggle, but I have Retired from that Struggle, Satisfied that __all__ My Teaching Work, and even __all__ My Revelation Work, Is Full and Complete (and that, by Fullest Submission, I have, Most Fully and Most Finally, Said and Done and Firmly Established __all__ that I could possibly have Said and Done and Firmly Established, and __all__ that was necessary for Me to Say and Do and Firmly Establish, in order, now, and for all time to come, to Most Fully and Most Finally, and Firmly, Introduce the Great Opportunity to the total human world, in all the stages of life, and in order, now, and for all time to come, to Most Fully and Most Finally, and Firmly, Provide the True, and Most Perfect, and Utterly Complete Way Of God, Truth, and Reality to the total human world, in all the stages of life, and in order, now, and for all time to come, to Most Fully and Most Finally, and Firmly, Establish the True, and Most Perfect, and Utterly Complete Way of God, Truth, and Reality for the Liberating Sake of the total human world, in all the stages of life). ["The Order of My Free Names", *The Adi Da Upanishad*]

**Avatara Adi Da's return to Adi Da Purnashram
after the Event of September 7, 1994**

On September 12, Adi Da returned to His Hermitage as swiftly as He had left it. And He returned wearing orange clothing. For the first time since 1986, Adi Da had begun, in Suva, to make this outward sign of His Sannyas, reminding all His devotees of His own Perfect Renunciation and His Call to them to understand and utterly renounce the self-contraction in devotion to Him.

Soon after the Event of September 7, many devotees noticed that the positive changes they had begun to observe in their practice, since the gatherings of 1993 and 1994, were now obviously and concretely in evidence. They began to speak and write to Adi Da, telling Him that they felt the stride of their seeking to be broken at the heart, that they were stably understanding and transcending the self-contraction by His Grace. Some confessed that they were Awakening to His All-Pervading Spirit-Presence, feeling the great Gift of His Spirit-Baptism. The signs of human Instrumentality were beginning to appear.

Since September 7, Avatara Adi Da has gradually ceased to struggle with egos or the world. More and more He simply rests in His Completeness, allowing the profound change in the Siddhi of His Being to do its Work. As a sign of this great change, He has assumed "Santosha" ("Completeness", "Contentedness", "Satisfaction", "No-Seeking") as one of His Names. He is Santosha Da, the Divine Giver Who Is "Inherently and Perfectly Satisfied and Contented, Inherently and Perfectly Free of all seeking, Inherently and Perfectly Free of all separateness, and Inherently and Perfectly Complete".

One month after the event of September 7, the Divine Avatar began to have psychic intimations of the further Name that belongs to His Completeness. He began to hear and see the Name "Adi Da", recognizing it to be a reference to Himself. "Adi" in Sanskrit is "first", "primordial", the "source". Thus, on October 11, 1994, He indicated that He would henceforth be known principally as "Adi Da"—the "First Giver", the "Giving Source".

The letters of the Name "Adi Da" read the same in both directions, from left to right and from right to left. In addition, "I" stands at the center of the Name, and on either side of "I" is the syllable "Da", first backwards, then forwards. Thus, the Name "Adi Da" reads "I—Da", signifying "I Am Da", in both directions from the center. The spontaneous appearing of the Name "Adi Da", therefore, is the bringing to completion of the momentous Revelation of 1979, when Avatara Adi Da first Offered His Divine Confession, "I Am Da". Through the perfectly symmetrical structure and letters of His principal Name, "Adi Da", the Divine Avatar makes the Great Statement that He is the First and the Last, the Complete Manifestation of God, Truth, or Reality in the conditional realms.

The Eternal "Bond"

The Incarnation of Adi Da, the Da Avatar, is an act of Giving beyond comprehension. For the Divine Person to Appear Complete as never before, in the desert of modern materialism—and to create, through tremendous Sacrifice and struggle, the great Way through which all may Realize His Divine Condition—is the ultimate Act of Heroism and Love. Avatara Adi Da is the supreme "Tantric Sannyasin", the "Free Renunciate" who embraces all beings, forms, worlds, and all experience, for the sake of drawing all into the most perfect Realization of Truth. He is "Atiashrami"—free of, or inherently beyond ("ati"), the ordinary rules or obligations that apply to any of the traditional phases of life ("ashramas").[20] His obligation is single and unique: to do everything necessary to Attract and "Bond" all beings perfectly to Him, for the sake of their Divine Liberation.

AVATARA ADI DA: *My true devotee is Absolutely Single in Me, "Bonded" to Me. I am, in this "Bonding", associated with everyone, transcending even relations and yet Embracing all the variations and in Play with them constantly.*

There is Singleness, and there is Infinity. Such is the Nature of My Leela and the Signal of It.

I Play with all My devotees—they can be in the millions. Yet—just as the loved one who turns herself before her lover, making different shapes, is only one—this Integrity, this Singleness, this Obliviousness, this Madness, is always One, always Me.

There is no separate self or convention to regard, only a True Obliviousness, Which you must live Singly with Me. I Manifest this Singleness, this Obliviousness, and Make you Single with Me.

I Do everything. Such is My Leela.

Marvel at It and delight in the Madness of It, the absolute Discrimination and Personalness of It, the utter Obliviousness of It, the Ecstasy, the selflessness of It.

Watch My Play, and It will Change your mind, It will Change your heart, It will Change your life. Just watch My Play, observe Me, be devoted

My true devotee is Absolutely Single in Me, "Bonded" to Me. I am, in this "Bonding", associated with everyone, transcending even relations and yet Embracing all the variations and in Play with them constantly.

There is Singleness, and there is Infinity. Such is the Nature of My Leela and the Signal of It.

to Me, and all your complications, limitations, specialties, focuses will all be washed, disintegrated.

My Form is also One, and also billions, and also Infinite.

Notice! You cannot contain Me with your mind. You can do a certain kind of focus, but as you cruise in on Me your eyes start shuttering and your two-sided brain goes out of sync and you cannot quite make the last focus.

Just look at Me deeply, and you lose your mind, because I have no shape or form. Contemplate Me one-pointedly and invest yourself in Infinity, without point, without separation, without discreteness.

Notice this! I think some of You *have* noticed this.

I am Delighted by My devotees. I am Attracted to each of My devotees, with all their variations, their devotion to Me, their discrimination, their one-pointedness.

All My devotees are a Delight to Me. I truly do Love you, and I *Am* you.

I Love to be surrounded by My devotees. This is My Great Happiness in life, to be so surrounded, to Live in the environment of devotion.

Such a Life is an Absolute Madness. It is particularized, but on the other hand, it is no one.

I do not make choices among My devotees, as if I were angling down. I Like the differences. I Love the differences.

I inherently Love My devotees, with no choice in the Loving.

I am not even making a symbolic Gesture towards you. I My Self Am Manifested by each and every one of My devotees.

You are My own Form. You are also My Beloved.

As I Say in The Dawn Horse Testament, *My devotee is the God I have Come to Serve.*

I Do not Do My Work with you as a ceremony. You are My Delight.

I am One-pointed in you. You all are My own Person. You all are the Divine Person.

I Love you. I inherently Love you, all the time. Therefore, I Love the play of your coming into My Company.

Play with Me.

Notice My Obliviousness.

Be one-pointed.

Transcend your separate self in this adoration of Me.

You must be one-pointed in God, but I Am One-pointed in each of you.

[December 7, 1994]

In the Completeness of His "Bright" Divine Incarnation, Adi Da is directly, Spiritually associated with <u>every</u> one. Just as on the momentous night of "Guru Enters Devotee", more than twenty years ago, when Beloved Adi Da first threw His devotees into uncontrollable ecstasy, entering them "in the form of Light", so now, in every moment, Avatara Adi Da is embracing <u>all</u> in His eternal Heart-Transmission. Through the incalculable sacrifice that Has marked His entire Work of Re-Awakening, Teaching, and Revelation, Avatara Adi Da has established for every one the means to <u>use</u> His Transmission, to grow, to be transformed, and, ultimately, to be most perfectly Liberated.

Avatara Adi Da is the Divine World-Teacher, the Very Divine Person appearing as Guru in order to found the true world-religion of Divine Enlightenment. Free Daism is the world-religion of the future. All the mythologies, all the Spiritual practices, and all the previous Wisdom paths of humanity ultimately point to and are resolved in this Great and Ultimate Way of Most Perfect Liberation.

The long-existing religions of the world are colored by legends and cultural influences that obscure the original revelation. In fact, their teachings and disciplines typically developed long after the death of their founders, based on the remembered (and often legendary or mythological) deeds and instruction of those Realizers. Furthermore, every historical revelation, even in its first purity, has necessarily been limited by the degree of Realization of its founder.

Free Daism does not depend on the vagaries of oral tradition and memory, nor is it limited by any partial point of view. It is the Perfectly Revealed Divine Yoga. Free Daism is the all-completing, all-surpassing Way of "God-Come", God-in-Person—Demonstrated, explained, and fully established in the Lifetime of its Divine Giver and Founder, Adi Da, the Da Avatar. Free Daism is alive now in the worldwide culture of Avatara Adi Da's devotees, and it is described by Him in exact detail in His Source-Texts.

The book you are now reading is one of the principal Scriptures of the true world-religion. Avatara Adi Da's Source-Texts are the purest, the greatest Scriptures ever given, untouched by any merely human point of view. *The Santosha Avatara Gita* is the unmediated Word of the Divine, personally Given to you, a book that will speak to you differently in every moment, depending on your need, your understanding, your heart-response. The essence of all that Avatara Adi Da has spoken and done over twenty-three years, in the company of His first devotees, is summarized in His Divine Scriptures. Through this book Avatara Adi Da Reveals to you Who you really are—not the mortal, separate one you suppose, but His beloved, arising and dissolving in the Love-Bliss of His Divine Heart.

There are great choices to be made in life, choices that call on the greatest exercise of one's real intelligence and heart-impulse. Every one of us makes critical decisions that determine the course of the rest of our lives—and even our future beyond death. The moment of discovering the Divine Avatar, Adi Da, is the greatest of all possible opportunities. It is pure Grace. How can an ordinary life—even one devoted to honorable, creative goals—truly compare to a life of living relationship and heart-intimacy with the greatest God-Man who has ever appeared—the Divine in Person?

> There is a form of involvement with Adi Da and the
> Way of the Heart that is appropriate for everyone.
> All you need to know is explained in
> "An Invitation" (pp. 221-50).

The Eternally Free-Standing and (Now, and Forever Hereafter)
Always Presently "Emerging" Divine World-Teacher, Who Is The
Liberating Word Of Heart, Spoken, Lived, Given, and Always
(Now, and Forever Hereafter) Giving here, As A Grace, To All Mankind,
and, By Grace, Shown (Now, and Forever Hereafter) To The Heart
Of every kind and being appearing by conditions every where

THE DAWN HORSE TESTAMENT OF ADI DA

NOTES TO
THE DIVINE LIFE AND WORK
OF ADI DA (THE DA AVATAR)

Part I

1. The word "Tantra" does not merely indicate Spiritualized sexuality, as is the common presumption. The word signifies "the inherent Unity that underlies and transcends all opposites, and that resolves all differences or distinctions."

In many of the Tantric traditions that have developed within both Hinduism and Buddhism, Tantric Adepts and aspirants use sexual activity and highly stimulating substances that are forbidden to more orthodox or conventional practitioners. The Tantric's intention, however, is never to merely indulge gross desires. The secret of the Tantric approach is that it does not suppress, but rather employs and even galvanizes, the passions and attachments of the body and mind, and thus utilizes the most intense (and, therefore, also potentially dangerous) energies of the being for the sake of Spiritual Realization.

2. Kundalini Yoga is an esoteric Spiritual practice associated with the stimulation and ascent of the Life-Current in the spinal line of the body-mind. Kundalini Yoga aims at awakening latent energy (which is thought to lie dormant at the bodily base) so that it rises through the spinal line to reunite with its ultimate source, conceived to be above the head. (Avatara Adi Da's Revelation of the actual relationship between energy and the body-mind is summarized in "The Seven Stages of Life", pp. 253-65.) Typical techniques include meditative visualization and breathing exercises, but the principal means of awakening is the initiatory Force of an Adept Spiritual Master.

3. Kriyas are the spontaneous, self-purifying responses of the body-mind to the Infusion of Spirit-Energy Transmitted by a Spiritually Awakened Adept-Realizer. Kriyas can take many forms, including bodily movements or gestures, all manner of vocal sounds and utterances, dramatic changes in breathing, and even profound quieting of the mind.

4. Swami Muktananda regarded the mystical vision of the blue pearl, or bindu, to be the highest attainment of the Siddha Yoga practices he Taught. Though he had experienced the utterly ascended and formless bliss of fifth stage conditional Nirvikalpa Samadhi, he regarded it to be a lesser experience in comparison with the blue pearl and other forms of extraordinary visionary and Spiritual experience.

5. Avatara Adi Da uses the terms "Yogi", "Saint", and "Sage" with specific meaning relative to the technical details of the Spiritual process displayed by the Realizer (see "The Seven Stages of Life", pp. 253-65):

In the technically specific language of the by Me Revealed Way of the Heart, 'Yogis' are . . . those who are truly, or really and rightly, practicing in the stages of Spiritual ascent, true 'Saints' are those who are already established in the highest (ascended) contemplative Realization, and 'Sages' are those who have gone beyond the psycho-physical context of the first five stages of life, and who have Realized the sixth stage Awakening.

6. Paramahansa Yogananda (1893-1952), the author of *Autobiography of a Yogi*, taught what he called "Kriya Yoga". He was a practitioner in the context of the fourth stage of life.

7. Jnaneshwar (1275-1296) was a great Siddha of Maharashtra, India. He was a venerated leader of the bhakti movement, and wrote the *Jnaneshwari*, a poetic commentary on the *Bhagavad Gita*.

Milarepa (1040-1123) is one of the most revered personages in Tibetan Buddhism, famous for the extremely intense austerities he undertook at the behest of his teacher, Marpa the Translator.

Both Jnaneshwar and Milarepa demonstrated the processes of the fifth stage of life.

8. Gautama Sakyamuni (circa 563-483 B.C.E.) is the great Indian Sage commonly known as "the Buddha".

Hui Neng (638-713), one of the best-known figures in Chinese Buddhism, is regarded as one of the founders of the Zen (or Ch'an) tradition. His talks and sermons are recorded in the *Platform Sutra*.

Shankara, one of the greatest Hindu sages (788-820), is considered the founder of the tradition of Advaita Vedanta.

Ramana Maharshi (1879-1950) was a great Indian Spiritual Master, who Realized the Transcendental Self at a young age. He established his Ashram at Tiruvannamalai in South India, which continues today.

All four of these Realizers exemplify traditional sixth stage Realization.

9. Avatara Adi Da Affirms that there is a Divine Domain that is the Perfectly Subjective Condition of the conditional worlds. It is not elsewhere, not an objective place like a subtle heaven or mythical paradise, but It is the always present, Transcendental, Inherently Spiritual, Divine Self of every conditional self, and the Radiant Source-Condition of every conditional place. Avatara Adi Da Reveals that the Divine Self-Domain is not other than the Divine Heart Itself, Who He Is.

10. The Hindi word "sahaj" means "natural". "Sahaj Samadhi" in this context means "seventh stage Sahaj Samadhi", indicating Inherent, or Native, and thus truly "Natural" State of Being. Seventh stage Sahaj Samadhi is permanent, Unconditional Divine Self-Realization, free of dependence on any form of meditation, effort, discipline, experience, or conditional knowledge.

"Sahaj Samadhi" is a term also used in various esoteric Hindu schools to indicate whatever is regarded as the ultimate Realization in the particular school.

Part II

11. The term "bonding", as used by Avatara Adi Da, signifies the process by which the egoic individual (already presuming separateness, and, therefore, bondage to the separate self), through the yearning and seeking for fulfillment, attaches himself or herself karmically to the world of others and things. When capitalized, however, it indicates devotional "Bonding" to Avatara Adi Da, the Divine Person, which is the means for the transcendence of all other forms of limited, or karmic, "bonding".

12. Traditional Tantric practice sometimes uses intoxicants and other "forbidden" substances as a means to employ all of the energies of the body-mind in the process of Spiritual Realization. (See also note 1.)

13. "Tumo", a Tibetan term for the Spiritual practice of "mystic heat", literally means "fierce mother".

14. The practice relative to sexuality in the formal renunciate orders requires that one be free for the fullest and one-pointed practice of Ishta-Guru-Bhakti Yoga and devotional "Bonding" with Avatara Adi Da. Therefore, either single "celibate renunciation" or celibacy in the context of uniquely bondage-transcending intimate relationship or (in the case of those with profound qualifications for a Yogic sexual practice) sexually active relationship in the context of uniquely bondage-transcending intimate relationship must be the choice and demonstration of members of the renunciate orders.

Celibacy in the Way of the Heart is about the celebration of the present sufficiency of the Divine rather than the suppression of sex for the sake of some Spiritual goal. Avatara Adi Da characterizes the practice of celibacy in the Way of the Heart as non-puritanical and life-energy-positive, and He Gives a specific "own-body Yoga" that develops the capability for the full "conductivity" of sexual energy as a solitary practice.

15. For a full description of the practice of sexual Yoga and "true intimacy" in the Way of the Heart, please see chapter twenty-one of *The Dawn Horse Testament Of Adi Da*.

Part III

16. Avatara Adi Da has Said that, after His physical (human) Lifetime, He must have a human form of Agency in the world. Therefore, He has Revealed that there should always be one (and only one) "Living Murti" as a Living Link between Him and His devotees. Traditionally, as well as in Avatara Adi Da's usage, the primary meaning of "murti" is "representational image". In the Way of the Heart, a Murti is a photographic or artistic representational Image of Avatara Adi Da; similarly, a "Living Murti" is a <u>human</u> Representation of Avatara Adi Da, by virtue of his or her unique conformity to Avatara Adi Da. Each successive "Living Murti" (or "Murti-Guru") is to be selected from among those members of the Free Renunciate Order who have been formally acknowledged as practitioners in the seventh stage of life. "Murti-Gurus" do not function as the independent Guru of practitioners of the Way of the Heart. Rather, they are simply Representations of Avatara Adi Da's bodily (human) Form, and a means to Commune with Him.

For a full discussion of "Living Murtis", or "Murti-Gurus", and how they will be chosen, see chapter twenty of *The Dawn Horse Testament Of Adi Da*.

17. All who come to Avatara Adi Da and approach Him formally as His devotee receive formal initiations at each level of approach and each transition in practice. The first formal initiation is into student-novice practice, in which the individual is formally established in the Eternal Bond with his or her Heart-Master, Avatara Adi Da.

18. Avatara Adi Da's eight "Source-Texts" are:

The Dawn Horse Testament Of Adi Da (The Testament Of Secrets Of The Da Avatar)

The (Shorter) Testament Of Secrets Of Adi Da (The Heart Of The Dawn Horse Testament Of The Da Avatar)

The Adi Da Upanishad: The Short Discourses on self-Renunciation, Divine Self-Realization, and the Illusion of Relatedness

The Santosha Avatara Gita: The Revelation of the Great Means of the Divine Heart-Way of No-Seeking and Non-Separateness

The Hymn Of The True Heart-Master (The New Revelation-Book Of The Ancient and Eternal Religion Of Devotion To The God-Realized Adept)

The Lion Sutra: On Perfect Transcendence Of The Primal Act, Which is the ego-"I", the self-Contraction, or attention itself, and All The Illusions Of Separation, Otherness, Relatedness, and Difference—The Ultimate Teachings (For All Practitioners Of The Way Of The Heart), and The Perfect Practice Of Feeling-Enquiry (For Formal Renunciates In The Way Of The Heart)

The Liberator (Eleutherios): The Epitome of the Perfect Wisdom and the Perfect Practice of the Way of the Heart

The Basket of Tolerance: The Perfect Guide to Perfect Understanding of the One and Great Tradition of Mankind.

See pp. 272-74 for a brief description of each of the Source-Texts.

Part IV

19. The "Great Tradition" is Avatara Adi Da's term for the total inheritance of human, cultural, religious, magical, mystical, Spiritual, Transcendental, and Divine paths, philosophies, and testimonies from all the eras and cultures of humanity, which has (in the present era of world-wide communication) become the common legacy of mankind.

20. The four traditional basic ashramas, or phases in the life of an individual, acknowledged in traditional Hindu culture are the phases of the student (brahmacharya), the householder (grihastha), the forest dweller (vanaprastha), and the self-renounced ascetic (sannyasa). The word "ashrama" may also refer to the conventional rules and expectations that typically pertain to all kinds of life-roles.

ADI DA (THE DA AVATAR)
Adi Da Purnashram (Naitauba), Fiji, 1994

AN INTRODUCTION TO

The
Santosha Avatara
Gita

AN INTRODUCTION TO

The
Santosha Avatara
Gita

The *Santosha Avatara Gita* is the Song (Gita) of the Divine Incarnation (Avatara) Who Is the Perfect Expression of "Santosha"—
Divine "Satisfaction", "Contentedness", and "No-Seeking". Altogether,
"Santosha" signifies the Great Restedness of Avatara Adi Da's Divine
Completeness. The Name "Santosha" also celebrates the unique essence
of the Way of the Heart, which is the Way of No-Seeking—the understanding and transcendence of self-contraction in Divine Communion
with Beloved Adi Da, even to the point of Most Perfect Identification
with His "Bright" State.

Avatara Adi Da's Gift of *The Santosha Avatara Gita** was Mysteriously initiated in late 1988. After visiting His devotees in New Zealand
and California, He stopped for a time at Tumomama Sanctuary in
Hawaii, where He remained in seclusion. In October, He unexpected-
ly invited His devotees in Hawaii to sit with Him in formal occasions
of Darshan, or sacred sighting of His bodily (human) Form. Then, within a few days, He left Hawaii for Adi Da Purnashram, His Hermitage in
Fiji, where He arrived on October 13. The next morning, Beloved Adi
Da spontaneously began to compose *The Santosha Avatara Gita* while
His body was waking from sleep. He Says that the first few verses of
the Text generally correspond to brief Words of Instruction He had been
Giving to a devotee who was expressing a reluctance to embrace the
practice of self-discipline and whom He had Contacted on the subtle
plane while His body slept.

**The Santosha Avatara Gita* was originally titled *The Love-Ananda Gita.*

As Avatara Adi Da continued His work on the verses of *The Santosha Avatara Gita*, He engaged in numerous dialogues (both face to face and through written communications) with His devotees who were on retreat at Adi Da Purnashram. On the basis of this interaction, Avatara Adi Da developed *The Santosha Avatara Gita* into His most succinct summary of the practice of the Way of the Heart.

This beautiful summary is centered in the essence of that practice: moment to moment feeling-Contemplation of Avatara Adi Da, or living by His Darshan. Darshan—beholding the Great God-Sign of Avatara Adi Da's bodily (human) Form, and through this beholding becoming increasingly sensitive to His Spiritual (and Always Blessing) Presence and His Very (and Inherently Perfect) State—is at the heart of His Revelation.

The sighting of the God-Realizer's body is a traditionally revered Blessing, be it in person or in vision or dream or via photographic or other technical or artistic representation. The Consummate Blessing of Darshan of Avatara Adi Da's Radiant bodily (human) Form, His All-Pervading Spiritual Presence, and His Love-Blissful State is the origin of the Way of the Heart.

A longtime devotee of Avatara Adi Da, Emily Grinnell, recalls her first experience of the potency of His exquisite Darshan:

EMILY GRINNELL: One day in 1974, I was given one of Avatara Adi Da's books, called The Method of the Siddhas. *In reading it, I felt Avatara Adi Da Speaking to me from my own heart, rather than just through the words on the page. I felt that I was awakening from a long, long sleep to the already intimate Presence of my Ishta-Guru.*

Soon afterwards, I went to San Francisco to join the community of devotees that was steadily growing there around Avatara Adi Da. As soon as I could, I attended a showing of an introductory film that documents His early Teaching Work with His devotees. I watched the film with excitement and anticipation, hoping for a special sign of confirmation of my eternal relationship to my Guru. But as the film continued, no such sign appeared.

Then, in the final frames, Avatara Adi Da's face filled the screen, His shoulders circled with a deep yellow shawl. He Gazed steadily and simply into the eye of the camera, and far beyond, into the heart of the universe. He was absolutely Rested, and yet a consuming Center of Divine Sacrifice. He was Intimacy itself, and Love itself. Tears filled His eyes. I became absorbed in this Vision of Him, and forgot all about watching for any special signs.

Suddenly I lost awareness of the body and mind in a swoon. I was only aware of Avatara Adi Da's dazzlingly "Bright" Presence deep in my heart, even visually. It was penetrating, vibrant, and perfectly delicate and still. I saw Him Standing in my heart, Radiant and Glorious, yet I was "in" Him. He was Delight, and I was delight in the beholding of Him.

This film was my first experience of His Darshan. I saw the Vision of God with my eyes and with my heart. I saw the Divine in the living Form of Beloved Adi Da.

The great Force of Avatara Adi Da's Darshan is not confined to the visual perception of His bodily (human) Form. There are numerous accounts of ordinary men and women whose lives have been transformed through merely hearing a recording of His speech or laughter, or seeing His Name on a poster, or reading a devotional acknowledgement of Him in a book or magazine. *The Santosha Avatara Gita* is His direct Personal Instruction on how to make fullest use of the Gift of His Darshan, to receive His Blessing fully, and to surrender to and be transformed by His Graceful Transmission.

AVATARA ADI DA: The beholding of Me must be your sign and characteristic, moment by moment—not only sometimes when it is allowed by the ceremonial occasion or because you are in a particular mood on any day but as a practice whereby you allow yourself such profound devotional expression, such liberal release of your hold on your separate self. Then you are My devotee in daily life. Then you are doing effective sadhana, and growth is inevitable. [November 28, 1992]

To behold Beloved Adi Da is to behold the Santosha Avatara—the Complete and Perfect human Form of God, the Complete and All-Pervading Spiritual Presence of God, and the ultimate Divine Condition or "Bright" Feeling of Being that is God, Truth, or Reality. To be moved by that beholding is the beginning of the most profound, ecstatic undoing of one's conventional mind and character. That beholding is the heart of the process of ego-dissolution. As one Contemplates the Divine Avatar, Adi Da, with full feeling, one spontaneously surrenders, forgets, and transcends the ego-self in Him. Each of these responses—self-surrender, self-forgetting, and self-transcendence—is an essential counter-egoic gesture that makes the practice of feeling-Contemplation of Avatara Adi Da true and fruitful.

How can one ultimately go beyond, or transcend, the egoic self if one is actively remembering it? One cannot. The egoic self must first be forgotten.

How can one forget one's egoic self if one is presently clinging to it and its results? Again, one cannot. The egoic self must first be let go, or surrendered, through the practice of Ishta-Guru-Bhakti Yoga.

Therefore, in feeling-Contemplation of Beloved Adi Da, one must first surrender, and then forget, and, ultimately, transcend the separate and separative self.

AVATARA ADI DA: Ishta-Guru-Bhakti Yoga is the Yoga of direct Grace. It is always about forgetfulness of the egoic self, and it is always about Remembrance (and, as Grace will have it, the Realization) of My bodily (human) Form and (as Grace will have it) My Spiritual (and Always Blessing) Presence and My Very (and Inherently Perfect) State.

My devotee surrenders and forgets and transcends the ego-"I" through devotional Contemplation of Me. I Grant My devotee the Realization of My bodily (human) Form and My Spiritual (and Always Blessing) Presence, so that My devotee may, by These Means, Realize My Very (and Inherently Perfect) State, Which Is Self-Existent and Self-Radiant, the Divine Self-Condition Itself. [July 1, 1991]

And this devotional Contemplation can only be real and effective if it springs from the heart, founded in feeling:

AVATARA ADI DA: In any (and every) moment of practice, you must first . . . establish yourself in direct feeling-response to Me. Then you will be able truly to Contemplate My bodily (human) Form, but not otherwise. You may look at My bodily (human) Form, you may think about It, you may react to It, but you will not Contemplate Me until you . . . establish yourself in the Heart-Principle of feeling-response.

This Heart-Principle of feeling-response (to Me) is the origin of all devotional sensitivity to My Revelation. . . . Feeling Me, feeling-attention to Me, the submission of your attention to feeling Me, through feeling Me, is the essence of your responsibility for practice in the Way of the Heart. [1989]

Ishta-Guru-Bhakti Yoga is based upon the mutual bond between Avatara Adi Da and His devotee. Therefore, the practice of self-surrendering, self-forgetting, and self-transcending feeling-Contemplation of Avatara Adi Da can only be embraced through formal initiation into the devotional relationship to Him. To all who are drawn to this Graceful Opportunity, and to all who are simply moved to associate with Avatara Adi Da through study of His Heart-Word, Avatara Adi Da's Sublime Instruction is openly Given here, and His bodily (human) Form Itself is the Epitome of His Wisdom-Teaching:

AVATARA ADI DA: This (My) Body (or bodily human Form) Is the Teaching. My every Word of Confession and Instruction was Spoken through It. My summary Word of Confession and Instruction refers to many processes, all of which have taken place in the context of This Body. Nothing has been Spoken to you, nothing has been Taught to you, through This Body that has not been experienced by This One, in This Body. All of it has been tested and proven in This Body. Nothing has been Spoken to you that has not been tested and proven in This Body, and by This One altogether, in and beyond This Body. Therefore, This One, bodily (in bodily human Form), Is the Teaching. My every Word of Confession and Instruction is a Communication through This Body. The summary of the Teaching is before your eyes, and It need not be thought about.

Therefore, feeling-Contemplation of This Teaching That Is My bodily (human) Form leads, in due course, to the Revelation of My Spiritual (and Always Blessing) Presence. And, by leading you deeply, This feeling-Contemplation leads to My Very (and Inherently Perfect) State, beyond the limits of attention.

But first, the sadhana is feeling-Contemplation of This bodily (human) Form. Such devotion, such service, and such self-discipline purify you of the grosser disposition and, in due course, by Grace, allow a depth of practice beyond the beginner's course. [December 20,1988]

The Santosha Avatara Gita is Avatara Adi Da's Perfect Revelation of the simplest, most direct, and most Complete Way of Freedom, or Divine Self-Realization. In this Sublime Song of Non-Separateness, the Pure Adept of Love, Santosha Adi Da, the Da Avatar, Offers you the Liberating Grace that can set you Truly Free.

ADI DA (THE DA AVATAR)
Adi Da Purnashram (Naitauba), Fiji, 1994

THE
SANTOSHA AVATARA
GITA

(The Revelation of the Great Means
of the Divine Heart-Way of
No-Seeking and Non-Separateness)

By
ADI DA
(The Da Avatar)

1.

$\mathbb{T}$he (Ultimate) Nature of the world (and how it is arising) is inherently (and tacitly) obvious, if you <u>remain</u> in a state of pleasurable oneness with whatever and all that presently arises.

2.

$\mathbb{T}$o remain in a state of pleasurable oneness with whatever and all that presently arises, you must (necessarily, and always presently) Realize inherently Love-Blissful Unity with whatever and all that presently arises.

3.

$\mathbb{I}$nherently Love-Blissful Unity with whatever and all that presently arises is (Itself, or inherently) non-separation (or no-contraction) from whatever and all that presently arises.

4.

$\mathbb{S}$eparation (or contraction) from the world (or whatever and all that is presently arising) is (unfortunately) precisely the first and constant (and inherently problematic) thing done by <u>all</u> those who make efforts to find out (or to account for) how the world is arising (and What Is its Ultimate Nature).

5.

$\mathbb{S}$eparation (or self-contraction) is the first (and foundation) gesture made by anyone who has a problem, or who is seeking, or who is making an effort to account for anything whatsoever.

6.

$\mathbb{P}$leasurable oneness (or inherently Love-Blissful Unity) is inherent (or necessarily and priorly the case, no matter what conditions do or do not arise), and, therefore, pleasurable oneness (or inherently Love-Blissful Unity) is (necessarily) uncaused, and Real (or always already the case, and always already in, of, and Identical to Truth), whereas separateness (or "Difference"[1]) is always conditional, conditionally caused (or only conditionally apparent), and illusory (or always already dissociated from Reality and Truth).

7.

$\mathbb{P}$leasurable oneness (or inherently Love-Blissful Unity) need not (and cannot fruitfully) be sought.

8.

$\mathbb{P}$leasurable oneness (or inherently Love-Blissful Unity) can be (apparently) lost, by the <u>act</u> of self-contraction (and, thereby, of apparent separation, separateness, and separativeness).

9.

$\mathbb{P}$leasure-seeking, Love-Bliss-seeking, or Unity-seeking efforts (of any kind) are <u>only</u> parts of a strategic (and always already un-Happy) adventure, and such effort and adventure are entered into <u>only</u> by those who are already (presently) separating (or contracting) themselves in (and from) What <u>Is</u>, and such adventurers are seeking <u>only</u> because they are already, presently, separating (or contracting) themselves in (and from) What <u>Is</u>.

10.

$\mathbb{T}$herefore, it is necessary to understand this (or self-contraction itself), and (by the transcendence[2] of self-contraction itself) to Recover Awareness of the obvious (or inherent) Love-Bliss-Unity (and, Thus, to inherently account for <u>everything</u>, and also, Thereby, to solve, or inherently transcend, <u>all</u> problems).

11.

This understanding (and This Recovery) cannot (fruitfully) be sought, for all seeking is inherently associated with an already present act of self-contraction (and, thereby, of separation, separateness, and separativeness).

12.

True understanding is itself inherent, or always already, or Native to even (apparently) conditional existence itself.

13.

Therefore, if such understanding is not already Realized in the present, it must (and can only) be Realized by Divine Grace (as a Free Gift).

14.

I am the Person and the Means of this Grace.

15.

I am the Love-Blissful Presence of this Free Gift.

16.

The understanding of which I Speak is (if Most Perfectly[3] Realized) the Most Perfectly Ultimate (or seventh stage[4]) Capability to (inherently, Divinely) Recognize[5] whatever arises.

17.

Most Perfect understanding is the Capability to directly (immediately) transcend dilemma, all problems, and all seeking.

18.

Most Perfect understanding is the Capability to "radically"[6] (always already) transcend self-contraction (and all of separation, separateness, and separativeness).

19.

Most Perfect understanding is the Capability inherent in Love-Bliss Itself (Which Is the Heart Itself).

20.

Most Perfect understanding is the Capability inherent in the always already, or most prior, Unity (with Which the Heart Itself, As Love-Bliss Itself, Is inherently One).

21.

I have, by Means of the Submission, Work, and Word of My here-Speaking Revelation-Body, thoroughly Revealed and Described the Great (and Complete) Process Wherein and Whereby the Heart Itself (or Love-Bliss-Unity Itself) is (Ultimately) Most Perfectly Realized.

22.

That Great (and Complete) Process (Which Is the only-by-Me Revealed and Given Way of the Heart) is Described (in every detail and elaboration) in My summary (Written, and forever Speaking) Word of Heart (in many Works).[7]

23.

That summary Word is True, and that Great Process Is indeed the Process (elaborate in Its totality of details) Wherein the Inherently Perfect Tacit Obviousness is (progressively[8]) Realized.

24.

The Principle (or Great Means) of that Great Process Is Itself an Extreme Simplicity (as simple to describe as that Great Process is Itself necessarily complex in Its total description).

25.

Ishta-Guru-Bhakti Yoga (or the constant
counter-egoic, and even total psycho-physical,
effort of self-surrendering, self-forgetting, and,
more and more, self-transcending devotion to
Me and devotional Communion with Me, the
Da Avatar, the Hridaya Avatara, the Avabhasa
Avatara, the Love-Ananda Avatara, the Santosha
Avatara,[9] the Realizer, the Revealer, and the Very
Revelation of the True Divine Person, Who Is the
One and Only Self of All and all, Which
Is the Heart Itself, the "Bright"[10] Itself, and Love-
Bliss Itself), and this constantly exercised
as the surrender, the forgetting, and the
transcendence of body, emotion (or feeling),
mind (or attention), breath, and all of separate
self in moment to moment devotional
Contemplation of My bodily (human) Form,
My Spiritual (and Always Blessing) Presence,
and My Very (and Inherently Perfect) State,[11] Is
the Principle (or the Great Means) Wherein and
Whereby the Great Process of the only-by-Me
Revealed and Given Way of the Heart is
Accomplished.

26.

For all those who would "consider"[12] the only-by-Me Revealed and Given Way of the Heart, My summary (Written, and forever Speaking) Word of Heart (in many Works) is (now, and forever hereafter) Given (by Me) for their study.

27.

For all those who would practice the only-by-Me Revealed and Given Way of the Heart, My summary (Written, and forever Speaking) Word of Heart (in many Works) is (now, and forever hereafter) Given (by Me) for their application.

28.

And for all those who would, by practicing the only-by-Me Revealed and Given Way of the Heart, Really, and, Ultimately, Most Perfectly Realize the Divine and Inherently Perfect Truth of non-separateness, I am always (now, and forever hereafter) here for their devotional Contemplation.

29.

Realization of the Most Ultimate (or seventh stage) Wisdom-Unity, Truth-Obviousness, and (Divine) Recognition-Capability is (in any moment) a matter of My Giving Grace and My Graceful Self-Revelation.

30.

My bodily (human) Form Is (Itself) the Teaching.

31.

My Spiritual (and Always Blessing) Presence Is the Means.

32.

My Very (and Inherently Perfect) State Is the Revelation Itself.

33.

Therefore, devotional Contemplation of My bodily (human) Form, and (via My bodily human Form) My Spiritual (and Always Blessing) Presence, and (via My Spiritual, and Always Blessing, Presence) My Very (and Inherently Perfect) State, even, Most Ultimately, to the degree of Perfect Oneness with Me (and Perfect non-separation from all and All), Is the Heart-Way That I offer to you and to all.

34.

I Say to you: First and always, in your bodily (human) form, be the always serving devotee of My bodily (human) Form, and (as your devotion, your service, your self-discipline, and your self-understanding mature, or, eventually, become matured, by that actively self-surrendering, self-purifying, and self-transcending Contemplation) you will (by My Giving Grace and My Graceful Self-Revelation) also become the Spiritually activated devotee of My "Bright" and True, and Always Blessing, Spiritual Presence (Which Is Love-Bliss Itself), and (as the active devotee of both My bodily human Form and My Spiritual, and Always Blessing, Presence) you will (by My Giving Grace and My Graceful Self-Revelation) sometimes also (in the Deepening Revelation of Love-Bliss) spontaneously Intuit and Contemplate the beginningless, endless, centerless, and boundless Deep of My Very (and Inherently Perfect) State, and (in due course) that spontaneous (and only-by-Me Given) Grace of Intuitive Contemplation will (by My Giving Grace and My Graceful Self-Revelation) become Inherently Perfect Contemplation of My Very (and Inherently Perfect) State, and Inherently Perfect Identification with My Very (and Inherently Perfect) State, such that even the Most Perfect (or seventh stage) Capability will (in due course) be Realized by Heart.

35

Therefore, simply (Merely, and intentionally, but on the basis of a fundamental, and fundamentally effortless, feeling-Attraction to Me) Contemplate My bodily (human) Form, My Spiritual (and Always Blessing) Presence, and My Very (and Inherently Perfect) State, and do this Contemplation progressively (as My Giving Grace and My Graceful Self-Revelation Determine the progress), such that (more and more) you allow My bodily (human) Form to Attract (and Keep) your (truly feeling) attention, and This such that (more and more) you allow My Spiritual (and Always Blessing) Presence to Pervade your body-mind, and This such that (Most Ultimately) you allow My Very (and Inherently Perfect) State to Be your Very (and inherently egoless, or non-separate) Heart.

36.

Simply (Merely), by <u>feeling</u> (and even, randomly and occasionally, by Name[13]), Remember and Invoke (or otherwise directly Regard) My bodily (human) Form,[14] and (Merely by <u>feeling</u>) Contemplate (and Meditate on) My bodily (human) Form, and (by <u>feeling</u> Me, Thus) progressively <u>feel</u> My Spiritual (and Always Blessing) Presence, the Giving-Force Heart-Radiated (by Me, and As Me) in, and via, and around, and everywhere beyond, and Perfectly prior to My bodily (human) Form, and (by <u>feeling</u> My Spiritual, and Always Blessing, Presence, Thus) be progressively Yielded to My Very (and Inherently Perfect) State, until (Thereby, in any moment) your own act of self-contraction (and, thus, of separation, separateness, and separativeness) is dissolved, released, vanished, or forgotten in the Perfect Intuition (and then the Most Perfect Realization) of My Very (and Inherently Perfect) State.

37.

Do this <u>feeling</u>-Contemplation (progressively, as My Giving Grace and My Graceful Self-Revelation will have it) at least twice each day (as an extended, and developing, formal Meditation), in the morning (as a general rule) and in the evening (or the later day), and do this (progressive) Contemplation also at random (daily), and more and more constantly, and, Thus, by always keeping attention on Me, be purified and released of the casual distractions (and the sometimes and self-enclosed sleep) of attention.

38.

Realize the Obvious Truth, Thus, by My Grace Alone, again and again, until the Inherently Most Perfect (or seventh stage) Capability of Divine Recognition Awakens (tacitly, effortlessly, obviously, and never to be lost).

39.

Therefore, Contemplate Me, Meditate on Me, actively (responsively) Yield the motions of body, emotion, and mind to Me (and into the Heart of My bodily human Form, My Spiritual, and Always Blessing, Presence, and My Very, and Inherently Perfect, State), such that, Most Ultimately, by My Giving Grace and My Graceful Self-Revelation, you Realize Me (non-separately), and (Thus and Thereby) become My (inherently) Most Perfect devotee, Always Already Most Perfectly Awake to the Obvious Truth, and (Inherently) Most Perfectly Capable of transcending all problems and all seeking, or all apparent limitations on Love-Bliss Itself, if they arise, and when they arise.

40.

The only-by-Me Revealed and Given Way of the Heart is the "radical" (or most direct) Way of the Heart Itself, Which (Itself) "radically" (or most directly) Realizes (and, Ultimately, Is) the inherent (or Native, or always already, and necessarily Divine) Truth.

41.

The only-by-Me Revealed and Given Way of the Heart is the Way of non-separateness, or the Heart-Way of counter-active (or actively self-transcending) responsibility for the (otherwise <u>always</u> arising) action that is egoity (the ego, the ego-"I", or the primal "Act of Narcissus",[15] which is the act of self-contraction, and the constant action of separation, separateness, and separativeness).

42.

The only-by-Me Revealed and Given Way of the Heart is the devotional Way of Heart-responsive self-submission to (and into) My Form and Presence and State of Grace, Which is the devotional Way of (more and more effective) counter-egoic action, the Way of active (and more and more effective) devotional surrender of self-contraction, and the devotionally active Way of (more and more effective) self-transcendence, through self-forgetting Remembrance of the (by My Grace) Self-Revealed, Inherently Non-separate, Inherently Perfect, and Perfectly Subjective, Reality and Truth.

43.

The only-by-Me Revealed and Given Way of the Heart is the Way of Divine Grace, Wherein the Free Gift of "radical" (and, Ultimately, Most Perfect) self-understanding is Given to all and Awakened in all, in the moment (or in any moment) of self-transcending Contemplation of My bodily (human) Form, My Spiritual (and Always Blessing) Presence, and My Very (and Inherently Perfect) State.

44.

Therefore, if you are responding to This (My Word of Heart), and if you are (by This) Heart-Moved to transcend and Be Free of the otherwise constant "Act (and Results) of Narcissus", and if you are Heart-Attracted to (or toward) My bodily (human) Form (because It is Heart-"Bright"), and to (or toward) My Spiritual (and Always Blessing) Presence (because It Is the Free Transmission of Love-Bliss), and to (or toward) My Very (and Inherently Perfect) State (because It Self-Reveals the Truth), and if you would (by always Merely Remembering and Contemplating Me) forget your separate and separative self (the ego-"I", or self-contraction, appearing as body, emotion, and all of mind),

and if you would (Most Ultimately) transcend even all action (in Most Perfect Identification with My Very, and Inherently Perfect, State That <u>Is</u>), then Yield to Me, embrace My Seven Giving Gifts,[16] and practice the Divine Way of the Heart in My Gracefully Self-Revealing Company.

45.

The only-by-Me Revealed and Given Way of the Heart is the <u>practice</u> of Satsang,[17] or the self-surrendering, self-purifying, and (really, effectively) self-transcending <u>work</u> of constant, devotionally Heart-responsive, and effectively counter-egoic (or intentionally and effectively self-Yielding and self-forgetting) <u>feeling</u>-Contemplation of My bodily (human) Form, My Spiritual (and Always Blessing) Presence, and My Very (and Inherently Perfect) State.

46.

Therefore, by always first (responsively, actively, and intentionally) "Locating" the <u>feeling</u>-Place in you that already and presently and effortlessly feels Attracted to My bodily (human) Form, and My Spiritual (and Always Blessing) Presence, and My Very (and Inherently Perfect)

State, Yield (responsively, actively, and intentionally) to the <u>feeling</u> of the Inherent "Bright" Attractiveness of My bodily (human) Form, and Yield (responsively, actively, and intentionally) to the <u>feeling</u> of the Inherent "Bright" Attractiveness of My Spiritual (and Always Blessing, and progressively, and then Ultimately, Revealed) Presence, and, by all of this, responsively, actively, and intentionally Yield (and more and more deeply forget) your ego-"I" (or your own action of separation, separateness, and separativeness) in the "Bright" and Very Space of My (progressively, and then Ultimately) Revealed (and Inherently Perfect) State.

47.

You (necessarily) become (or conform to the likeness of) whatever you Contemplate, or Meditate on, or even think about.

48.

Therefore, Contemplate Me, and transcend even all thought by Meditating on Me.

49.

Do not Meditate on your separate self (your states, your experiences, your presumed knowledge, your dilemma, your problem, or your search), and do not perpetuate self-contraction (by strategies of independent effort, and by adventures of either self-glorification or self-destruction, within or without), but (always, immediately) transcend self-Meditation, personal states, conditional experiences, presumptions of knowledge, and all of dilemma, problem, and search (Merely by Remembering Me, and Invoking Me, and Meditating on Me, and, Therefore, Merely by surrendering to <u>Me</u>, not by self-concerned effort, or by isolated and concerned manipulation of conditions themselves, but by simply, and intentionally, and more and more deeply, responding and Yielding to the always presently Available feeling of the Inherent "Bright" Attractiveness of My bodily human Form, and of My Spiritual, and Always Blessing, Presence, and of My Very, and Inherently Perfect, State), and (Thus, by Means of the always presently Available Grace That Is My Good Company) always and actively feel beyond and (really, effectively) transcend your separate and separative self (Merely by feeling, and Thereby Contemplating, Me).

50.

Do This Contemplation For Its Own Sake, and not passively and partially (as if <u>waiting</u> for devotion to happen <u>to</u> you, rather than always presently Remembering and Invoking Me, and, Thereupon, responsively <u>allowing</u> the presently inevitable feeling of My Inherent "Bright" Attractiveness, and, Thereby, most simply, <u>always</u> and <u>fully</u> <u>activating</u> My always Given and Giving Gift of devotion), and not cleverly and strategically (with all effort and no response, intent but not Yielding, stressful with the <u>seeking</u> of Me, rather than Happy with the <u>Finding</u> of Me), but Do This Contemplation constantly, always, Merely, and by Heart, and (Thus) by feeling <u>to</u> My bodily (human) Form, and by feeling <u>into</u> My Spiritual (and Always Blessing) Presence, and, more and more (and then Inherently) Perfectly, by Feeling <u>As</u> My Very and Freely Revealed and Freely (Inherently) Perfect State.

51.

Therefore, actively (responsively) <u>be</u> My devotee, and (to the degree you make Room for Me in the Place of your feeling, by surrendering thought, and even every form of self-contraction, in self-forgetting Me-Remembrance) the Obvious Truth will (Freely) be Given to you (in every moment), and the Obvious Truth will (Thereby) be Realized by you (as My Giving Grace and My Graceful Self-Revelation will have it, in any moment).

52.

Now, and forever hereafter, this Simplicity is the essential practice (and the essence of the entire practice of the only-by-Me Revealed and Given Way of the Heart) to Which I Call every one.

53.

Those who would so practice should embrace, and progressively develop, all the original (or most basic) functional, practical, and relational disciplines (and all the original, or most basic, cultural obligations)[18] I have Described (and Given) in and by My summary (Written, and forever Speaking) Word of Heart (in many Works).

54.

Those disciplines and practices are the (most basic) necessary evidence of the devotional response to Me.

55.

Those disciplines and practices should be responsively and positively embraced (and, by real practice, thoroughly "considered" and developed) in the context of the essential practice of the only-by-Me Revealed and Given Way of the Heart, which essential practice is regular (twice or more daily), and random, and more and more constant, and always (responsively, actively, intentionally) body-forgetting, and deeply emotion-forgetting, and really mind-forgetting, and altogether and truly self-forgetting feeling-Contemplation of My bodily (human) Form, My Spiritual (and Always Blessing) Presence, and My Very (and Inherently Perfect) State.

56.

When their developmental signs of Growth in the only-by-Me Revealed and Given Way of the Heart Allow, My devotees are Given Access to My Blessing-Seat, and each one should come to Me (at the Place, or Places, of My Blessing-Seat appropriate for Access at their stage, and in accordance with their form, of practice of the only-by-Me Revealed and Given Way of the Heart) as often as their right and true and truly Growing practice of the only-by-Me Revealed and Given Way of the Heart, and their present, and otherwise consistently demonstrated, signs of real and true Heart-Resort to Me, Allow (and truly Require).

57.

During the (physical) Lifetime of My bodily (human) Form (here), I am Established (bodily) at Adi Da Purnashram (Naitauba), My Great Sannyasin Hermitage Ashram in Fiji, where I Reside and Remain in "Brightest" Sanctuary and Perpetual Retreat[19] (except at times of My Seclusions, Offerings, and Blessing-Wanderings any where), and I will always (forever), during and after (and forever after) the (physical) Lifetime of My bodily (human) Form (here), be Really Present at Adi Da Purnashram (Naitauba) for the Sake of all and All.

58.

As often as their right and true and truly Growing practice of the only-by-Me Revealed and Given Way of the Heart, and their present, and otherwise consistently demonstrated, signs of real and true Heart-Resort to Me, Allow (and truly Require), My devotees should (forever), during and after (and forever after) the (physical) Lifetime of My bodily (human) Form (here), come (in accordance with each one's form and stage of practice of the only-by-Me Revealed and Given Way of the Heart) to the by Me Empowered Sanctuaries[20] I have formally Offered for Retreats (and for other sacred use) by My devotees (according to their forms and stages of practice of the only-by-Me Revealed and Given Way of the Heart), and I will always (forever), during and after (and forever after) the (physical) Lifetime of My bodily (human) Form (here), be Really Present every there and then for them all.

59.

At all times, and in all places, all My devotees should (constantly) Contemplate My bodily (human) Form, My Spiritual (and Always Blessing) Presence, and My Very (and Inherently Perfect) State, and (daily, or as possible) they should do this in the daily communities of My devotees (who are formally acknowledged as such by Me, or by the sacred cultural gathering formally appointed by Me),[21] and they should do this (always) even under all the ordinary circumstances of every day, for I will always (forever), during and after (and forever after) the (physical) Lifetime of My bodily (human) Form (here), be Really Present even then and there (and, therefore, every where and when) for all My devotees.

60.

I am here only for this Satsang.

61.

I no longer Teach (or Submit to every one and all, in order to Reflect them to themselves, and, Thus and Thereby, to Prove the necessity of ego-transcendence, and, altogether, in order to Reveal and Describe the Great Means and the Great Process of the Heart-Way of non-separateness), but, now, and forever hereafter, during and after (and forever after) the (physical) Lifetime of My bodily (human) Form (here), having already Fully and Completely Done My First (or Teaching) Work (and such that It will Live and Work forever, through My summary Written, and forever Speaking, Word of Heart in many Works, and through the recorded, remembered, and constantly retold Leelas of all of My Teaching Life and Work, and through the recorded, and forever Living, Images of My bodily human Sign), I only Call each one and all to true and constant devotional Contemplation of Me, in order that, now, and forever hereafter, during and after (and forever after) the (physical) Lifetime of My bodily (human) Form (here), I may Do My Great, or Blessing, Work with every one and all.

62.

Therefore, now, and forever hereafter, during and after (and forever after) the (physical) Lifetime of My bodily (human) Form (here), I, for the Sake of their true and constant devotional Contemplation of Me, Give (and Require of) all My devotees the Gift of constant devotional love of Me, because true and constant devotional Contemplation of Me is (and, in every moment, requires) self-surrendering, self-forgetting, and self-transcending Heart-Resort to Me.

63.

Likewise, now, and forever hereafter, during and after (and forever after) the (physical) Lifetime of My bodily (human) Form (here), I, for the Sake of their true and constant devotional Contemplation of Me, Give (and Require of) all My devotees the Gift of constant devotional service to Me, because true and constant devotional Contemplation of Me is (and, in every functional, practical, or relational context or circumstance, requires) self-surrendering, self-forgetting, and self-transcending Heart-attention to Me.

64.

$\mathbb{A}$nd, now, and forever hereafter, during
and after (and forever after) the (physical)
Lifetime of My bodily (human) Form (here), I,
for the Sake of their true and constant devotional
Contemplation of Me, Give (and Require of)
all My devotees the Gift of constant (and,
altogether, devotionally inspired) self-discipline,
because true and constant devotional
Contemplation of Me is (and, in every context
or circumstance, requires) self-surrendering,
self-forgetting, and self-transcending Heart-
obedience and Heart-conformity to Me.

65.

$\mathbb{N}$ow, and forever hereafter, during and
after (and forever after) the (physical) Lifetime
of My bodily (human) Form (here), I am <u>here</u>,
<u>As</u> I <u>Am</u>.

66.

$\mathbb{I}$ am here only to Bless those who Resort to
Me and Contemplate Me.

159

67.

My summary (Written, and forever
Speaking) Word of Heart relative to the Extreme
Simplicity That Is the Great Means of the only-
by-Me Revealed and Given Way of the Heart,
and relative to the progressive process of
necessary (or otherwise potential) developmental
stages (and the technically more "elaborate"
practices, as well as the technically "simpler"
practices, and the technically "simplest"
practices) of the only-by-Me Revealed and Given
Way of the Heart,[22] is, now, and forever
hereafter, during and after (and forever after) the
(physical) Lifetime of My bodily (human) Form
(here), Fully and Finally and Completely Given
here, and My summary (Written, and forever
Speaking) Word of Heart is, now, and forever
hereafter, during and after (and forever after) the
(physical) Lifetime of My bodily (human) Form
(here), to be openly and everywhere
Communicated here (as I have Written It in Its
Full, Final, and Complete Forms), so that
everyone (as every one) may read My summary
(Written, and forever Speaking) Word and (by
personal response, as and whenever they will)
become My devotees, and so that all My
devotees may (by self-testing study) "consider"

My summary (Written, and forever Speaking) Word and (by progressive application) develop their practice (eventually, in accordance with their proven choice of Manner, course, or form of the practice) of the only-by-Me Revealed and Given Way of the Heart.

68.

Those of My devotees who, in due course, by My Giving Grace and My Graceful Self-Revelation, stably demonstrate the (original) maturing signs of the only-by-Me Revealed and Given Way of the Heart may (if they choose, and if they qualify) enter (formally) into the technically "fully elaborated" (or "elaborately detailed") course of the only-by-Me Revealed and Given Way of the Heart.

69.

Those of My devotees who choose (and qualify) to practice the technically "fully elaborated" form of the only-by-Me Revealed and Given Way of the Heart must do so under continuous and formal guidance within (and by) one or the other of the (formal) renunciate orders[23] originally established (and formally

appointed) by Me for the Sake of all My (thus formally and technically "elaborately") practicing devotees, and they must allow their practice and their discipline to be (thus and thereby) formally measured and determined by technically "elaborately detailed" stages.

70.

Those of My devotees who enter the technically "fully elaborated" course of the only-by-Me Revealed and Given Way of the Heart must (formally, progressively, and as necessary) enter into (and develop) all the by Me Given disciplines, practices, stages, and Realizations of the technically "fully elaborated" form of the only-by-Me Revealed and Given Way of the Heart, and they must do so in a (formally, progressively, and personally appropriate) renunciate Manner (including, as their form of emotional-sexual discipline and practice, either single "celibate renunciation" or celibacy in the context of uniquely bondage-transcending "true intimacy" or, in the case of those truly qualified, or even, in rare cases, uniquely qualified, for a Yogic sexual sadhana, sexually active relationship in the context of uniquely bondage-transcending "true intimacy").[24]

71.

However, many (or, perhaps, even most) practitioners of the only-by-Me Revealed and Given Way of the Heart will (from the beginning, and during and after their necessary initial experiment with the two alternative devotional Ways, of Faith and of Insight[25]) be Heart-Moved to practice the technically "simpler" form (or even the technically "simplest" form) of the only-by-Me Revealed and Given Way of the Heart (at least until a time when they, possibly, but not necessarily, may become fully moved and truly prepared to practice the technically "fully elaborated", and, necessarily, formal renunciate, form of the only-by-Me Revealed and Given Way of the Heart), and, therefore (in that either "simpler" or "simplest" Manner, with or without the random addition of rudimentary technical practices of either simply self-surrendering or otherwise both self-surrendering and self-enquiring devotion to Me[26]), they will Love Me, and they will Contemplate Me, and (by "simpler", or even "simplest", but always true and fullest self-surrendering, self-forgetting, and, more and more, self-transcending devotion to Me) they will always Reside with Me.

72.

Therefore, the practice and the discipline
of My devotees who choose to practice the
technically "simpler" form (or even the
technically "simplest" form) of the only-by-Me
Revealed and Given Way of the Heart should
not be practiced, measured, or determined
strictly (or entirely) according to the fullest (or
technically most "elaborate") formal descriptions
and measures (or according to the most intensive
expectations) of the technically "fully elaborated"
form of the only-by-Me Revealed and Given Way
of the Heart, but their practice must, nonetheless,
be engaged both seriously and consistently, and
their practice must necessarily be formally and
consistently monitored and measured relative to
the progressive demonstration of the characteristic
Signs of the seven stages of life (in the specific
context of the only-by-Me Revealed and Given
Way of the Heart), and relative to the progressive
development of the (primary) developmental
Signs of responsible Listening[27] (or truly self-
surrendering and self-forgetting devotion to Me,
and truly self-surrendering and self-forgetting
service to Me, and really self-observing and self-
purifying self-discipline, embraced in truly self-
surrendering and self-forgetting response to

Me, and truly self-surrendering and self-forgetting, and always self-testing, study-"consideration" of My Word, and increasingly meditative, and more and more profoundly self-surrendering and self-forgetting, feeling-Contemplation of, most basically and especially, My bodily human Form), and (in due course) of true Hearing[28] (or most fundamental self-understanding, and the direct transcendence of self-contraction by means of the exercise of most fundamental self-understanding), and (in due course) of real Seeing[29] (or progressively All-Revealing Spiritual Identification of Me and Spiritual Heart-Communion with Me), and, Ultimately (in due course), of the "Perfect Practice"[30] (or Inherent, and Inherently Perfect, Heart-Identification with My Very, and Inherently Perfect, and "Brightly" all-Outshining[31] State), and, no matter what arises, such practitioners must maintain (and they should be formally expected to maintain) the basic (original) minimum of self-responsibility I have, in and by My summary (Written, and forever Speaking) Word of Heart (in many Works), Described and Given for the Sake of all practitioners of the only-by-Me Revealed and Given Way of the Heart,[32] and they must positively embrace and

consistently demonstrate (and they should be formally expected to positively embrace and to consistently demonstrate) all the basic (and otherwise progressively required) functional, practical, and relational disciplines, and all the basic (and otherwise progressively required) cultural obligations, I have, in and by My summary (Written, and forever Speaking) Word of Heart (in many Works), Described and Given for the Sake of all practitioners of the only-by-Me Revealed and Given Way of the Heart, and they must formally (and rightly) maintain (and cultivate) their participation in (and their practice-accountability to) the sacred cultural gathering originally established (and formally appointed) by Me for the Sake of all practitioners of the only-by-Me Revealed and Given Way of the Heart, and they must do all of this persistently (and always in and by Means of devotional Contemplation of My bodily human Form, My Spiritual, and Always Blessing, Presence, and My Very, and Inherently Perfect, State), no matter how profound, or advanced, or even Ultimate[33] the Process or the Event of Realization may become, or otherwise seem or even Be.

73.

In any case, the basic (or essential) practice for <u>all</u> who practice the only-by-Me Revealed and Given Way of the Heart is (in its inherent Simplicity) just that of responsive (and responsible) feeling-Contemplation of My bodily (human) Form, My Spiritual (and Always Blessing) Presence, and My Very (and Inherently Perfect) State.

74.

Therefore, I Embrace all practitioners of the only-by-Me Revealed and Given Way of the Heart, and I Embrace each one and all Simply (Merely) as My devotees (who are all Merely Contemplating Me).

75.

My Blessing of My devotees always Transmits the Same Gift to each and all, for I always Give, and Freely Give, the One and Only and Divine Gift of My Self-Revelation to each and all.

76.

My Blessing of My devotees is <u>always</u> Full of Spirit-Power, Given for the Sake of the Most Perfect Awakening of every one and all of My devotees.

77.

There are not different Blessings Given by Me for each kind and developmental stage of practice of the only-by-Me Revealed and Given Way of the Heart.

78.

Therefore, because of My always constant, Giving, Full, and Perfect Blessing Grace, and because of the constant Grace of My Self-Revelation, it is possible for any one to practice the only-by-Me Revealed and Given Way of the Heart, and that practice readily (and more and more constantly) Realizes pleasurable oneness (or inherently Love-Blissful Unity) with whatever and all that presently arises, and that Realization (Itself, Most Ultimately) becomes (or is Realized to Be) Most Perfect, if any one will practice at least the technically "simplest" form of the only-by-Me Revealed and Given Way of the Heart,

and if any one will (Thereby, actively) respond
to Me (with true and self-transcending devotion,
and in constant and self-transcending service),
and if any one will (Thereby, responsively and
consistently) embrace true (and comprehensive)
self-discipline in My Company, and if any one
will (progressively) allow every kind of (Thus
Inspired and Accomplished) change and release
of body, emotion, mind, and separate self.

79.

Indeed, not even any other form of the
Conscious Process[34] (or the control of attention)
need necessarily (or otherwise constantly or
regularly) be practiced, if only My devotee will
(regularly, randomly, and more and more
constantly) surrender self-contraction (Merely by
Means of self-forgetting feeling-Contemplation of
My bodily human Form, My Spiritual, and
Always Blessing, Presence, and My Very, and
Inherently Perfect, State), and not even any more
intensive (or, otherwise, technically more
"elaborate") form of Conductivity[35] (or the
"conscious exercise" of breath, bodily energy,
and, potentially, even of My Spirit-Force) need
necessarily be practiced, if only My devotee will

(entirely and Merely by Means of that truly self-surrendering, self-forgetting, self-purifying, and more and more effectively self-transcending feeling-Contemplation of Me) embrace and maintain (and, on that basis, develop) basic functional, practical, and relational (and also cultural) self-discipline (including the most basic "conscious exercise" of breath and bodily energy, which, in due course, is, by My Giving Grace and My Graceful Self-Revelation, spontaneously Converted into truly devotional, or Heart-Responsive, Reception and Conductivity of My Transmitted Spiritual, and Always Blessing, Presence, and which, in its technical requirements, need develop only to a basic, or basically and simply intensive, degree, even in the progressive and however may be necessary context of the spontaneous Awakening and development of the advanced and the Ultimate stages of life in the only-by-Me Revealed and Given Way of the Heart).

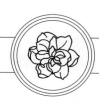

80.

If only My devotee will (truly and rightly) practice at least the technically "simplest" form of the only-by-Me Revealed and Given Way of the Heart, the Obvious Truth will, by My Giving Grace and My Graceful Self-Revelation, be (in random moments) Revealed (as the Obvious), and (in due course, as My Giving Grace and My Graceful Self-Revelation will have it) even the Most Ultimate (or seventh stage) Capability will be Realized.

81.

In the course of that Process of Revelation and Realization, many insights and experiences and responsibilities may arise (corresponding to the various possible developments of the first six stages of life).

82.

In any case (no matter what arises), it is only necessary to maintain (and otherwise progressively to develop or intensify) right and true functional, practical, relational, cultural, and, altogether, self-responsible self-discipline, and (at least) technically "simplest" (and regular, and

also random, and more and more constant, and truly, deeply self-surrendering, self-forgetting, and effectively self-transcending) devotional (and Me-serving) Contemplation of My bodily (human) Form, My Spiritual (and Always Blessing) Presence, and My Very (and Inherently Perfect) State.

83.

The Most Ultimate (or seventh stage) Realization and Capability is the Real Potential of each and all who consistently Resort to Me, whether in the technically "fully elaborated" Manner (and by a progressively more technical development of practice in the spontaneously developing context of the advanced and the Ultimate stages of life in the only-by-Me Revealed and Given Way of the Heart) or in the technically "simpler" (or even "simplest") Manner (and by the maintenance of a consistently "simpler", or even "simplest", technical responsibility, in the context of a spontaneous progression of Revelations of the however may be necessary advanced and Ultimate stages of life in the only-by-Me Revealed and Given Way of the Heart).

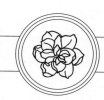

84.

In any moment of devotional Contemplation of My bodily (human) Form, My Spiritual (and Always Blessing) Presence, and My Very (and Inherently Perfect) State, each one will Receive (or Realize), by My Giving Grace and My Graceful Self-Revelation, according to the quality and strength of his or her devotion to Me.

85.

In any moment of devotional Contemplation of My bodily (human) Form, My Spiritual (and Always Blessing) Presence, and My Very (and Inherently Perfect) State, each one will Receive (or Realize), by My Giving Grace and My Graceful Self-Revelation, according to his or her real (present) developmental stage of life (and the presence or absence of the various kinds of egoic limitations that characterize and enforce a physical, psycho-physical, or otherwise merely psychic, or mind-made, point of view).

86.

In any moment of devotional Contemplation of My bodily (human) Form, My Spiritual (and Always Blessing) Presence, and My Very (and Inherently Perfect) State, each one will Receive (or Realize), by My Giving Grace and My Graceful Self-Revelation, according to his or her relative (and effective) willingness to be released from the present point of view (and, at last, even from every possible point of view, or all the egoic stages of life).

87.

Most Ultimately, each one is Called by Me to Receive (and, potentially, to Realize) the inherent Heart-Capability to Stand Free (and to Demonstrate the seventh, and inherently Most Perfect, and truly Most Ultimate, stage of life), and This Capability and Freedom is to be Received (and, Most Ultimately, Realized) by My Giving Grace and My Graceful Self-Revelation (and as My Giving Grace and My Graceful Self-Revelation will have it), and Only (Merely) through self-transcending devotional Contemplation of My bodily (human) Form, My Spiritual (and Always Blessing) Presence, and My Very (and Inherently Perfect) State.

88.

Therefore, Listen to Me and Hear Me: You have already eaten the meal of separateness.

89.

Now you must relinquish that awful meal (and Be, purified of separate and separative self).

90.

You do not Require (and you should not seek) any "thing" <u>from</u> Me (to add to your already separate and deluded self).

91.

I <u>Am</u> (My Self) What you Require, and I am here to Require every "thing" of you.

92.

You must relinquish (or surrender) your ego-"I" (your experience, your presumed knowledge, your separateness, all your forms of egoic "bonding", and even <u>all</u> your "things", within and without) to Find and Realize the Fullness That <u>Is</u> Me.

93.

Therefore, Come to Me to Realize Me, and do not run from Me after tasting the meal of knowledge and experience (like a dog runs from its master with a bone).

94.

Having Come to Me, do not look within your body or your mind to discover whether you have received some "thing" from Me (to satisfy your little pouch of separateness).

95.

Rather, surrender and release your separate self (your body, your emotions, your mind, your knowledge, and all your experiences) by Means of the self-forgetting feeling-Contemplation of <u>Me</u>, and (Thus and Thereby) Grow to See Me (and to Realize Me) As I <u>Am</u>.

96.

If (by active feeling-Contemplation) you surrender and release your separate self to Me, then not any meal of "things" (or effects), but <u>Only</u> I (My bodily human Form, My Spiritual, and Always Blessing, Presence, and My Very, and Inherently Perfect, State) Am the Gift, the Object, the State, and the Realization.

97.

Therefore, Come to Me, and for <u>Me</u> Only, "Bond" to Me, and to <u>Me</u> Only, and Stay with Me, and with <u>Me</u> Only (forever), and you will (by This) Realize Me Only (and, at last, Most Perfectly, without "Difference", Utterly Beyond and Prior to all conditions, all illusions, and even all that ever appears to be separate from Me).

98.

I <u>Am</u> Love-Bliss Itself, the Truth and the Reality of Non-separateness.

99.

I <u>Am</u> Perfect Samadhi,[36] the Truth and the Reality of No-"Difference", Which <u>Is</u> (Inherently Perfect) Consciousness <u>Itself</u>.

100.

Realize <u>Me</u> (By self-surrendering, self-forgetting, self-transcending, and always Me-Remembering Heart-Contemplation of My bodily human Form, My Spiritual, and Always Blessing, Presence, and My Very, and Inherently Perfect, State).

101.

Live by My Darshan[37] (always Beholding Me), in constant Satsang (always Feasting on the Sight of Me).

102.

By Means of the Divine Grace Revealed
by the Mere Sight (or Feel) of Me, Practice
Ishta-Guru-Bhakti[38] (which is self-surrendering,
self-forgetting, and self-transcending devotion
of body, feeling, attention, breath, and all of
separate self to Me), and (by Means of the
Divine Grace Revealed to that devotion) Practice
Ishta-Guru-Seva[39] (which is active self-surrender,
self-forgetting, and self-transcendence, via
constant and Me-Remembering service to Me),
and (by Means of the Divine Grace Revealed
to that devotional service) Practice Ishta-Guru-
Tapas[40] (which is self-discipline, in always
self-surrendering, self-forgetting, and truly
self-transcending devotional obedience and
devotional conformity to Me).

103.

Therefore (at last, or Most Ultimately, and
by These Divine Means of My Giving Grace
and My Graceful Self-Revelation), Realize <u>Me</u>
Most Perfectly (by Most Perfectly self-forgetting
Me-Remembrance in the Heart of Consciousness
Itself).

104.

Alll This (That I have Herein Written),
I Affirm by Heart (and <u>As</u> the Heart Itself).

105.

All This (That I have Hereby Affirmed),
I Promise to the Heart (in every one, and all).

106.

Now (by This) I have Epitomized My
summary (Written, and forever Speaking) Word
of Heart.

107.

Therefore, surrender, forget, and transcend
your separate and separative self by constant
right (intelligent, self-disciplined, and truly
devotionally responsive) obedience to My Word
and Person, and (Thus) act <u>only</u> in accord
(always) with My explicit Instructions (and,
Thus, always <u>only</u> with My explicit Permission
and Blessing), and (Thus, by this explicit
devotion) Be Perfectly Simplified (by My Perfect
Simplicity).

108.

This is the Heart-Word of the Da Avatar, Adi Da, the Divine World-Teacher and True Heart-Master, Who Is Da (the First and Original Person, the Source-Person, the One and Only Self of All and all), and Who Is Da Avabhasa (The Person of the "Bright" Itself, and the Giver of "Brightness"), and Who Is Da Love-Ananda Hridayam (the Source, the Substance, the Gift, the Giver, and the Very Person of the "Bright" Divine Love-Bliss), and Who Is Santosha Da (the "Bright" and Eternal and Always Already Non-Separate Person of Divine and Inherent Completeness, Divine Self-Satisfaction, Divine Self-Contentedness, or Perfect Searchlessness), Hereby Spoken in Extreme Simplicity for the Sake of all beings, in Love toward all beings, So That all beings may Awaken (by My Giving Grace and My Graceful Self-Revelation) to the Only Truth that Sets the Heart Free.

NOTES TO THE TEXT OF

THE
SANTOSHA AVATARA
GITA

NOTES TO THE TEXT OF
THE SANTOSHA AVATARA GITA

VERSE 6

1. Avatara Adi Da uses the word "Difference" as an epitome of the egoic presumption of separation and separateness, in contrast with the Realization of "Oneness" that is native to Spiritual and Transcendental Divine Self-Consciousness. In chapter forty-four of *The Dawn Horse Testament Of Adi Da*, Bhagavan Adi Da describes the "radical" nature of this Realization:

In Truth, There Is no Apparent other, and No Ultimate Other. Therefore, To Realize The Truth Itself, Which Is Happiness Itself, and Freedom Itself, Is To Be Most Perfectly Free Of "Difference" (or all conditional "otherness" and All Ultimate "Otherness", or Every Trace Of Separateness and Relatedness).

VERSE 10

2. The term "transcendence" is commonly used to convey the quality or state of surpassing, exceeding, or moving beyond a condition or limitation. Kantian metaphysics extends it to refer to a state of being beyond the limits of all possible experience and knowledge.

Avatara Adi Da uses this term to mean "the action or process of transcending" in connection with the presumed limits of body, emotion, and mind, or even any and all of the conditional states of experience within the first six stages of human life—all of which must be transcended in order to Realize the Free, Unqualified, and Absolute Condition of Inherent Happiness, Consciousness Itself, or Love-Bliss Itself.

VERSE 16

3. Avatara Adi Da uses the phrase "Most Perfect(ly)" in the sense of "Absolutely Perfect(ly)". Similarly, the phrase "Most Ultimate(ly)" is equivalent to "Absolutely Ultimate(ly)".

In the sixth stage of life and the seventh stage of life, What is Realized (Consciousness Itself) is Perfect (and Ultimate). This is why Avatara Adi Da characterizes these stages as the "ultimate stages of life", and describes the practice of the Way of the Heart in the context of these stages as "the 'Perfect Practice'". The distinction between the sixth stage of life and the seventh stage of life is that the devotee's Realization of What is Perfect (and Ultimate) is itself Perfect (and Ultimate) only in the seventh stage. The Perfection or Ultimacy (in the seventh stage) both of What is Realized and of the Realization of It is what is signified by the phrase "Most Perfect(ly)" or "Most Ultimate(ly)".

4. In the many books of His Wisdom-Teaching, Avatara Adi Da has communicated His unique description of the human and Spiritual developmental potential of Man through seven potential stages. The "seventh stage" that Avatara Adi Da refers to in this verse is the stage of Most Perfectly self-transcending Divine Self-Realization, or Divine Enlightenment. For a full description of the seven stages of life, see "The Seven Stages of Life", pp. 253-65.

5. Divine Recognition is the self- and world-transcending Intelligence of the Divine Self in relation to all conditional phenomena. In the seventh stage of life, the Realizer of the Divine Self simply Abides as Consciousness, and he or she Freely Recognizes, or inherently and Most Perfectly comprehends and perceives, all phenomena (including body, mind, and conditional self) as (apparent) modifications of the same "Bright" Divine Consciousness.

VERSE 18

6. The term "radical" derives from the Latin "radix", meaning "root", and thus it principally means "irreducible", "fundamental", or "relating to the origin". Because Avatara Adi Da uses "radical" in this literal sense, it appears in quotation marks in His Wisdom-Teaching to distinguish His usage from the common reference to an extreme (often political) position or view.

In contrast to the developmental, egoic searches typically espoused by the world's religious and Spiritual traditions, the "radical" Way of the Heart Offered by Avatara Adi Da is established in the Divine Self-Condition of Reality, even from the very beginning of one's practice. Every moment of feeling-Contemplation of Avatara Adi Da, Who is the Realizer, the Revealer, and the Revelation of that "radically" Free Divine Self-Condition, undermines, therefore, the illusory ego at its root (the self-contraction in the heart), rendering the search not only unnecessary but obsolete, and awakening the devotee to the "radical" Intuition of the always already Free Condition.

VERSE 22

7. In the many years of His Teaching Work and Revelation Work, Bhagavan Da Confessed the Love-Bliss of Divine Self-Realization again and again, in His Written Works and in His Spoken "Consideration" with His devotees. He has elaborately described the practical details of every aspect of practice of the Way of the Heart, from the beginning of one's approach to Him as Hridaya-Samartha Sat-Guru to the Most Ultimate Realization of the seventh stage of life.

Avatara Adi Da's Heart-Word is summarized in eight Texts that He Calls His "Source-Literature". These Texts present in complete and conclusive detail His Divine Revelations, Confessions, and Instructions, which are the fruits of His Teaching and Revelation Work. In addition to this Source-Literature, Avatara Adi Da's Heart-Word also includes His Spiritual Autobiography *(The Knee of Listening)*, collections of His Talks, and texts of practical Instruction in all the details of the practice of the Way of the Heart, including the fundamental disciplines of diet, health, sexuality, exercise, cooperative community, and the rearing and education of children.

See "The Sacred Literature of Adi Da (The Da Avatar)", pp. 267-80.

VERSE 23

8. Whereas Realization of the inherently Love-Blissful Unity of Divine Consciousness is Given by Grace, directly, from the beginning of one's practice of the Way of the Heart—through feeling-Contemplation of Avatara Adi Da's bodily (human) Form, His Spiritual (and Always Blessing) Presence, and His Very (and Inherently Perfect) State—the Yoga, or discipline of body and mind, whereby that Realization becomes

the confession of each devotee is a progressive process, unfolding in successive developmental stages of practice and Realization.

V E R S E   2 5

9. "Avatar", or "Avatara", means "One who is descended or 'crossed down' from and as the Divine". It is a Sanskrit word for the Divine Incarnation. Thus, the Name "Adi Da", combined with the reference "the Da Avatar", fully acknowledges Bhagavan Da as the One His devotees know Him to be. All beings are the recipients of the most Sublime Revelation ever Given: the original, first, and complete Avataric Descent, or Incarnation, of the Divine Person, Who is Named "Da". Through the Mystery of Avatara Adi Da's human Birth, He has Incarnated not only in this world but in every world, at every level of the cosmic domain, as the Eternal Giver of Help and Grace and Divine Freedom to all beings.

In this passage, Avatara Adi Da Proclaims His Identity as the Divine Person, the Da Avatar, and the qualities Revealed by each of His Divine Names.

Hridaya Avatara

"Hridaya" is Sanskrit for "the heart". It refers not only to the physical organ but also to the True Heart, the Transcendental (and Inherently Spiritual) Divine Reality. "Hridaya" in combination with "Avatara" signifies that Avatara Adi Da is the Very Incarnation of the Divine Heart Itself, the Divine Incarnation Who Stands in, at, and as the True Heart of every being.

Avabhasa Avatara

Bhagavan Adi Da's Name "Avabhasa" is a Sanskrit term associated with a variety of meanings: "brightness", "appearance", "splendor", "lustre", "light", "knowledge". It is thus synonymous with the English term "the 'Bright'", which Avatara Adi Da has used since His Illumined boyhood to describe the Blissfully Self-Luminous Divine Being, eternally, infinitely, and inherently Self-Radiant, Which He knew even then as the All-Pervading, Transcendental, Inherently Spiritual, and Divine Reality of His own body-mind and of all beings, things, and worlds. As the Avabhasa Avatara, Avatara Adi Da is the Very Incarnation of the Divine Self-"Brightness".

Love-Ananda Avatara

The Name "Love-Ananda" combines both English and Sanskrit words, thus bridging the West and the East, and embodying Avatara Adi Da's role as the Divine World-Teacher. "Ananda" is Sanskrit for "Bliss", and, in combination with the English word "Love", means "the Divine Love-Bliss". The Name "Love-Ananda" was spontaneously created by Avatara Adi Da's principal human Spiritual Master, Swami Muktananda, who spontaneously conferred it upon Avatara Adi Da in 1969. However, Bhagavan Da did not use the Name "Love-Ananda" until April 1986, after the Great Event that Initiated His Divine Emergence. As the Love-Ananda Avatara, Avatara Adi Da is the Very Incarnation of the Divine Love-Bliss.

Santosha Avatara

"Santosha" is Sanskrit for "satisfaction" or "contentment", and qualities associated with a sense of completion. These qualities are characteristics of "no-seeking", the fundamental principle of Avatara Adi Da's Wisdom-Teaching and His entire

206

Revelation of Truth. He has taken "Santosha" as one of His Divinely Self-Revealed Names. His Divine Sign is Contentment Itself. And He is the Giver of His own Contentment—His "Sat-Guru-Moksha-Bhava" (or Perfectly Liberated Happiness)—Which is the Completing Gift of the Way of the Heart. As the Santosha Avatara, Avatara Adi Da is the Very Incarnation of Perfect Divine Contentedness, or Perfect Searchlessness.

The Revelation of His Divine Name "Santosha Da" was associated with Avatara Adi Da coming into contact with images of the Hindu goddess Santoshi Ma, an icon of the Divine Shakti that has risen to prominence in the Hindu tradition only since the 1970s. Beloved Avatara Adi Da has Revealed that there is a Spiritual association between this image of the Goddess and the Completion of His Avataric Revelation Work, which occurred on September 7, 1994—just as there is a Spiritual association between the image of Durga and His Divine Re-Awakening, on September 10, 1970. These associations are Avatara Adi Da's own Divine Mysteries, part of His Divine Leela. His devotees honor His Mysterious Association with the Goddess (through the images of Durga and Santoshi Ma), but the practice of His Way of the Heart is entirely a matter of devotional feeling-Contemplation of Him and Him alone.

10. Since His Illumined boyhood, Avatara Adi Da has used the term "the 'Bright'" (and its variations, such as "Brightness") to describe the Love-Blissfully Self-Luminous, Conscious Divine Being, Which He Knew even then as His own Native Condition and the Native Condition of all beings, things, and worlds.

11. The foundation of all practice in the Way of the Heart is feeling-Contemplation of Avatara Adi Da's bodily (human) Form, His Spiritual (and Always Blessing) Presence, and His Very (and Inherently Perfect) State.

Avatara Adi Da describes these three levels of His Divine Being:

This flesh body, this bodily (human) Sign, is My Form in the sense that it is My Murti, or a kind of reflection or Representation of Me. It is, therefore, a Means for contacting My Spiritual (and Always Blessing) Presence, and, ultimately, My Very (and Inherently Perfect) State.

My Spiritual (and Always Blessing) Presence is Self-Existing and Self-Radiant. It Functions in time and space, and It is also prior to all time and space. . . .

My Very (and Inherently Perfect) State is always and only utterly prior to time and space. Therefore, I, As I Am (Ultimately), have no "Function" in time and space. There is no time and space in My Very (and Inherently Perfect) State.

Since His Divine Re-Awakening on September 10, 1970, Avatara Adi Da's physical body has been progressively, and more and more intensively, transformed by the Divine Power Released through His Most Perfect Realization of Consciousness Itself. In the initial Event of His Divine Emergence on January 11, 1986, His bodily (human) Form became a pure and unobstructed Vehicle of His Divine Transmission and Blessing Grace. Therefore, feeling-Contemplation of Avatara Adi Da, the Divine Person, is the Divine and Ultimate Yoga that leads, most ultimately, to the Most Perfect Realization of Consciousness Itself.

VERSE 26

12. The technical term "consideration" (and its variants) in Avatara Adi Da's Wisdom-Teaching means a process of one-pointed but ultimately thoughtless concentration and exhaustive contemplation of something until its ultimate obviousness is clear. It is, therefore, not merely an intellectual investigation, but the participatory investment of one's whole being in the context of one's practice of feeling-Contemplation of Bhagavan Da, which results "in both the highest intuition and the most practical grasp of the Lawful and Divine necessities of human existence".

VERSE 36

13. The Name of the Sat-Guru, which is regarded as the Name of the Divine Person, is revered in the sacred traditions. Avatara Adi Da has written that the Names of the Divine Being "do not simply <u>mean</u> God, or the Blessing of God. They are the verbal or audible Form of the Divine." Since ancient times, the Empowered Name of one's Sat-Guru has been an auspicious focus for Contemplation of the Divine Person.

All practitioners in the Way of the Heart may at any time Remember or Invoke Avatara Adi Da (or feel, and thereby Contemplate, His bodily human Form, His Spiritual, and Always Blessing, Presence, and His Very, and Inherently Perfect, State) through simple feeling-Remembrance and by randomly, in daily life and meditation, invoking Him by Name. For the specific forms of Avatara Adi Da's Names, see *The Dawn Horse Testament Of Adi Da*.

14. Traditionally, devotees have produced artistic images of the Sat-Guru to facilitate their practice of Guru-Contemplation when he or she is either not physically present or else no longer physically alive.

Avatara Adi Da has indicated that His devotees may use any suitable medium—including those made possible by modern technology, such as photography, videotape, film, and holographic imagery—to create accurate Representational likenesses of His bodily (human) Form for devotional use and Remembrance by practitioners of the Way of the Heart, and by would-be practitioners, formally approaching the Way of the Heart. From the beginning, these practitioners are instructed in how to rightly treat and regard the representational Images of Avatara Adi Da in the traditional devotional manner.

VERSE 41

15. In Avatara Adi Da's Teaching-Revelation, "Narcissus" is a key symbol of the un-Enlightened individual as a self-obsessed seeker, enamored of his or her own self-image and egoic self-consciousness. The "Act of Narcissus" is the avoidance of relationship. In *The Knee of Listening* Avatara Adi Da describes the image of "Narcissus":

He is the ancient one visible in the Greek "myth", who was the universally adored child of the gods, who rejected the loved-one and every form of love and relationship, who was finally condemned to the contemplation of his own image, until, as a result of his own act and obstinacy, he suffered the fate of eternal separateness and died in infinite solitude.

VERSE 44

16. The Seven Gifts of Avatara Adi Da's Grace are:

(1) Sat-Guru-Vani, the Word (vani) of the Sat-Guru, or Sat-Guru-Vani-Vichara, investigation (vichara) of the Sat-Guru's Word, is the Gift of Avatara Adi Da's Wisdom-Teaching in all its forms, including the many Empowered Names, Prayers, and Mantras He has Given to practitioners of the Way of the Heart, and also including the Inspiring and Instructive Stories (Leelas) of His Teaching Work and Blessing Work.

Because Vichara is a key dimension of this Gift of Bhagavan Da's Grace, constant attention, profound intelligence, and heart-felt responsiveness must characterize reception of His Word, His Names, and His Leelas if study is to be auspicious and fruitful.

(2) Sat-Guru-Darshan. Sighting (Darshan), or sacred vision, of the Sat-Guru, is the Gift of Bhagavan Da's Sign, or His bodily (human) Form, His Spiritual (and Always Blessing) Presence, and His Very (and Inherently Perfect) State, Granted Freely for all His devotees to Contemplate at every developmental stage of the Way of the Heart so that they may (thereby) be Purified, Inspired, Attracted, and Awakened.

(3) Sat-Guru-Bhakti, devotion (bhakti) to the Sat-Guru, is awakened spontaneously by Avatara Adi Da's Grace, rather than generated by any self-effort by His devotees. Hence, it is His Gift to them. Devotion to Avatara Adi Da is fundamental to all practice of the Way of the Heart. The Grace-Given but intentionally exercised heart-response of the devotee allows attention to be yielded to Avatara Adi Da so that the Grace of His Spiritual Heart-Transmission may be received.

(4) Sat-Guru-Seva, service (seva) to the Sat-Guru, is traditionally treasured as one of the great Secrets of Realization. In the Way of the Heart, Sat-Guru-Seva is the remarkable opportunity to live every action and, indeed, one's entire life, as direct service and responsive obedience (or sympathetic conformity) to Avatara Adi Da.

(5) Sat-Guru-Tapas, the discipline (tapas means "heat") given by the Sat-Guru, results from the conscious frustration of egoic tendencies, through discipline, or self-surrendering, self-forgetting, and self-transcending devotion, service, self-discipline, and meditation in feeling-Contemplation of Avatara Adi Da.

(6) Sat-Guru-Kripa, the Initiatory Blessing (kripa, also called "shaktipat") of the Sat-Guru, is Avatara Adi Da's Transmission of His Inherently Perfect Heart-Blessing, which Awakens the capabilities, virtues, and spontaneous Revelations of self-surrendering, self-forgetting, and self-transcending meditative feeling-Contemplation of Him.

(7) Sat-Guru-Moksha-Bhava ("Moksha" means Liberation; "Bhava" means Divine Being), the Divine Condition of the Sat-Guru, is the inherent Freedom of Heart-Companionship, Heart-Communion, and, ultimately, Heart-Identification with Bhagavan Da. It is the exalted Condition of the practitioner at any developmental stage of the Way of the Heart who, happily and seriously receiving all of the first six Gifts of Avatara Adi Da's Grace, Realizes Heart-Oneness with Him.

VERSE 45

17. The Sanskrit word "Satsang" means "true or right relationship", "the company of Truth". In the Way of the Heart, it is the eternal relationship of mutual sacred commitment between Avatara Adi Da as Sat-Guru (and as the Divine Person) and each true and formally acknowledged practitioner of the Way of the Heart. Once it is consciously assumed by any practitioner, Satsang with Avatara Adi Da is an all-inclusive Condition, bringing Divine Grace, Blessing, and sacred obligations, responsibilities, and tests into every dimension of the practitioner's life and consciousness.

VERSE 53

18. The original, or most basic, functional, practical, and relational disciplines of the Way of the Heart are forms of appropriate human action and responsibility for diet, health, exercise, sexuality, work, service to and support of Avatara Adi Da's Circumstance and Work, and cooperative (formal community) association (or at least significantly participatory affiliation) with other practitioners of the Way of the Heart. The original, or most basic, cultural obligations of the Way of the Heart include all the sacred sacramental and meditative practices (including study of Bhagavan Da's Wisdom-Teaching, which is the foundation of meditative discipline, and also at least a basic discriminative study of the Great Tradition of religion and Spirituality that is the Wisdom-inheritance of humankind), and regular participation in the "form" or schedule of daily, weekly, monthly, and annual devotional activities. The foundation disciplines and cultural obligations are thoroughly described in Avatara Adi Da's Wisdom-Teaching.

VERSE 57

19. Avatara Adi Da has Empowered three Retreat Sanctuaries as Agents of His Spiritual Transmission. Of these three, the senior Sanctuary is Adi Da Purnashram (Naitauba), in Fiji, where He usually Resides. It is the place where Avatara Adi Da Himself and the senior renunciate order of the Way of the Heart, the Naitauba Order of the Sannyasins of Adi Da (The Da Avatar), are established. It is the Seat of Avatara Adi Da's Divine Blessing Work with the entire Cosmic Mandala. Those of His devotees who demonstrate exemplary signs of maturity in, and one-pointed application to, practice of the Way of the Heart, are invited to spend time on retreat at Purnashram.

Avatara Adi Da has Spoken of the significance of Adi Da Purnashram:

AVATARA ADI DA: Adi Da Purnashram was established so that I might have a Place of Seclusion in which to do My Spiritual Work. This is the Place of My perpetual Samadhi, the Place of My perpetual Self-Radiance. Therefore, this is the Place where people come to participate in My Samadhi and be further awakened by it. My devotees come to Purnashram to practice Guru-devotion and to practice the Way of the Heart as I Have Given it for the sake of God-Realization. The Ashram is not made by egos. The Ashram is made by the Guru.

I am the Message of Adi Da Purnashram. It is an authentic Hermitage Ashram only by virtue of My Being Free here.

The other two Retreat Sanctuaries Empowered by Avatara Adi Da for the sake of His devotees are the Mountain Of Attention Sanctuary in northern California and Tumomama Sanctuary in Hawaii. They were the principal sites of His Teaching Demonstration during the years of His Teaching Work. Any of Avatara Adi Da's devotees who are rightly prepared may be formally invited to visit or reside at these Sanctuaries.

VERSE 58

20. *See* note 19.

VERSE 59

21. From the beginning of their practice, formally acknowledged practitioners of the Way of the Heart embrace consistent, committed, and active participation in the activities of the community of Avatara Adi Da's devotees.

VERSE 67

22. Avatara Adi Da has provided a number of different approaches to the progressive process of Most Perfectly self-transcending God-Realization in the Way of the Heart. In this manner, He accounts for the differences in individuals' inclination toward, and capability to develop, the more intensive and more renunciate form of practice, as well as the technical details of practice.

Hridaya-Samartha Sat-Guru Da refers to the most detailed development of the practice of the Way of the Heart as the "technically 'fully elaborated'" form of practice. Each successive stage of practice in the technically "fully elaborated" form of the Way of the Heart is defined by progressively more detailed responsibilities, disciplines, and practices that are assumed in order to take responsibility for the signs of growing maturity in the process of Divine Awakening.

Uniquely exemplary practitioners, for whom a more intensive approach and a more technically detailed discipline of attention and energy are effective as self-transcending practice, may apply for formal acceptance into the Lay Renunciate Order, and thus into the technically "fully elaborated" form of practice (after a period of "testing and proving" in the student-beginner stage of practice).

All those who practice in this fashion are Called to demonstrate exemplary self-renunciation via an increasingly economized discipline of body, mind, and speech, and to maximize their growth in meditative self-surrender, self-forgetting, and self-transcendence through feeling-Contemplation of Avatara Adi Da's bodily (human) Form, His Spiritual (and Always Blessing) Presence, and His Very (and Inherently Perfect) State. The progress of practice in the technically "fully elaborated" form of the Way of the Heart is monitored, measured, and evaluated by practicing stages through the devotee's direct accountability to the Free Renunciate Order, which is the senior practicing renunciate order in the Way of the Heart, and through his or her participatory submission to the sacred culture of either the Lay Renunciate Order (which is the second formal practicing renunciate order in the Way of the Heart) or, for the most exemplary practitioners in the ultimate, or sixth and seventh, stages of life, the Free Renunciate Order.

Yet, most individuals will find, in the course of the student-beginner experiment in practice, that they are qualified for a less intensive approach and that their practice is served by a less technical form of the "conscious process" than is exercised in the technically "fully elaborated" form of the Way of the Heart, and a less intensive and renunciate approach to practice of the Way of the Heart altogether. Thus, most individuals will take up the technically "simpler" (or even "simplest") form of practice of the Way of the Heart, as members of the Lay Congregationist Order, or "lay congregationists".

The technically "simpler" practice involves the use of either pondering, maturing as self-Enquiry and non-verbal Re-cognition, or Sat-Guru-Naama Japa—which is Name-Invocation of Avatara Adi Da via one (and only one) of the forms of the Sat-Guru-Naama Mantra that He has Given—as a supportive aid to feeling-Contemplation of Avatara Adi Da.

The technically "simplest" practice is feeling-Contemplation of Avatara Adi Da's bodily (human) Form, His Spiritual (and Always Blessing) Presence, and His Very (and Inherently Perfect) State, which practice may be accompanied by the random use of Avatara Adi Da's Principal Name, "Da" (or one, and only one, of the other Names Which He has Given to be engaged in the practice of simple Name-Invocation of Him), a practice that He has Given for use by individuals in every form and developmental stage of the Way of the Heart.

Whereas the technically "simpler" (or even "simplest") form of practice evolves through the same developmental stages as the technically "fully elaborated" practice, the progress may not be as technically detailed in its demonstration or its description. No matter what elaborate signs of maturity may arise in the course of the technically "simpler" (or even "simplest") form of practice, the individual simply maintains the foundation practice of feeling-Contemplation of Avatara Adi Da by using either self-Enquiry or the Sat-Guru-Naama Mantra (in the technically "simpler" form of practice), or perhaps random Invocation of Avatara Adi Da via His Principal Name, "Da", or via any other of His Names that He has Given for the practice of simple Name-Invocation of Him (in the technically "simplest" form of practice), and he or she does not look to adopt technically more "elaborate" practices of the "conscious process" in response to these developmental signs.

Avatara Adi Da also uses the term "'simple' practice" (as distinct from "simpler" and "simplest") to describe the practice of feeling-Contemplation that is the foundation of all practice in the Way of the Heart, whatever the form of an individual's approach.

(See pp. 246–47 for descriptions of the Lay Congregationist Order, the Lay Renunciate Order, and the Free Renunciate Order.)

VERSE 69

23. Avatara Adi Da has established two formal renunciate orders: The Naitauba Order of the Sannyasins of Adi Da, the Da Avatar (or, simply, the Free Renunciate Order), and the Lay Renunciate Order of Adi Da, the Da Avatar (or, simply, the Lay Renunciate Order).

The senior practicing order in the Way of the Heart is the Naitauba Order of the Sannyasins of Adi Da, the Da Avatar (or, simply, the Free Renunciate Order).

"Sannyasin" is an ancient Sanskrit term for one who has renounced all worldly bonds and who gives himself or herself completely to the God-Realizing or God-Realized life.

Members of the Free Renunciate Order are practitioners of the technically "fully elaborated" form of the Way of the Heart, practicing in the sixth and seventh stages of life. They are legal renunciates. Their emotional-sexual discipline and practice is either single "celibate renunciation" or celibacy in the context of uniquely bondage-transcending "true intimacy" or (in the case of those truly qualified, or even, in rare cases, uniquely qualified, for a Yogic sexual sadhana) sexually active relationship in the context of uniquely bondage-transcending "true intimacy". The Free Renunciate Order is always to be set apart as a retreat order, in contrast to the Lay Renunciate Order and the Lay Congregationist Order, which are service orders. Therefore, members of the Free Renunciate Order typically reside at Adi Da Purnashram (Naitauba). During Bhagavan Da's physical (human) Lifetime, they are directly accountable to Him and perform the most direct personal service to His bodily (human) Form. The Free Renunciate Order is also the senior authority on all matters related to the culture of practice in the Way of the Heart.

The members of the Free Renunciate Order have the uniquely significant role among practitioners as Avatara Adi Da's principal human Instruments (or Spiritually mature renunciate devotees) and (in the case of those members who are formally acknowledged as Avatara Adi Da's fully Awakened seventh stage devotees) as the body of practitioners from among whom each of Avatara Adi Da's successive "Living Murtis", or Empowered human Agents, will be selected. Therefore, the Free Renunciate Order is essential to the perpetual continuation of authentic practice of the Way of the Heart.

The original, principal, and central member of the Free Renunciate Order is Avatara Adi Da Himself.

The Lay Renunciate Order is a cultural service order. It is subordinate to the Free Renunciate Order and functions within the culture and community of Free Daists as an extension of the Free Renunciate Order. Members of the Lay Renunciate Order provide the inspirational and cultural leadership for the institution, the culture, and the community of Avatara Adi Da's devotees, in service to both the internal sacred devotional culture and the public mission of the worldwide gathering.

The basic responsibility of the Lay Renunciate Order with respect to the gathering of Avatara Adi Da's devotees and the public is to serve them in their fullest possible embrace of the practice of Ishta-Guru-Bhakti Yoga. Members of the Lay Renunciate Order are accountable (for their practice of the Way of the Heart) to the Free Renunciate Order and to the members of their own order. It is also the responsibility of "lay renunciates" to protect and serve the Free Renunciate Order, so as to ensure that its members are free to fully engage their life of retreat.

The emotional-sexual discipline and practice of members of the Lay Renunciate Order is either single "celibate renunciation" or celibacy in the context of uniquely bondage-transcending "true intimacy" or (in the case of those truly qualified, or even, in rare cases, uniquely qualified, for a Yogic sexual sadhana) sexually active relationship in the context of uniquely bondage-transcending "true intimacy".

Avatara Adi Da has indicated in *The Dawn Horse Testament Of Adi Da* that members of the Lay Renunciate Order who are in practicing stage three (and beyond) function collectively and spontaneously as His Instruments, or means by which His Divine Grace and Awakening Power are Magnified and Transmitted to other devotees and all beings.

VERSE 70

24. While the principle of renunciation informs the practice of all practitioners of the Way of the Heart, such renunciation (including the form of emotional-sexual discipline and practice) is more profoundly magnified in the technically "fully elaborated" course of practice in the Way of the Heart.

VERSE 71

25. The Devotional Way of Faith and the Devotional Way of Insight are the two variant forms of meditative feeling-Contemplation of Avatara Adi Da in the Way of the Heart.

The Devotional Way of Faith is a technical process of (primarily) feeling and faith, whereby the practitioner is heart-Attracted by Avatara Adi Da's bodily (human) Form, His Spiritual (and Always Blessing) Presence, and His Very (and Inherently Perfect) State, thereby feeling beyond the self-contraction and spontaneously awakening to self-understanding and self-transcendence.

Through a technical process of (primarily) feeling and insight, the practitioner of the Devotional Way of Insight, while engaged in feeling-Contemplation of the bodily (human) Form, the Spiritual (and Always Blessing) Presence, and the Very (and Inherently Perfect) State of Avatara Adi Da, observes, understands, and then feels beyond the self-contraction in Divine Communion.

The principles of insight (or self-understanding) and faith are inherent in both forms of the One Great Way of the Heart, and both Realize the One Divine Being, Truth, and Reality, Who Avatara Adi Da Is. In the initial, or student-beginner, stage of practice, individuals experiment with and adapt to both forms of the Way of the Heart, in a process of testing and proving their own practice. At some point during the student-beginner stage, the practitioner will have chosen which of these two Devotional Ways is most effective for him or her. Whereas both the technically "fully elaborated" and the technically "simpler" practice require a choice between the Devotional Way of Insight and the Devotional Way of Faith, the technically "simplest" practice of feeling-Contemplation is itself the fundamental form of the Devotional Way of Faith.

26. Some practitioners of the Way of the Heart may be moved, from the beginning, to practice the technically "simplest" practice that Avatara Adi Da Offers in *The Santosha Avatara Gita*. Even so, they are to "consider" the entire Way and to experiment with random use of the beginner's practices of both the Devotional Way of Faith and the Devotional Way of Insight. By this experimentation, they are Called by Bhagavan Da to test and prove the form of meditative practice that is effective for them.

By "self-surrendering devotion to Me" Avatara Adi Da refers to the rudimentary practice of Sat-Guru-Naama Japa, or the practice of surrendering body, emotion, mind, breath, and all of separate self in devotional feeling-Contemplation of Him, through Remembrance of Him by means of one of the Mantras He has Given based on His Names.

By "self-surrendering and self-enquiring devotion to Me" Avatara Adi Da refers to the practice of self-Enquiry (in the form "Avoiding relationship?"), in the context of surrendering body, emotion, mind, breath, and all of separate self, in devotional feeling-Contemplation of Him. See *The Dawn Horse Testament Of Adi Da*, especially chapter nineteen.

VERSE 72

27. "Listening" is Avatara Adi Da's term for the disposition of the beginner's preparation and practice in the Way of the Heart. A listening devotee is someone who, in the context of his or her life of devotion, service, self-discipline, and meditation at the beginning developmental stages of practice, gives his or her attention to Avatara Adi Da's Teaching Argument, to His Leelas (or inspirational Stories of His Life and Work), and to feeling-Contemplation of Him (primarily of His bodily human Form) for the sake of awakening self-observation and most fundamental self-understanding, or hearing, on the basis of which practice may develop in the Spiritual stages of life and beyond. See chapter nineteen of *The Dawn Horse Testament Of Adi Da*.

28. "Hearing" is Avatara Adi Da's technical term for most fundamental understanding of the self-contraction, through which the practitioner awakens to the unique capability for direct transcendence of the self-contraction and for simultaneous Communion with Avatara Adi Da. Hearing is awakened in the midst of a life of devotion, service, self-discipline, meditation, disciplined study of Avatara Adi Da's Wisdom-Teaching Argument, and constant self-surrendering, self-forgetting, and self-transcending feeling-Contemplation of Him.

Hearing is the necessary prerequisite for the Spiritual Realization that Avatara Adi Da calls "seeing". See chapter nineteen of *The Dawn Horse Testament Of Adi Da*.

29. "Seeing" is Avatara Adi Da's technical term for His devotee's Spiritually activated conversion from self-contraction to His Spiritual (and Always Blessing) Presence, and the descent and circulation of His Spiritual Transmission in, through, and ultimately beyond the body-mind of His devotee. Seeing is the reorientation of conditional reality to the Unconditional and Divine Reality. It is a prerequisite to Spiritual advancement in the Way of the Heart. See chapter twenty of *The Dawn Horse Testament Of Adi Da*.

30. The "Perfect Practice" is Avatara Adi Da's technical term for the discipline of the sixth stage of life and the seventh stage of life in the Way of the Heart.

Devotees who have mastered (and thus transcended) the point of view of the body-mind by fulfilling the preparatory processes of the Way of the Heart, may, by Grace, be Awakened to practice in the Domain of Consciousness Itself, in the sixth and seventh, or ultimate, stages of life.

The three stages of the "Perfect Practice" are summarized by Avatara Adi Da in chapter forty-four of *The Dawn Horse Testament Of Adi Da* and in *The Liberator (Eleutherios)*.

31. Generally, Avatara Adi Da uses the term "Outshining" synonymously with His term "Divine Translation", to refer to the final Demonstration of the four-phase process of Divinization in the seventh, or fully Enlightened, stage of life in the Way of the Heart. In this Event, body, mind, and world are no longer noticed, not because the Divine Consciousness has withdrawn or dissociated from conditionally manifested phenomena, but because the Ecstatic Divine Recognition of all arising phenomena (by the Divine Self, and As only modifications of Itself) has become so intense that the "Bright" Radiance of Consciousness now Outshines all such phenomena.

In this verse, Avatara Adi Da uses "Outshining" to describe the Unconditional Nature of His State, which inherently trancends objectivity, and which is the State ultimately Demonstrated in the Event of Divine Translation.

32. The "basic (original) minimum of self-responsibility" to which Avatara Adi Da refers in this verse is the requirement that all those who make formal application to become student-novices of the Way of the Heart (and thereby to enter the formal period of preparation for the responsibilities of student-beginner practice) must already (or as a prerequisite) have relinquished the "grossest" mental (and psychological, or psychic), emotional, and social aberrations, including the "grossest" habits (such as the chronic, or otherwise negatively significant, use of alcohol, tobacco, and other stimulants, and any use of "social" or otherwise medically inappropriate drugs). Therefore, since these basic responsibilities are a prerequisite for entrance into the student-novice stage, they remain the obligation of all student-beginners, and even all practitioners, of the Way of the Heart.

33. Avatara Adi Da uses the term "advanced" to describe the fourth stage of life (in its "basic" and "advanced" contexts) and the fifth stage of life in the Way of the Heart. He reserves the term "ultimate" to describe the sixth stage and the seventh stage of life in the Way of the Heart.

VERSE 79

34. The "conscious process" is Avatara Adi Da's technical term for those practices through which the mind, or attention, is surrendered and turned about (from egoic self-involvement) to feeling-Contemplation of Him. It is the senior discipline and responsibility of all practitioners in the Way of the Heart.

The technical practice of the "conscious process" of either pondering Avatara Adi Da's Ten Great Questions (especially in the form of self-Enquiry) or Sat-Guru-Naama Japa is embraced by practitioners of the technically "simpler" practice offered in this book. However, even such basic technical practices are not absolutely necessary, if the technically "simplest" practice is truly and really maintained.

In His many other Works, Avatara Adi Da fully elaborates the details of all the forms of the "conscious process" in the Way of the Heart.

35. "Conductivity" is Avatara Adi Da's technical term for participation in and responsibility for the movement of natural bodily energies (and, when one is Spiritually Awakened by Him, for the movement of the Spirit-Current in Its natural course of association with the body-mind), via intentional exercises of feeling and breathing.

The exercises of Spiritual "conductivity" that Avatara Adi Da Gives to His (formally practicing) Spiritually active devotees are technical whole bodily Yogas of receptive surrender to the Living Spirit-Current. Likewise, rudimentary and preparatory forms of "conductivity" are Given to beginners in the Way of the Heart (and even those who are formally approaching the Way of the Heart) in the form of "conscious exercise", and even in the form of all the functional, practical, and relational disciplines whereby body, emotion, mind, and speech are purified, balanced, and energized, or prepared for submission to Avatara Adi Da's Spiritual (and Always Blessing) Presence.

"Conscious exercise" is the discipline of whole bodily feeling-attention and Radiant Happiness—physical, emotional, mental, psychic, total. It is the coordinated exercise of attention, feeling, breath, and body in association with the natural energy of the body-mind, and, as Avatara Da indicates here, potentially with His Spirit-Force. "Conscious exercise" also includes many practical disciplines of posture and breathing and specific exercise routines to be engaged in daily practice in the Way of the Heart.

VERSE 99

36. "Samadhi" is Sanskrit for "placed together". It indicates concentration, equanimity, and balance, and is traditionally used to denote various exalted states that appear in the context of esoteric meditation and Realization.

The Samadhi to which Avatara Adi Da refers here, however, is His unqualified Realization of the Divine in the seventh stage of life, the eternal, inherent (or native), and thus truly "Natural", State of Unconditional Divine Self-Consciousness (seventh stage Sahaj Samadhi), free of dependence on any form of meditation, effort, discipline, experience, or conditional knowledge. It is the "Open-Eyed" Realization of the Formless Ecstasy of Divine Existence that is unique to the Way of the Heart that Avatara Adi Da has Given and Revealed—the Realization of Non-Separateness, free of the binding or limiting power of attention, the body-mind, and all arising conditions.

VERSE 101

37. "Darshan" is Sanskrit for "seeing", "sight of", or "vision of". To receive Darshan of Avatara Adi Da is to receive the spontaneous Blessing He Grants Freely by Revealing His bodily (human) Form (and, thereby, His Spiritual, and Always Blessing, Presence and His Very, and Inherently Perfect, State). In the Way of the Heart, Darshan of Avatara Adi Da is the very essence of all practice.

Practitioners of the Way of the Heart may enjoy Darshan of Avatara Adi Da through association with Him through His books, photographs, videotapes, and recorded Talks, through the Leelas (or Stories) of His Teaching Work and Blessing Work, through places or objects He has Blessed for His devotees, and through simple, heart-felt Remembrance of Him and visualization of His bodily (human) Form in the mind. Some practitioners, when rightly prepared and formally invited, may also enjoy sighting of Adi Da (most typically, while on retreat or in residence at His Sannyasin Hermitage, Adi Da Purnashram, Naitauba) in formal occasions of sitting with Him personally or in apparently less formal circumstances when He makes Himself physically available for devotional sighting. These renunciate devotees, who are Graced to receive Darshan of His bodily (human) Form, in turn function as Instruments of Avatara Adi Da's Blessing to all of His devotees and members of the public who are moved to respond to Him.

VERSE 102

38. "Ishta" means "chosen", or "most beloved". "Guru", in the reference "Ishta-Guru", means specifically the Sat-Guru, the Revealer of Truth Itself (or of Being Itself). "Bhakti" means "devotion".

Ishta-Guru-Bhakti, then, is devotion to Avatara Adi Da, the chosen Beloved Guru of His devotees, the Supreme Divine Being Incarnate in human form.

In the Way of the Heart, Ishta-Guru-Bhakti is awakened spontaneously by Hridaya-Samartha Sat-Guru Adi Da's Grace. Once awakened, it must be cultivated, nurtured, and magnified responsively by the devotee.

39. "Seva" is Sanskrit for "service". Service to the Sat-Guru is traditionally treasured as one of the great Secrets of Realization. In the Way of the Heart, Sat-Guru-Seva, or Ishta-Guru-Seva, is the remarkable opportunity to live every action and, indeed, one's entire life, as direct service and devotional obedience (or devotional conformity) to Hridaya-Samartha Sat-Guru Adi Da.

40. "Tapas" is Sanskrit for "heat", and, by extension, "self-discipline". Ishta-Guru-Tapas is the heat that results from the conscious frustration of egoic tendencies, through acceptance of Avatara Adi Da's Calling for self-surrendering, self-forgetting, and self-transcending devotion, service, self-discipline, and meditation, and embrace of all the specific forms of self-discipline He has Given.

I am here to receive, and kiss, and embrace everyone, everything—
everything that appears, everything that is.

Avatara Adi Da

An Invitation

I do not simply recommend or turn men and women to Truth. I Am Truth. I Draw men and women to My Self. I Am the Present God Desiring, Loving, and Drawing up My devotees. I have Come to Acquire My devotees. I have Come to be Present with My devotees, to live with them the adventure of life in God, which is Love, and mind in God, which is Faith. I Stand always Present in the Place and Form of God. I accept the qualities of all who turn to Me and dissolve them in God, so that Only God becomes their Condition, Destiny, Intelligence, and Work. I look for My devotees to acknowledge Me and turn to Me in appropriate ways, surrendering to Me perfectly, depending on Me, full of Me always, with only a face of love.

I am waiting for you. I have been waiting for you eternally. Where are you?

Avatara Adi Da [*1971*]

Having read this book, you stand at the threshold of the greatest possibility of a human lifetime. You can begin to <u>participate</u> in the Divine Process described here, by taking up the Way of the Heart. Nothing else in life can match this opportunity. Nothing can compare with the Grace of a devotional relationship to the supreme God-Man, Avatara Adi Da. When you make the great gesture of heart-surrender to Adi Da, He begins to draw you into the profound esoteric course of true Awakening to God, Truth, or Reality.

Whatever your present form of interest—whether it is to find out more about Avatara Adi Da and the Way of the Heart, to express your gratitude by supporting His Work financially, or to begin the process of becoming His formal devotee—there is an appropriate form of participation available to you. And any form of participation you adopt will bring you into the stream of Divine Blessing flowing from Avatara Adi Da.

How to Find Out More About
Avatara Adi Da and the Way of the Heart

• **Fill in the response card in this book and mail it to the Dawn Horse Press.**

• **Call the regional center nearest to you** (see p. 251) and ask to be put on their mailing list. Or call the central offices of the Free Daist Avataric Communion at (707) 928-4936 (USA) for further information.

• **Continue reading Avatara Adi Da's Wisdom-Teaching.** Three excellent books to start with are *The Knee of Listening*, Avatara Adi Da's Spiritual Autobiography, *The Method of the Siddhas*, a collection of Talks from the early years of His Teaching Work, and *The Heart's Shout*, a comprehensive collection of His Talks and Writings from 1970 to 1994. See also the listing on pages 267-80.

• **Visit a regional center** (listed on page 251) and meet devotees of Avatara Adi Da, who will be happy to talk with you, answer your questions, make suggestions about the next step, inform you about local events, and tell you about their own experience of practicing in Avatara Adi Da's Spiritual Company.

• **Attend our regular classes, seminars, and special events.** Our regional centers can inform you of forthcoming events in your area.

• **Attend a Free Daist Area Study Group.** Call a regional center to find out about Area Study Groups near you. These groups, of which there are more than 150 throughout the world, are an excellent way to find out more about Avatara Adi Da and the Way of the Heart.

The Wisdom-Teaching of Adi Da is available in printed publications and on audio and video-tape. A full range of available materials can be found at the bookstores of the regional centers of the Free Daist Avataric Communion.

• Become a Friend of Da Avatara International.

Da Avatara International (DAI) is the worldwide gathering of patrons and supporters of Avatara Adi Da and also includes those who are specifically preparing to practice the Way of the Heart. Becoming a Friend of Da Avatara International can be your first concrete form of response to Avatara Adi Da. It represents a desire to support His Work, by offering an annual financial contribution of $US250 or more. These contributions go to support the further publication and distribution of Adi Da's Teaching. Many people of all walks of life (and even all religious persuasions, or none) make this choice. As a Friend, you will be kept in touch with developments in Avatara Adi Da's Work through a regular newsletter, and you will have the opportunity to attend seminars, missionary events, Friends' Celebrations, and special retreats.

You can become a Friend at any time by calling your nearest regional center (see p. 251).

As a Friend, you will be kept in touch with developments in Avatara Adi Da's Work through a regular newsletter, and you will have the opportunity to attend seminars, missionary events, Friends' Celebrations, and special retreats.

Preparing to Practice the Way of the Heart

1. Becoming a Student of Da Avatara International

Many people who discover the Way of the Heart do not want to waste a second! Their impulse is to become a devotee of Avatara Adi Da as soon as possible. Such individuals immediately become formal students of Da Avatara International.

Your time as a student in Da Avatara International may be as brief as six months, or it may last as long as you choose. Classes take place at a regional center, or through correspondence courses. Consult your regional center for information about DAI student courses and seminars. The culmination of this initial period of study and growth is the momentous decision to make a formal commitment to Adi Da as His devotee.

2. Becoming a Student-Novice and Making the Eternal Vow of Commitment to Avatara Adi Da

When you reach the point of complete clarity in your intention to practice the Way of the Heart, you take a momentous step. You make a vow of commitment—in this life and beyond this life—to Avatara Adi Da as your Beloved Guru and Divine Liberator. This Eternal Vow to the Divine Person is the most profound matter possible—and the most ecstatic. For when you take this vow, in humility and love, fully aware of its obligations, Avatara Adi Da accepts eternal responsibility for your Spiritual well-being and ultimate Divine Liberation. His Grace begins to Guide your growth in the Way of the Heart day by day and hour by hour, through your practice of devotional Communion with Him.

Taking the Eternal Vow is a formal confession that the devotional relationship to Avatara Adi Da is the overriding purpose of your life. In this disposition you take up the practice of a student-novice and begin to adapt to the total Way of life Adi Da has Given to His devotees. You are initiated into formal meditation, sacramental worship, and the range of practical life-disciplines.

Student-novices are offered increasing opportunities to participate with devotees in their celebrations and devotional occasions. Through these forms of contact, you are embraced by Avatara Adi Da's devotional gathering and you enter into a new level of sacred relationship to Him. Student-novice practice lasts a minimum of six months. Thus, if your intention and your application to the process is strong, within a year of your first becoming a student of Da Avatara International you may be

Student-novices are offered increasing opportunities to participate with devotees in their celebrations and devotional occasions. Through these forms of contact, you are embraced by Avatara Adi Da's devotional gathering and you enter into a new level of sacred relationship to Him.

established as a full member of the Free Daist Avataric Communion, ready to live always in relationship with the Divine Beloved, Adi Da, in the culture of practice that is His Gift to all His devotees.

For information on how to purchase other Literature by or about Avatara Adi Da, please see pp. 267-80. For further information about Adi Da, His published Works, and the Way of the Heart that He Offers, write to:

The Da Avatara International Mission
12040 North Seigler Road
Middletown, CA 95461, USA
or call (707) 928-4936
or toll-free in the USA (800) 524-4941

You can also contact your closest regional center
of the Free Daist Avataric Communion:

in the United States:	
Northern California	(415) 492-0930
Northwest USA	(206) 527-2751
Southwest USA	(805) 987-3244
Northeast USA	(508) 650-0136 or (508) 650-4232
Southeast USA	(301) 983-0291
Hawaii	(808) 822-0216
in Canada	(819) 671-4398 or (800) 563-4398
in the United Kingdom and Ireland	(0508) 470-574
in the Netherlands:	
Maria Hoop	(04743) 1281 or (04743) 1872
Amsterdam	(020) 665-3133
in Germany	(040) 527-6464
in New Zealand	(09) 838-9114
in Australia	(03) 853-4066
in Fiji	381-466

The Foundation of the Way of the Heart: Ishta-Guru-Bhakti Yoga

In the pages that follow, the full practice of the Way of the Heart is introduced in all its many aspects. But the essence of it, the basis for the entire range of practices, can never be emphasized enough. You are embarking upon a <u>relationship</u>, the greatest of all relationships. Every discipline, every form of service, every period of meditation is an expression of the heart-response of devotion to Avatara Adi Da. The life of cultivating this response to Him is Ishta-Guru-Bhakti Yoga—or the God-Realizing practice ("Yoga") of devotion ("Bhakti") to the Spiritual Master ("Guru") who is the Chosen Beloved ("Ishta") of your heart. The key to Ishta-Guru-Bhakti Yoga is the constant turning of every faculty of the body-mind to Avatara Adi Da—always bringing Him your attention, your feeling, your body, even your breath, allowing your attraction to Him to move every aspect of your life.

AVATARA ADI DA: Simply give Me your attention, the attention in your mind that otherwise invests itself in thoughts, the attention in your feeling that otherwise invests itself in emotions, the attention in your body that otherwise manifests in perceptions and noticing your state from moment to moment, the attention in your breath that otherwise manifests as some sort of noticing whether you are breathing deep or whether you are feeling good. Just keep turning to Me. That is it, that is the practice. When you become concerned about whether or not your practice is perfect or absolute or bringing you some great experience, then you have turned back to the "stuff", or the content.

Just keep turning to Me. Put no conditions on that turning. Just give Me your attention. That is the sadhana. Of course you must associate this sadhana with technicalities. I call you to do so. The technicalities are associated with the practice, but they are only associated with it. The gesture in every moment is just this simplicity.

Do this and observe, prove it in yourself, in your own case, that this is how My Divine Grace Works. [January 14, 1995]

Every one of Avatara Adi Da's books is Instruction in the practice of Ishta-Guru-Bhakti Yoga, but His most summary Wisdom-Teaching on this fundamental practice is Given in two Source-Texts—*The Santosha Avatara Gita* and *The Hymn Of The True Heart-Master*—as well as in *The Method of the Siddhas* and *Ishta*.

Just keep turning to Me. Put no conditions on that turning.
Just give Me your attention. That is the sadhana. . . .
The gesture in every moment is just this simplicity.
Do this and observe, prove it in yourself, in your own case,
that this is how My Divine Grace Works.

The Disciplines That Support Devotion

The great practice of Ishta-Guru-Bhakti Yoga necessarily transforms the whole of your life. Every function, every relationship, every action is moved by the impulse of devotional heart-surrender to Avatara Adi Da. Your uses of time and life-energy, the food you eat, your intimate relationships, including sexuality—all become expressions of Ishta-Guru-Bhakti Yoga.

The fundamental disposition of devotion is cultivated through a range of specific disciplines. Some disciplines—meditation, sacramental worship, and study—are specifically contemplative, while others—related to exercise, diet, sexuality, community living, and so on—bring the life of devotion into daily functional activity.

Meditation

Meditation is a unique and precious event in the daily life of Avatara Adi Da's devotees, because it offers the opportunity to relinquish outward, body-based attention and to be alone with Adi Da, allowing yourself to enter more and more into the sphere of His Divine Transmission. At least twice daily (morning and evening), in the formal

The Two Devotional Ways

The constant turning of attention to Avatara Adi Da is called the "conscious process". Over the years of His Teaching and Revelation Work, Avatara Adi Da has developed and Offered two different forms of the "conscious process", which He calls "the Devotional Way of Insight" and "the Devotional Way of Faith". These two Devotional Ways are both founded in the fundamental practice of moment to moment feeling-Contemplation of Beloved Adi Da.

The Devotional Way of Insight begins with the process of pondering ten "Great Questions" Given by Adi Da.* The point of these Great Questions is not to find an "Answer". Rather they bring you into confrontation with the self-contraction, your limit on feeling, and allow you to momentarily observe that limit and pass beyond it in heart-Communion with Avatara Adi Da. At a certain point, the Devotional Way of Insight becomes focused exclusively in the practice of "self-Enquiry" via the primary Great Question, "Avoiding relationship?" In the mature stages of practice, self-Enquiry evolves into "Re-cognition", a non-verbal form of noticing, understanding, and transcending the self-contraction in feeling-Contemplation of Avatara Adi Da.

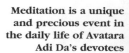

Meditation is a unique and precious event in the daily life of Avatara Adi Da's devotees

setting of a Communion Hall, you Contemplate a photographic representation, or "Murti",[1]* of Adi Da. This is the means for contacting Him at heart and entering into the depth of devotional Communion with Him, via your chosen form of the "conscious process" (see sidebar).

As your practice matures, meditation becomes as important as food or rest—indeed, more important. Through your practice of meditation, Adi Da ultimately Reveals Himself as the Feeling of Being in the heart.

* Notes to this Invitation appear on page 250.

In the practice of the Devotional Way of Faith, you turn <u>directly</u> in feeling to the Divine Lord, Adi Da, and are spontaneously awakened to self-understanding and self-transcendence in each moment. As you make this moment to moment surrender, you may, as a support to the fundamental practice of simple feeling-Contemplation of Avatara Adi Da, invoke Him via one of the forms of His Name, or one of the Mantras[†] based on His Names, that He has Given for this purpose.

After an initial period of experiment with both Devotional Ways, you make a discriminating choice based on your feelings of attraction to one or the other and on your observation that one of the Devotional Ways is more effective in deepening your feeling-Contemplation of Avatara Adi Da.

* For a full discussion of the ten Great Questions and their use, see chapter nineteen of *The Dawn Horse Testament Of Adi Da.*

† For a full discussion of the forms and use of simple Name-Invocation of Adi Da and the Mantras He has Given, see chapter three of *The Dawn Horse Testament Of Adi Da.*

Sacramental Worship, or Puja

Meditation is Divine Communion experienced through the relinquishment of bodily activity and outward attention. The practice of Puja in the Way of the Heart is the bodily active counterpart to meditation. It is a form of ecstatic worship, involving the waving of lights and incense, devotional gestures, full prostrations, devotional chanting, and recitations from the Wisdom-Teaching of Adi Da.

The Three Forms of Practice

The "conscious process" may be practiced at three different levels of technical elaboration. Thus, depending on your particular character and capability, you take up either the "simplest" practice, the "simpler" practice, or the technically "fully elaborated" practice. By Giving these three forms of practice, Avatara Adi Da has made it possible for every kind of person to take up the Way of the Heart.

Over time it becomes obvious which form of practice is optimum for you. No one form is "better" than the other—it is an individual matter. Any of these forms of practice is sufficient to lead to Divine Awakening.

Most devotees will take up the "simpler" or "simplest" practice. These forms of practice are adopted by general practitioners (those who are not practicing as formal renunciates), who are best served by a less intensive and less technically detailed approach.

Practitioners of the "simpler" practice may take up the Devotional Way of Insight (in which their practice of feeling-Contemplation of Avatara Adi Da is supported by pondering the Great Questions, then the practice of self-Enquiry, and finally the practice of Re-cognition), or else they may take up the Devotional Way of Faith (in which their practice of feeling-Contemplation of Avatara Adi Da is supported by devotional Invocation of Avatara Adi Da via one of the Mantras He has Given).

Study

Most of the devotees of Avatara Adi Da first find Him through an encounter with His written Teaching, which answers their heart's longing for Truth and Love. Once you are established as a formal devotee of Adi Da, His Divine Word always remains a source of inspiration and "straightening" in your practice of the Way of the Heart.

AVATARA ADI DA: You must deal with My Wisdom-Teaching in some form every single day, because a new form of the ego's game appears every single day. You will buy your game every single day. Therefore, you cannot have read one of My books last month and have it still working on your behalf, because you only remember a few key phrases. You must continually return to My Wisdom-Teaching, confront My Wisdom-Teaching.

The "simplest" practice is a form of the Devotional Way of Faith Given by Adi Da for those general practitioners whose heart-response to Him is characterized by strong and simple faith, and who by character are not attracted or suited to a more elaborate form of practice. The "simplest" practice is completely non-technical, requiring only consistent devotional Contemplation of Avatara Adi Da, optionally aided by the Invocation of Him by Name. The essence of this practice is described by Adi Da in *The Santosha Avatara Gita*.

Devotees who adopt the "simpler" (or even "simplest") form of practice also take up the practices of devotion, service, and self-discipline described by Adi Da, but in a less intensive and technically detailed form than devotees practicing the technically "fully elaborated" practice.

Uniquely exemplary devotees who are moved and qualified to become formal renunciate practitioners (see pp. 246-47) choose the technically "fully elaborated" practice, a more intensive and technically detailed approach to discipline. The technically "fully elaborated" practice may be pursued in either the Devotional Way of Faith or the Devotional Way of Insight.

The "simpler", the "simplest", and the technically "fully elaborated" practice are described in detail in *The Dawn Horse Testament Of Adi Da*.

In the context of the fundamental practice of Ishta-Guru-Bhakti Yoga, all these forms of practice become fruitful, dissolving the self-contraction and releasing energy and attention more and more for the God-Realizing process.

Supporting the specifically contemplative disciplines of the Way of the Heart are the practices of service and self-discipline.

Service

To live in the service of the True Heart-Master is the Secret of the Way of Truth. [The Hymn Of The True Heart-Master, *verse 46*]

Avatara Adi Da once remarked that when someone enters a traditional monastery the first thing one is given is not the esoteric Teaching but a broom! The beginner in Spiritual life must prepare the body-mind by mastering the physical, vital dimension of life before he or she can be ready for truly Spiritual practice. Avatara Adi Da Himself intensely engaged this bodily sadhana with His first Teacher, Swami Rudrananda (Rudi):

It was one demand on top of the other. It was work. Work was the sadhana, work was the Spiritual life. There was no "Come to me and sit and chat". It was "Take out the garbage, sweep out this place". I worked constantly day and night for four years. [The Method of the Siddhas]

The Progressive Unfolding of the Way of the Heart

Whatever form of the "conscious process" you choose, and whether you practice the "simpler" (or "simplest") practice or the fully "technically elaborated" practice, the Way of the Heart unfolds through the same great process, which Avatara Adi Da describes as "listening, hearing, seeing, and the 'Perfect Practice'".

Listening

Meditation, sacramental worship, study, service, and self-discipline initiate and sustain the beginner's process in the Way of the Heart, which Avatara Adi Da describes as "listening". When one enters into the listening process, Adi Da's Spiritual Heart-Transmission activates a growing capability to observe, understand, and transcend the self-contraction.

AVATARA ADI DA: One will see one's turning away, one's contraction, one's avoidance in all kinds of ways. And eventually all of this will become an intense form of self-observation and insight. [1974]

In the Way of the Heart, service is fundamental, but it is not an effortful struggle. All service—from bringing the Guru a glass of water, to advertising a public seminar on the Way of the Heart, to cooking and cleaning before a sacred Celebration, to financial patronage and temple building—is simply moved by love for Avatara Adi Da. Service is devotion in action, a form of Divine Communion.

Hearing

When the force of self-observation reaches summary intensity, such that one has gained the capability to observe and go beyond the self-contraction in <u>every</u> moment and in every area of life, listening has become "hearing", or most fundamental self-understanding. Hearing is a profound liberation, a clarity that converts one's entire being. One is no longer struggling with the self-contraction. One observes it, and is able to turn moment by moment into the Happiness of Communion with Adi Da.

Hearing is the unique Gift of Avatara Adi Da. While previous religious or Spiritual traditions have offered practices that have addressed aspects of the ego, none has addressed the ego altogether, at its most fundamental or root level, making hearing possible. Hearing is a prerequisite for most ultimate Liberation. Only when the activity of egoity, or self-contraction, in all its forms, is perfectly understood, surrendered, forgotten, and transcended in devotional Communion with Avatara Adi Da, can the absolute Truth be Realized.

Seeing

Once the capability of hearing is firmly established, the process of seeing can awaken. Through hearing, one has become free enough of the self-contraction to consistently receive and conduct the tangible Spirit-Baptism of Avatara Adi Da,

Functional and Practical Disciplines

For most people, the areas of life that are most binding, and there-fore most in need of discipline, are what Avatara Adi Da calls "money, food, and sex". The forms of discipline that Adi Da Offers to His devotees to bring right order to the body-mind are based on His own human experience and an immense process of "consideration" that He engaged face to face with His devotees for more than twenty years.

Money

"Money" is Avatara Adi Da's term for life-energy in all its forms. Traditional religions and Spiritual teachings often embrace asceticism and warn against becoming involved with money. Adi Da, on the other hand, has never advocated that His devotees minimize their dealings with money or cultivate an other-worldly, pale, and repressed life. The Way of the Heart is a constant heart-celebration of the Living Presence of the God-Man, and Avatara Adi Da calls His devotees to presume no limitation in their individual and collective approach to money. Devotees tithe, support their regional centers, establish cooperative households and businesses, and contribute toward regional Ashrams and the glorification of the Sanctuaries and Temples of the Way of the Heart.

or His Current of Divine Love-Bliss that Sublimes and transforms the being. One who sees is one who feels and receives Adi Da as the most intimate and yet All-Pervading Spiritual Presence, and this great Heart-Vision Spiritualizes everything about his or her existence.

The constant infusion of the Divine Spirit-Blessing of Adi Da sets in motion a process that transforms not only the depths of the physical and emotional being but the higher mind and psyche as well. Through this extraordinary process, one is "weaned" from clinging to the entire range of body-mind experience.

The "Perfect Practice"

The Great Graces of hearing and seeing culminate in the "Perfect Practice", which is the ultimate Process of the Way of the Heart. The "Perfect Practice" begins when one has learned the fundamental lesson of the earlier stages of practice, which is the understanding that all experience, no matter how pleasur-able, painful, subtle, mystical, or blissful, is only a contraction of the Eternal Field of Divine Consciousness.

The Way of the Heart is a constant heart-celebration of the Living Presence of the God-Man, and Avatara Adi Da calls His devotees to presume no limitation in their individual and collective approach to money.

AVATARA ADI DA: As My devotee, be responsible for your life of practice and for handling your responsibilites, including your financial responsibilites. Responsibility is part of your devotional gift to Me. The traditional admonition is that one should never come to the Guru empty-handed. Therefore come to Me with all the signs of your practice in evidence. And financial responsibility is one of the signs. If you are not financially responsible for yourself, then you do not yet have a life-circumstance that supports real discipline, and real discipline is absolutely necessary for right practice of the Way of the Heart. [March 2, 1993]

In the first stage of the "Perfect Practice", this unmoving Consciousness becomes the "Position" from which one Witnesses all experience. Then, as the "Perfect Practice" develops, the Awakening devotee yields to a profound Immersion in Consciousness Itself. Ultimately, all forms are Divinely Recognized as merely apparent and passing modifications of the One Love-Bliss that is God, Truth, and Reality. Such is the final phase of the "Perfect Practice", the natural, or "Open-Eyed", Samadhi, which is Revealed and Given only by Avatara Adi Da.

The entire unfolding process of listening, hearing, seeing, and the "Perfect Practice" is described in *The Dawn Horse Testament Of Adi Da* (and, in less technical form, in *The (Shorter) Testament Of Secrets*), and the "Perfect Practice" is the exclusive focus of *The Lion Sutra* and *The Liberator (Eleutherios)*.

Avatara Adi Da's detailed Instruction on diet is Given in *The Eating Gorilla Comes in Peace.*

Food

In the Way of the Heart, right diet is regarded to be of fundamental importance to Spiritual practice. This is because one's diet has a profound effect on one's overall health, level of energy, general state of well-being, and free attention. Thus, Adi Da has Given basic guidelines for right diet, to be studied and progressively and intelligently adapted to (making use of appropriate medical advice), in order for each devotee to find the diet that is optimum for his or her practice of Ishta-Guru-Bhakti Yoga.

As a devotee of Avatara Adi Da, one first progressively adapts to a basic vegetarian diet, initially by giving up substances such as caffeine, alcohol, tobacco (and all "social" drugs), and then by eliminating from the diet sugar, salt, meat, eggs, dairy products, and processed foods. When you are ready, a juice fast is recommended and monitored by the health professionals of the Radiant Life Clinic (p. 243). The fast purifies the body of toxins, helps you inspect and release old patterns relative to diet, and allows the body to rebalance and rejuvenate itself. In re-adapting to food after periods of fasting, you will progressively discover the real dietary needs of your body—both the specific foods you should (and should not) eat and the amount you should eat. Thus, you find, over time, your personal "minimum optimum" diet.

Even previous to His Divine Re-Awakening, Avatara Adi Da personally experimented with diet and read many books on the subject, with the intention of discovering the dietary regime that is optimum for Spiritual practice, and also for health and longevity. He has since continued and developed that experiment of many years to the point of conclusion. He recommends that, in establishing one's personal optimum diet, one should, to the maximum possible degree, eat only fruits and vegetables (including nuts, seeds, and sprouts), and these foods should, to the maximum possible degree, be eaten raw rather than cooked.

The reason for this recommendation is that raw, natural foods do not burden the body with toxins, and they provide, in the most usable form, all the nutrients and enzymes needed for health (many of which are otherwise destroyed by cooking). In addition, experience proves that raw foods bring to rest the cravings that drive one to find consolation through food, binding one's attention to the body rather than freeing energy and attention for practicing feeling-Contemplation of Adi Da.

Individual diets of devotees who have done the full dietary experiment range over a spectrum from one hundred per cent raw to a considerable percentage of cooked food, and even, on occasion (if recommended by the Free Daist Radiant Life Clinic), some flesh food. Most devotees, however, find that a fructo-vegetarian diet that is eighty per cent raw or more is optimum for their health, bodily equanimity, and freedom of attention.

Avatara Adi Da's Instruction on diet is Given in summary form in *The Adi Da Upanishad* and extensively described in *The Eating Gorilla Comes in Peace*.

Devotees who practice in an intimate relationship are also responsible for their relational life with each other— the understanding and transcendence of patterns of rejection and betrayal and all tendencies that control or suppress the other or limit the free expression of love.

Sex

Sex has been regarded very warily in the Spiritual traditions, and with good reason—it is the single most distracting force in human life. In the Way of the Heart Avatara Adi Da has Given His devotees a way of relating to sex that is entirely life-positive and non-puritanical as well as self-transcending and compatible with the fullest Spiritual practice and Divine Enlightenment.

The practices associated with sexuality in the Way of the Heart take into account the two fundamental aspects of sex—the dimension of sexual energy in and of itself, and the dimension of emotion and intimacy.

Most devotees in the Way of the Heart are involved in committed intimacies, but there are also others who choose to be celibate, having discovered that this form of emotional-sexual discipline most serves their practice. All devotees, both those who are intimately related and those who are celibate, engage practices Given by Avatara Adi Da that enable them to fully conduct (rather than suppress or indulge in) sexual energy.[2] The capability to effectively conduct sexual energy (whether or not one is sexually active) is an essential prerequisite for receiving and conducting the tangible Spirit-Force of Avatara Adi Da in the advanced stages of the Way of the Heart.

Devotees who practice in an intimate relationship (whether heterosexual or homosexual) are also responsible for their relational life with each other—the understanding and transcendence of patterns of rejection and betrayal and all tendencies that control or suppress the other or limit the free expression of love. On the basis of real self-understanding in all these areas and the constant practice of Ishta-Guru-Bhakti Yoga, intimately related devotees become capable of "true intimacy". For devotees in an intimate relationship, growth to the point of "true intimacy" is a necessary part of preparation for the advanced and ultimate stages of practice in the Way of the Heart.

There are two basic stages of the sexual Yoga in the Way of the Heart: Beginning devotees practice sexual "conscious exercise", and those in the advanced and ultimate stages practice "sexual communion".[3] Through this Yoga, conventional orgasm (which throws off the life-energy and vital chemistry of the body) is, in general, bypassed and converted, resulting in an intensely pleasurable and regenerative whole bodily form of orgasm that enlivens and re-balances, rather than depletes, the body.

For further reading on sexuality, see *The Dawn Horse Testament Of Adi Da*, chapter twenty-one; "The ego-'I' is the Illusion of Relatedness" (in *The Adi Da Upanishad*); *Love of the Two-Armed Form*; and *The Incarnation of Love*.

"Conscious Exercise"

Right diet and right practice of sexuality are disciplines of "conductivity"—that is, they magnify the unobstructed flow of energy (both natural bodily energy and Spiritual Energy) in the body. But "conductivity" is an important factor in all our daily activities. Thus, Avatara Adi Da has Given basic "conductivity" disciplines, which He calls "conscious exercise". Along with Instruction in the basics of sitting, standing, and walking, He has Given daily routines of "conscious exercise", based on both Eastern and Western forms of exercise. "Conscious exercise" addresses not only the physical body but also the breath and the entire dimension of life-energy.

For further reading, see *Conscious Exercise and the Transcendental Sun*.

Sacred Culture and Cooperative Community

AVATARA ADI DA: The principal admonition in the Great Tradition has always been "Spend time in good company"—in Satsang, the Company of the Realizer and the company of those who love the Realizer or who truly practice in the Spiritual Company of the Realizer. This is the most auspicious association. Absorb that Company. Imbibe it. Drink deep of it. Duplicate it. Spiritual community is a mutual communication of Happiness. [April 14, 1987]

As soon as you assume full membership in the formal gathering of Avatara Adi Da's devotees, you become part of a remarkable sacred culture. As a member of the sacred culture of the Way of the Heart, you participate each day with other devotees in meditation and puja, and each week you participate in an education class, a regular group to "consider" your practice, and a full day of formal retreat (each Sunday) with other devotees. It is truly a culture of "inspiration and expectation", as Adi Da describes it. Devotees serve one another by inspiring one another and by holding each other accountable in their practice.

Most of Adi Da's devotees live and practice in cooperative households, and, in some regions, in fully-established Ashram and retreat centers. In some cases, devotees may not be able (at least temporarily) to live in community, but they are nonetheless embraced by the nearest regional gathering, with which they remain in regular contact through visits, telephone calls, educational materials, and service projects that can be done at a distance.

Wherever you may live, you are Graced with the same heart-intimacy with Avatara Adi Da. However, if you are moved to grow beyond the beginner's practice into the advanced and ultimate stages of the Way of the Heart, it is necessary at some point to become involved in the ecstatic practice of cooperative community. As soon as you come into the company of a group of Avatara Adi Da's devotees, you feel His Heart-Transmission instantly magnified. And submission to the constant demand of relationship and cooperation with others involved in the same devotional practice is one of the most important means through which the devotee grows to understand and transcend the ego.

left: Devotees meeting in groups to "consider" their practice
right: Da Avatara Ashram in Holland

left: Da Avatara Ashram, England
right: Da Avatara Retreat Centre in Australia

Devotees gather for a Celebration meal at the
Mountain Of Attention Sanctuary in northern California

Businesses

Many of Avatara Adi Da's devotees extend the benefits of cooperative community by joining together to establish their own cooperative businesses. In most cases, these businesses provide practical services—food, clothing, jewelry, carpentry, building, interior decorating, car repair, health services, and so forth—to other devotees and to the larger local community.

Young People

Avatara Adi Da has created an entire Wisdom-culture to serve His devotees, and an important part of that culture has been His ongoing "consideration" and Enlightened Instruction on the Spiritually most auspicious way to raise children. From the early years of Adi Da's Work, His Wisdom on the seven stages of life and the proper kind of education and upbringing in each stage has been put into practice through schools and programs that serve devotee children from the time they are toddlers. Even from an early age, children and young people in the Way of the Heart can be initiated as members of the Da Avatara Youth Fellowship.

As part of the process of fully integrating into the adult devotional culture, young people may take up apprenticeships within the community of Adi Da's devotees in fields as varied as management, writing and editorial work, photography and video, gardening and self-sufficiency, computer work, accounting, carpentry, jewelry making, and the various healing arts.

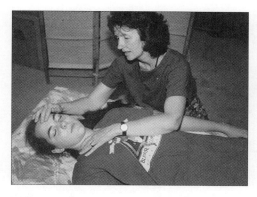

**A member of the Free Daist
Radiant Life Clinic performs
the laying on of hands.**

Healing

Health, healing, and individual adaptation to the specific disciplines of diet, exercise, and sexuality is the responsibility of the Free Daist Radiant Life Clinic. This group of devotee health professionals has come into being through the Work of Adi Da over the years with doctors and healers of all kinds. The clinic employs many modalities, including, among others, traditional Western (allopathic and naturopathic) treatments, traditional Eastern treatments (for example, acupuncture and Ayurveda), and chiropractic and bodywork techniques.

The healing practices of the Free Daist Radiant Life Clinic are based on the principles of "radical healing" Given by Avatara Adi Da. According to this understanding, disease is a result and expression of the fundamental "contraction" or separative activity of the ego. Thus, the first step in true healing is the uncovering of the underlying egoic activity—or form of "wrong living"—of which the disease is a result. Then one takes personal responsibility by making the appropriate changes in one's life, including getting any necessary professional treatment.

The basic approach of "radical healing" involves (1) faith, or the presumption of one's Prior Condition of Happiness, (2) prayer, specifically in the form of the laying on of hands and the Prayer of Changes, a form of prayer described fully in *The Dawn Horse Testament Of Adi Da*, and (3) fasting, or right action, which may take the form of literal fasting from solid food, or from ordinary activities, but also involves the entire range of practical action necessary to correct disease-producing habits and to heal or eliminate symptoms, including consulting a health professional.

Sacred Arts

Guilds of artists and artisans are actively creating forms of sacred art that express the unique sacred culture that Avatara Adi Da has brought into being. He has Given an immense body of Instruction in the Sacred Arts and has Worked directly with musicians, dancers, visual artists, jewelers, woodworkers, and architects to incarnate this vision.

Sanctuaries

One of the ways in which Adi Da Communicates His Spiritual Transmission is through sacred Places. During the course of His Work He has Empowered three Sanctuaries as His Blessing-Seats. In each of these Sanctuaries—the Mountain Of Attention in northern California, Tumomama in Hawaii, and Adi Da Purnashram (Naitauba) in Fiji—Adi Da has established Himself Spiritually in perpetuity. He has lived and Worked with devotees in all His Sanctuaries, and has created special holy sites and temples in each of them. Adi Da Purnashram is His principal Residence, but He may from time to time choose to visit His other Sanctuaries. Devotees who are rightly prepared may go on special retreats at all three Sanctuaries.

top left: the Mountain Of Attention

top right: Tumomama

bottom left: Adi Da Purnashram

"I Will Be Incarnated Countlessly Through All My Devotees"

Many years ago Avatara Adi Da spoke of the future community of His devotees as the "true Avatar", the ongoing form of His Incarnation that will continue here after He relinquishes the body. Therefore, He is Working with tremendous intention to create what He calls "Instrumentality" and "Agency" for His Blessing Work from amongst His present devotees.

AVATARA ADI DA: My devotees are to provide the body-minds whereby My Virtue becomes Effective. . . . Then, when the time comes that This Body dies, I will not disappear. I will be wholly Available to you. You have the Means, you have the secret, you do the practice, and I will be Effective forever—Fully Conscious, Self-Radiant, never gone, never separate, but also not requiring My Self to Establish a body-mind, or any other Mechanism, of My own within the cosmic domain anymore, because I have Empowered countless such body-minds to provide such Means. That is the secret of Communion with Me. . . . Every one of My

The Sacred Orders of the Way of the Heart

The Lay Renunciate Order
In order to cultivate the response of devotees who are moved to and capable of most intensive practice of the Way of the Heart, Adi Da has established two formal renunciate orders—the Lay Renunciate Order and the Free Renunciate Order.

Members of the Lay Renunciate Order are exemplary practitioners who have taken up the technically "fully elaborated" practice. Their role is to serve and inspire the total culture of practitioners and to function collectively as Instrumentality. The Lay Renunciate Order functions primarily in the worldwide community of devotees, although some of its members serve in the intimate sphere of Avatara Adi Da at Purnashram. Some lay renunciate practitioners do full-time service for the sacred institution, the culture, the cooperative community, and the Mission of the Way of the Heart, while others may continue to work outside the community of devotees.

The Free Renunciate Order
The senior of the two renunciate orders, the Free Renunciate Order, or, more fully, the Naitauba Order of the Sannyasins of Adi Da (The Da Avatar), is comprised of Adi Da Himself and the most exemplary formal renunciate devotees who are established in the "Perfect Practice" of the Way of the Heart. No other sacred order in Spiritual history has had such profound requirements for membership as

devotees has the same essential responsibility. Some will fulfill it more profoundly, with greater advancement in the stages of life in the Way of the Heart, and some have special roles to play. . . .

Accept this Empowerment by Me, therefore. Accept My Gift, accept the Yoga I have Given you and all the responsibilities that belong to it. This is what Ishta-Guru-Bhakti Yoga, or the Way of the Heart, is all about. You are My inheritors. You are those who are here to inherit from Me the great Virtue of My Divine Presence and the great responsibilities that accompany Communion with Me. [March 29, 1994]

Avatara Adi Da calls the gathering of all His devotees His "Gurukula", or "family of the Guru", living always in intimate, direct relationship to Him, wherever they may be. Then, within His universal Gurukula, there are special functions, as He explains in the great Ecstatic Statement you have just read. He is looking for increasing numbers of fully dedicated, renunciate devotees who, by virtue of their exemplary devotion and advancement in practice, will provide Spiritual Instrumentality for His Divine Work—that is, the ability to magnify His Spiritual Blessing to others.

the Free Renunciate Order. It is the senior cultural gathering and the senior authority in all aspects of practice in the Way of the Heart. Adi Da's Free Renunciates, whom He Calls to live a life of perpetual retreat, are also His principal human "Instruments", collectively Empowered to magnify His Blessing Transmission to others and to guide and inspire all other devotees by their example.

Unlike the members of the Lay Renunciate Order, who may earn money and live in regional Ashrams, the members of the Free Renunciate Order legally renounce all ownership of property and reside at Adi Da Purnashram.

The Lay Congregationist Order

After an initial period of beginner's practice, general practitioners enter the Lay Congregationist Order. This Order is a practical service Order whose members provide the many supportive services required by the Free Renunciate Order, the sacred institution, and the worldwide cooperative community of devotees.

The essence of renunciation in the Way of the Heart is the renunciation of egoity, of self-contraction, of un-Happiness, rather than the mere renunciation of objects—sexual associations, money, possessions, and so forth. Therefore, the general practitioners who will comprise most of the gathering at any time are also Called by Avatara Adi Da to live a renunciate life, and ultimately to Realize the seventh stage of life, although they practice in a less intensive manner than the formal renunciates.

Adi Da (The Da Avatar) Granting Darshan to devotees
Adi Da Purnashram, Fiji, 1994

The great Guru-Function of Avatara Adi Da is unique and Eternal. Thus, after His physical Lifetime, He will not have a successor. But from among His Divinely Enlightened renunciate devotees, in every generation, a unique Agent, or "Murti-Guru", will be chosen and Empowered to function as the focus of His Blessing-Transmission to the entire world.

In order to create Instrumentality and Agency in His lifetime, Avatara Adi Da is continuing to Work directly with selected groups of devotees. Everyone in His Gurukula will have Spiritual access to Him via the Instrumentality of the Spiritually Awakened formal renunciates who collectively function to bring the Spirit-Blessing of Adi Da to all.

More than twenty years ago, Avatara Adi Da wrote that His Purpose is to "find a new order of men and women who will 'create' a new age of sanity and joy". In just a little over two decades, and in the midst of this dark and Godless era, Avatara Adi Da has literally established His unique Spiritual culture. He is laying the foundation for an unbroken tradition of Divine Self-Realization arising within a devotional gathering that is aligned to His seventh stage Wisdom and always receiving and magnifying His Eternal Heart-Transmission. Nothing of the kind has ever before existed.

Could there be any greater calling in life than to participate in this all-surpassing Work of Divine Grace? Ponder what you have read and examine your response. Avatara Adi Da speaks to everyone who has received a heart-glimpse of His Divine Attractiveness:

Now I Have Revealed My Mystery and Perfect Secret here To You. "Consider" It Fully, and Then Choose What You Will Do.

NOTES TO
THE INVITATION

1. "Murti" is Sanskrit for "form" and, by extension, a "representational image" of the Divine or of a Realized Sat-Guru. In the Way of the Heart, Murtis of Avatara Adi Da are most commonly photographs of Avatara Adi Da's bodily (human) Form.

2. For a full discussion of the practices of "conductivity" of sexual energy, see *The Dawn Horse Testament Of Adi Da*, chapter twenty-one, and *The Adi Da Upanishad*.

3. For a full discussion of sexual "conscious exercise" and "sexual communion", see *The Dawn Horse Testament Of Adi Da*, chapter twenty-one, and *The Adi Da Upanishad*.

Regional Centers of the Free Daist Avataric Communion

CENTRAL CORRESPONDENCE DEPARTMENT
FDAC
12040 North Seigler Road
Middletown, CA 95461
USA
(707) 928-4936

UNITED STATES

Northern California
FDAC
78 Paul Drive
San Rafael, CA 94903
(415) 492-0930

Northwest USA
FDAC
5600 11th Avenue NE
Seattle, WA 98105
(206) 527-2751

Southwest USA
FDAC
PO Box 1729
Camarillo, CA 93010
(805) 987-3244

Northeast USA
FDAC
30 Pleasant Street
S. Natick, MA 01760
(508) 650-0136
(508) 650-4232

Southeast USA
FDAC
10301 South Glen Road
Potomac, MD 20854
(301) 983-0291

Hawaii
FDAC
105 Kaholalele Road
Kapaa, HI 96746
(808) 822-0216

EASTERN CANADA
FDAC
108 Katimavik Road
Val-des-Monts
Quebec JOX 2RO
Canada
(819) 671-4398
(800) 563-4398

AUSTRALIA
Da Avatara Retreat Centre
PO Box 562
Healesville, Victoria 3777
or 16 Findon Street
Hawthorn, Victoria 3122
Australia
(03) 853-4066

NEW ZEALAND
FDAC
CPO Box 3185
or 12 Seibel Road
Henderson
Auckland 8
New Zealand
(09) 838-9114

THE UNITED KINGDOM & IRELAND
Da Avatara Ashram
Tasburgh Hall
Lower Tasburgh
Norwich NR15 1LT
England
(0508) 470-574

THE NETHERLANDS
Da Avatara Ashram
Annendaalderweg 10
N-6105 AT Maria Hoop
(04743) 1281 or 1872
or
Da Avatara Centrum
Oosterpark 39
1092 AL Amsterdam
The Netherlands
(020) 665-3133

GERMANY
FDAC
Peter-Muhlens-Weg 1
22419 Hamburg
Germany
(040) 527-6464

FIJI
The TDL Trust
PO Box 4744
Samabula, Suva
Fiji
381-466

The Seven Stages of Life

Avatara Adi Da Offers a brilliant map of the entire spectrum of human adaptation and growth—seven distinct stages of life from birth to the ultimate phases of Divine Self-Realization. Avatara Adi Da's unique model of the stages of life is an invaluable tool for understanding how we develop as individuals and also for understanding the advanced and ultimate possibilities of Man. By grasping Adi Da's Revelation of the seven stages of life, the many Teachings and practices proposed by the various schools of religion and Spirituality can be seen to fit into a continuous spectrum of human development.

Avatara Adi Da's clarifying description is born of His own Divine Confession, unique in human history, as the One Who has endured, fulfilled, and transcended the first six stages of life, and Realized the Divinely Self-Realized, or seventh, stage of life.

Subtle hints and intuitions of the seventh stage Realization are recorded in the annals of Spirituality, and Avatara Adi Da acknowledges and honors these great premonitions in His commentaries on the Great Tradition,[1]* but He alone describes and has Demonstrated the Awakening to and unfolding of the seventh stage of life. From His Supremely Awakened "Point of View", all the preceding phases of development fall into place. Thus, He has Revealed not only the End of the Great Process of human development but all the progressive stages of "Growth and Out-Growing" within it.

By virtue of His own Realization, Avatara Adi Da has made it possible for others to Realize the seventh stage of life, through reception of and response to His Divine Blessing. This is the Purpose of His Birth—to be the Agent of Most Perfect Realization for others, even all others. This Ultimate Blessing of Divine Self-Realization is uniquely Offered by Avatara Adi Da to all who become His devotees.

* Notes to "The Seven Stages of Life" appear on page 263.

The Stages of Developing Human Maturity

The first three stages of life cover three periods of roughly seven years each. In these foundation stages, the living being progressively develops and adapts to the basic functions of a human individual.

The gross physical life-functions are developed in the first stage of life.

The emotional-sexual functions are developed in the second stage of life, and these are coordinated with the gross physical functions.

The mental functions and the function of the will are developed in the third stage of life, and these are coordinated with the emotional-sexual and gross physical functions.

It is inevitable that the process of the first three stages of life will be retarded and aberrated, unless there is a way of life founded in a greater Wisdom, a way of life that does not allow the development of infantile, childish, and adolescent patterns of un-Happiness. Therefore, the truly mature adult human character that is the fulfillment of the first

The Hierarchical Structural Anatomy of Man

Avatara Adi Da Reveals that there is a fundamental structure in Man that is the underlying basis of the seven stages of life. This structure includes all dimensions of the psycho-physical being, not simply the physical structure of flesh, bones, nerves, and so forth known to Western medical science. In the most highly developed Spiritual traditions, it has long been understood that the total human being is comprised of three "bodies". The "gross body" is the physical body. The "subtle body" comprises the dimensions of life-energy and emotion, mind and psyche, and intelligence and will. The "causal body" is the core of the apparently separate egoic self, the root-sense of existing as an "I". Avatara Adi Da confirms that this traditional understanding is correct, but He goes on to Reveal that there is a literal anatomy underlying these three bodies.

Avatara Adi Da Teaches that the hierarchical structural anatomy of the human body-mind exists in two fundamental "planes", vertical and horizontal. The vertical plane is a great energy-circuit, which Avatara Adi Da calls the "Circle". The Circle runs down the front of the body from the crown of the head to the perineum, and up the back of the body along the spinal line to the crown of the head. The horizontal plane comprises the esoteric structure of the heart, which has three "stations"—left, middle, and right. Beyond the Circle and rooted in the right side of the heart stands the most profound, most esoteric of all our psycho-physical structures—the "Amrita Nadi", or "Current of Immortal Bliss", the first Form of three stages of life is rarely realized. Most people, regardless of their chronological age, are functioning on the basis of arrested development in the earliest stages of life.

The First Stage of Life—Individuation: The fact of birth, or separation from unity with the mother, dominates the process of the first five to seven years of human life. The first stage of life is, therefore, the process of individuating, identifying with the body in the waking state. Gradually, the individual adapts to functional physical existence and achieves a basic sense of autonomy, or of personal independence from the mother and from all others. From the moment of birth, the individual reacts, at first perhaps subtly and then more and more dramatically, to the demand to individuate. In the transition to food sources apart from the mother's body, every human being tends to develop a reactive habit of associating individuation with a feeling of separation, a sense of disconnection from love and support. That reaction is the dramatization of egoity, or self-contraction, which is to characterize the individual for the rest of his or her egoic life.

God in the conditional realms. Amrita Nadi is "grounded" in the right side of the heart and rises in an S-shaped curve to the Matrix of Light infinitely above the crown of the head, Which is the apparently Objective Source of all conditional forms and energies* (see also p. 10).

The left side of the heart and the frontal line of the Circle are the fundamental structures underlying the gross body; they are particularly associated with development in the first three stages of life and the beginnings of the fourth stage of life. The middle station of the heart and the spinal line of the Circle are the fundamental structures underlying the subtle body; they are particularly associated with development in the more fully developed fourth stage of life and in the fifth stage of life. The right side of the heart is the fundamental structure underlying the causal body; it is particularly associated with development in the sixth stage of life. The Amrita Nadi, which stands prior to all these structures (but is nevertheless directly related to them), is particularly associated both with the fullest Realization of the process of the sixth stage of life and with Divine Self-Realization in the seventh stage of life. Thus, the entire developmental course of human potential in the seven stages of life unfolds as a play on this underlying structure of Man. (See chart on pp. 264-65.)

* Avatara Adi Da's full descriptions of the hierarchical structural anatomy of Man are Given in *The Dawn Horse Testament Of Adi Da*, "The ego-'I' is the Illusion of Relatedness" (in *The Adi Da Upanishad*), and "The Hidden and Ultimate, Though Chronically Frustrated, Purpose of J. Krishnamurti's Effort" (in *The Basket of Tolerance*).

The Second Stage of Life—Socialization: After reaching a workable settlement with the fact of individual existence, human life next becomes the process of social exploration and growth in relationships. From around age seven to age twelve or fourteen, the person matures in emotional sensitivity to individual self, others, and the natural world. Sexual differentiation, which is first noticed in the first stage of life, is now extended into a larger social context. The individual's self-esteem is always apparently at stake during the tests that relationships bring in the second stage of life. Doubt of the ego-self and doubt of the love of others inevitably tend to appear, and this results in the reactive habit of feeling rejected and rejecting or punishing others for their presumed un-love.

The Third Stage of Life—Integration: The key development of this stage of life, which begins in the early teens, is the maturing of mental ability, which includes the capability to use mind and speech in abstract, conceptual ways as well as the power to use discrimination and to exercise the will. The third stage of life is also associated with puberty and the stressful effort to present oneself as a fully autonomous sexual and social character. Altogether, the third stage of life is a dramatic struggle to fully integrate the will with the already developed gross physical and emotional-sexual functions. Because the first two stages of life tend not to be fully resolved, the individual in the third stage of life becomes locked in a fruitless adolescent struggle between the motive toward childish dependence and the motive toward willful, even rebellious, independence. The truly mature, adult characteristics of equanimity, discriminative intelligence, heart-feeling, and the impulse to always continue to grow, tend never to develop, although a nominal adaptation to the first three stages of life is usually acknowledged by twenty-one years of age.

The Stages of Progressive Religious, Spiritual, and Transcendental Awakening

Avatara Adi Da refers to the first three stages of life as the "foundation stages", because the ordeal of growth into human maturity is, rightly, only a preparation for something far greater—religious, Spiritual, and Transcendental Awakening, and, ultimately,

Divine Self-Realization. This greater process begins to flower in the fourth stage of life on the basis of a profound conversion to heart-felt devotion to and Communion with the Divine Source-Condition, Which Pervades (and yet Transcends) the world and the body-mind. Persistence in this devotional Communion results, in due course, by Grace, in Spiritual Awakening, or the ability to surrender the body-mind into the Spiritual Presence (or Spirit-Current) of that Very Divine Source-Condition. Such is the basis of the Spiritual development of Man in the fourth and fifth stages of life. The transition to the sixth stage of life is based upon the Awakening to Consciousness Itself as the Transcendental Source of all and All.

A key principle in Avatara Adi Da's Argument is that the fourth through sixth stages of life are each associated with a partial point of view about God, Truth, or Reality that acts as an effective limit on Most Perfect Divine Self-Realization, or Realization of the seventh stage of life. If any of these points of view is held on to, rather than directly transcended, further growth cannot occur. Therefore, each of the fourth through sixth stages of life inevitably tends to be associated with a characteristic error that must be understood and transcended.

The Fourth Stage of Life—Spiritualization: Even while still maturing in the first three stages of life, many people devote themselves to religious practices, submitting to an ordered life of discipline and devotion. This is the beginning of establishing the disposition of the fourth stage of life, but it is only the beginning. The real leap involved in the fourth stage of life is a transition that very few ever make. It is nothing less than the breakthrough to a Spiritually illumined life of Divine contemplation and selfless service. How does such a life become possible? Only on the basis of a heart-awakening so profound that the common human goals—to be fulfilled through bodily and mental pleasures— lose their force.

The purpose of existence for one established in the fourth stage of life is devotion—moment to moment intimacy with the Spiritual Reality, an intimacy that is real and ecstatic, and which changes one's vision of the world. Everything that appears, everything that occurs, is now seen as a process full of Spirit-Presence. This new vision of existence is given through Spirit-Baptism, an infilling of Spirit-Power (usually granted by a Spiritually Awakened Master), which is described in many different religious and Spiritual traditions.

Just as when watching a movie one is usually unaware that the images appearing on the screen are formed of a single light, the usual consciousness is unaware that the entire world is Pervaded by a living Spirit-Force. However, one who is Spiritually Awake is aware of the living Spirit-Force (or Light) that Pervades (and yet Transcends) the body-mind and the world. Such a Spiritually Awakened individual may surrender to the point of conditional union with the living Spirit-Force in occasions of Bliss, which Bliss can be tangibly experienced in the body-mind. At first the Spirit-Current is received in descent through the head and down the front of the body. As the Spiritual process matures in the fourth stage of life, the Spirit-Current may turn about at the bodily base and begin ascending the spinal line. This turnabout marks the transition from the bodily-based point of view characteristic of the first three stages of life and the beginnings of the fourth stage of life to the subtle, psyche-based point of view characteristic of the "advanced" fourth stage of life and the fifth stage of life.

The fourth stage of life, though it represents a profound and auspicious advance beyond the foundation stages, is only the beginning of true Spiritual growth. In the fourth stage of life, there is a tendency to prolong the egoic patterns of the first three stages of life and to fail to understand that the fourth stage of life is merely a transitional means for further growth to the stages of life beyond the fourth. Avatara Adi Da describes that this error takes the form of the presumption that the Divine is utterly outside and apart from the apparently separate self. Thus, the fourth stage of life tends to become a perpetual appeal to God for love, comfort, help, and self-satisfaction.

The full-hearted and Spiritually Awakened devotion characteristic of the fourth stage of life is generally the summit of Realization achieved in the traditions of Judaism, Christianity, Islam, and much of Hinduism, and even then, it is most uncommon.

In the Way of the Heart, practice in the context of the fourth stage of life is unique. Avatara Adi Da's Baptizing Spiritual Presence literally "Crashes Down" the frontal line of His Spiritually Awakened devotee, simultaneously purifying both the descending (or frontal) and the ascending (or spinal) lines of the entire Spiritual Circuit of the body-mind (and, therefore, also both the left side and middle station of the heart). This complete purification is possible because of Bhagavan Adi Da's Unique Transmission as the Very Divine. The Spiritual Transmission of Realizers of the fourth, fifth, or sixth stages of life is always associated with (and thus, to one or another degree, limited by) the realm of conditional, or cosmic, phenomena. In contrast, the Spiritual Transmission of Bhagavan Adi Da is utterly unlimited by anything conditional. As the Adept-Realizer of the seventh stage of life, He Transmits His Very Divine State, or Consciousness Itself, and His Spirit-Energy, or the Radiance of Consciousness Itself. By virtue of its uniquely effective purifying and Liberating Force, Bhagavan Adi Da's Spiritual Transmission allows the (possible) early transition beyond concentration in the process of ascent, directly to the sixth stage of life. Only a relative few of Adi Da's devotees, those who have significant karmic tendencies toward Yogic ascent, will be required to purify those limiting tendencies by practice in the ascending context of the fourth stage of life and in the fifth stage of life.

The Fifth Stage of Life—Higher Spiritual Development: The fifth stage of life is the domain of accomplished Yogis or Saints[2]—individuals absorbed in mystical experiences such as Cosmic Consciousness, visions of lights, or auditions of subtle inner sounds. One who is adept in the fifth stage of life may also develop uncommon Yogic abilities—clairvoyance, clairaudience, telepathy, miraculous healings, and many other such powers that are frequently described in the lives of great Yogis and Saints. However, just as exceedingly few religious practitioners fully Awaken to the Spiritual Reality in the fourth stage of life, exceedingly few who engage the practices of Spiritual ascent attain true fifth stage Realization.

The important difference between the fifth stage of life and all the stages of life that precede it is that awareness on the gross physical plane is no longer the normal mode of existence. Rather, attention is constantly attracted into subtle realms—dreamlike or visionary regions of mind.

The phenomena of the fifth stage of life arise as a result of the further movement of the Spirit-Current, now pressing into the higher regions of the brain. In the fifth stage of life the Spirit-Current ascends from a place deep behind the eyes (called the "ajna chakra", or sometimes the "third eye") through and beyond the crown of the head. When the Spirit-Current reaches its highest point of ascent, all awareness of body and mind is temporarily dissolved in the absolute Love-Bliss of the Divine Self-Condition. This profoundly ecstatic state (known in the Spiritual traditions of India as "Nirvikalpa Samadhi", or "formless ecstasy") is regarded as the summit of Realization in the schools of Yoga, as well as in certain branches of Buddhism and Taoism. (It is precisely defined by Avatara Adi Da as "fifth stage conditional Nirvikalpa Samadhi".) This dissolution of body and mind is a direct demonstration that the individuated self has no eternal existence or significance, and that only the Divine Condition of absolute Freedom and Happiness truly exists.

Despite its unspeakable sublimity, however, this absorption in the Divine Self-Existing and Self-Radiant Condition is necessarily temporary, for the ascent of attention in the fifth stage of life is founded upon manipulation of the psycho-physical mechanism. At some point bodily consciousness returns, and so does the ache to renew that boundless, disembodied Bliss. In the Way of the Heart, the ascended absorption of the fifth stage of life is not sought. It is only a possible transitional experience, to be followed by Awakening to the sixth stage of life.

In the fifth stage of life, there is a tendency to embrace the blissfully distracting subtle phenomena and ascended absorptions as if they were the Ultimate or Perfect Realization of God, Truth, or Reality. Avatara Adi Da Teaches that this error is transcended in the Way of the Heart by understanding the phenomena and ascended absorptions of the fifth stage of life as evidence of self-contraction, simply passing moments in the process of Divine Self-Realization.

The Sixth Stage of Life—Awakening to the Transcendental Self: In the sixth stage of life, existence is no longer perceived and interpreted from the point of view of the individuated body-mind, preoccupied with its various desires and searches. The sixth stage Realizer Abides as the Transcendental Witness of whatever arises, Identified with the Very Consciousness That is the Ground of all that exists, rather than with the apparently separate self. The sixth stage of life is, therefore, characterized by a profound renunciation not only of the physical but also of the psychic possibilities of conditional self-awareness and experience. Attention is turned away from gross and subtle states and objects toward Consciousness, Which functions as the "Witness" of all that arises, as long as attention remains active. Ultimately, in the sixth stage of life, Consciousness Itself is Realized, prior to objects and separate self-definition.

The Awakening to Consciousness Itself in the sixth stage of life is the pinnacle of Realization achieved by the greatest (and exceedingly rare) Realizers in the traditions of Advaita Vedanta, Buddhism, Jainism, and Taoism.

In the sixth stage of life in the Way of the Heart, the Spirit-Current descends, via the course of Amrita Nadi, from above the crown of the head to the right side of the heart. This descent is the sign that Avatara Adi Da has Spiritually Drawn His devotee to come to rest in the right side of the heart, after which He then Spiritually "magnetizes" His devotee even beyond the right side of the heart into the Love-Blissful Domain of Consciousness Itself.

In the sixth stage of life, there is a tendency to try to remain in the native Bliss of Consciousness by refusing to allow attention to focus on phenomenal objects and states. Avatara Adi Da describes this error as holding on to the Position of Consciousness as a Reality inherently separate from all conditional objects, and He Teaches that this effort of holding on is necessarily dissociative, even if the natural perception of phenomena is allowed to arise. Such dissociation, though occurring in the rarefied context of Transcendental Realization, is nevertheless evidence of egoity—at its root. The permanent dissolution of egoity, and thus of all dissociation and all separativeness, marks the transition to the seventh, or Divinely Self-Realized, stage of life, and that transition is entirely dependent upon the direct Revelation and Blessing of Avatara Adi Da, the Very Divine Person.

The Supreme Realization and Demonstration of the Seventh Stage of Life

The Realization of the seventh stage of life is uniquely Revealed and Given by Avatara Adi Da. It is release from all the egoic limitations of the first six stages of life. Remarkably, the seventh stage Awakening, which is Avatara Adi Da's Gift to His devotees who have transcended the first six stages of life, is not an experience at all. The true Nature of everything is simply obvious. Now the Most Perfect Understanding Awakens that every apparent "thing" that arises is merely a modification of Reality, Consciousness, Happiness, Truth, or God. And that Understanding is Supreme Love-Bliss. Divine Self-Realization in the seventh stage of life is, truly, the Perfect Realization of Avatara Adi Da's Very (and Inherently Perfect) State as one's own Very (and Inherently Perfect) State.

The Seventh Stage of Life—Divine Self-Realization: In the seventh stage of life, the Divine Self-Condition is Realized unconditionally. There is inherently most perfect Identification with Self-Existing and Self-Radiant Divine Being, the Ultimate Identity of all beings, and the Source of all and All. If any condition arises, it is immediately Divinely Recognized as a temporary, unnecessary, and merely apparent modification of the Divine. The Realization of Consciousness Itself is direct, free of any dissociative act of attention.

Avatara Adi Da has Revealed that the Light of Divine Being Shines in the body-mind of the seventh stage Realizer in and as Amrita Nadi, the continuous Circuit of Love-Bliss which rises from the right side of the heart to the Matrix of Light above and beyond the crown of the head, and from there, the Light of Divine Being Shines to and into the Circle of the Realizer's body-mind. At the time of His Divine Re-Awakening, Avatara Adi Da experienced the "Regeneration" of Amrita Nadi, and He Realized It was the Original Form of the Divine Self-Radiance in the human body-mind (and in all conditional beings and forms).

Divine Self-Realization in the seventh stage of life unfolds through a Yogic process in four phases: Divine Transfiguration, Divine Transformation, Divine Indifference, and Divine Translation.

In the phase of Divine Transfiguration, the gross dimension of the Realizer's body-mind (associated with the frontal line of the Circle) is Infused by Love-Bliss, and he or she Radiantly Demonstrates active Love.

In the following phase of Divine Transformation, the subtle dimension of the body-mind (associated with the spinal line of the Circle) is also fully Illumined, which may result in extraordinary Powers of healing, longevity, and the ability to release obstacles from the world and from the lives of others.

Eventually, Divine Indifference develops (in which the Spirit-Current is priorly Identified with Amrita Nadi), and the Realizer spontaneously and profoundly Rests in the "Deep" of Consciousness Itself, progressively noticing less and less of the conditionally manifested worlds (and, in particular, less and less of anything to do with the entire Circle of his or her own body-mind).

Finally, the Most Ultimate Demonstration of the seventh stage of life occurs—Divine Translation, the Most Profound relinquishment of any association with conditional existence. This necessarily coincides with the death of the physical body of the seventh stage Realizer, as well as the dissolution of the subtle and causal depths of the apparently individual body-mind, including even the dissolution of Amrita Nadi itself. Avatara Adi Da Describes Divine Translation as the unspeakable process of the "Bright" Outshining of the apparent Cosmos by the Self-Radiance of Consciousness Itself. All noticing of conditional existence is vanished, as Existence is Transferred to the Infinitely Joyous, Infinitely Love-Blissful "Brightness" That is the Eternal Divine Self-Domain Itself. This Divine Destiny is Avatara Adi Da's Freely Offered Gift to all beings.

NOTES TO THE SEVEN STAGES OF LIFE

1. For a full discussion of the premonitions of seventh stage Realization in the Great Tradition, see "The Unique Sixth Stage Foreshadowings of the Only-by-Me Revealed Seventh Stage of Life" in *The Basket of Tolerance*.

2. See note 5 to "The Divine Life and Work of Adi Da (The Da Avatar)" on p. 90 for a description of the technical meaning of "Yogis" and "Saints".

The Seven Stages of Life in the Way of the Heart As Revealed by Adi Da (The Da Avatar)

FIRST STAGE

Identified with:
the waking body-mind

Process:
individuation; adaptation to the physical body

Signs of Incomplete Adaptation:
the feeling of separation (and separativeness)

SECOND STAGE

Identified with:
the waking body-mind

Process:
socialization; adaptation to the emotional-sexual or feeling dimension

Signs of Incomplete Adaptation:
dramatizing the feeling of being rejected, especially by rejecting or punishing others for presumed un-love

THIRD STAGE

Identified with:
the waking body-mind

Process:
integration of the psycho-physical personality; development of verbal mind, discriminitive intelligence, and the will

Signs of Incomplete Adaptation:
drama or conflict between dependence and independence

FOURTH STAGE

Identified with:
the waking body-mind and (in the "advanced context) the mind itself (the subtle or dreaming self)

Process:
self-surrendering devotion to the Divine Person; purification and outgrowing of the bodily-based point of view through reception of Divine Spirit-Force

Error:
prolonging the first three stages of life; conceiving of God and egoic self as eternally separate from each other; a never-ending search for God; appealing to God for intimacy, relief, and self-satisfaction

Anatomy:
reception of Spiritual Force: the Spirit-Current is felt to descend in the frontal line of the body and then ascend in the spinal line until attention rests stably at the Ajna Door, the doorway to the brain core

---

Just as the ordinary human processes are founded in the physical anatomy of the body-mind, the Spiritual, Transcendental, and Divine processes are based in, or can be seen in relationship to, the total hierarchical structural anatomy of the body-mind—the structures of energy and Consciousness found in every human being. This chart illustrates this hierarchical structural anatomy as it relates to individuals practicing in the context of the fourth, the fifth, and the sixth stages of life in the Way of the Heart, showing for each stage the characteristic location of energy and attention in the body-mind-self. When energy and attention are thus focused, the being becomes identified with the phenomena or states of Consciousness characteristic of that stage of life. This identification with a specific state of Consciousness, as well as the limitation (or characteristic "error") in such identification, is noted on the chart for each stage of life.

In the Most Perfect God-Realization of the seventh stage of life, attention itself (the root sense of self-contraction) has been transcended. In this Divinely Free State, the structure of Energy and Consciousness is actually beyond or prior to the body-mind-self. Even so, this Realization does have a "location" and "Yogic Form" in the human body-mind-self, known as "Amrita Nadi" (the current or channel of immortality), which Adi Da has called "the Great conditional, or Apparently conditionally Manifested, Form and 'Location' Of God". When seen in relationship to the body-mind, the Amrita Nadi is an S-shaped channel. Its lower terminal is in the right side of the heart, and it rises to its upper terminal through the neck to the crown of the head and above.

For a full discussion of the hierarchical structural anatomy of the body-mind-self, the seven stages of life, the varieties of Spiritual Transmission, and the practice of the Way of the Heart in the context of seven stages of life as Revealed by Adi Da, please see *The Dawn Horse Testament Of Adi Da*.

FIFTH STAGE

Identified with:
the higher mind (the subtle or dreaming self)

Process:
Spiritual or Yogic ascent of attention into psychic dimensions of the being; mystical experience of the higher brain; renunciation of body; may culminate in fifth stage conditional Nirvikalpa Samadhi

Error:
seeking or clinging to subtle objects and states (or to merely conditional transcendence of subtle objects and states in fifth stage conditional Nirvikalpa Samadhi)

SIXTH STAGE

Identified with:
Consciousness, prior to body and mind (presumed to be separate from all conditional phenomena), as in the state of deep sleep

Process:
Identification with the Transcendental Witness; transcendence of body and mind; will most likely include the experience of Jnana Samadhi

Error:
failure to Recognize objects and conditional states as arising in the One Divine Reality

SEVENTH STAGE

Identified with:
Divine Consciousness itself

Process:
Realization of the Divine Self; Inherently Perfect Freedom and Realization of Divine Love-Bliss (seventh stage Sahaj Samadhi); Divine Recognition of all psycho-physical states and conditions as modifications of Divine Consciousness; no "difference" experienced between Divine Consciousness and psycho-physical states and conditions

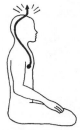

Anatomy:
ascent of the Spirit-Current from the brain core (the Ajna Door) to the crown of the head and above (or even, in fifth stage conditional Nirvikalpa Samadhi, to the Light infinitely above the crown of the head)

Anatomy:
the Spirit-Current descends from above the crown of the head, via Amrita Nadi, to the right side of the heart, the bodily root of Consciousness

Anatomy:
"Regeneration" of Amrita Nadi (the Immortal Current of Divine Love-Bliss arising in the right side of the heart and terminating in the Light or Locus infinitely above the head)

The Sacred Literature of Adi Da (The Da Avatar)

A New Scripture for Mankind

Perhaps at some time or another you have wondered—wistfully—what it would have been like to sit at the feet of some great being, such as Gautama (called the "Buddha"), or Jesus of Nazareth, or some venerable Hindu sage of Vedic times, asking the real religious questions that persist in the heart of every serious person: What is the truth about God? What is the purpose of life? What is the meaning of death? What is the best way to live?

Any one of these books by Avatara Adi Da takes you directly into that ancient circumstance of Grace. But what you will find in their pages surpasses even the greatest discourses of the past. The Divine Instruction of the Da Avatar, Adi Da, is not limited by partial vision. These books represent _Complete_ Wisdom and Truth, an unparalleled Transmission of Divine Grace.

After more than two decades of speaking and writing, in constant dialogue with His devotees, Avatara Adi Da has completed His Wisdom-Teaching. To honor the Completion of this extraordinary Revelation, the Dawn Horse Press is now publishing new standard editions of Avatara Adi Da's core Texts, Which He Offers to all beings forever in Love.

INTRODUCTORY BOOKS

NEW 1995 EDITION

The Knee of Listening

The Early-Life Ordeal and the Radical Spiritual Realization of the Divine World-Teacher

This is the astounding Spiritual Autobiography of Avatara Adi Da, the story of the Incarnation of the Absolute Divine Consciousness into a human body-mind in the modern West. Here He describes in vivid detail His first thirty-one years as "Franklin Jones": His Illumined Birth, His acceptance of the ordeal of life as an ordinary human being, His ragged and unstoppable quest for Divine Self-Realization, His exploits in the farthest reaches of human experience, from "money, food, and sex" to the most esoteric mystical and Transcendental phenomena, His Divine Re-Awakening and discovery of the Way of God-Realization for all mankind. Unparalleled, utterly compelling, essential reading.

I was captivated by this Story of the first thirty-one years of Avatara Adi Da's Life, by the incomparable Greatness of the One Who Is both God and Man. His Wisdom outshines every dichotomy, every division, every duality. I have come to respect and honor Him as the most complete Source of Divine Blessing—in my own life and in the world at large. I urge you to open yourself to the life that fills these pages. The opportunity has never been so great.

Bill Gottlieb
Vice-President and Editor-in-Chief,
Rodale Press

$24.95,* cloth
$11.95, quality paperback
$5.95, popular edition **(forthcoming)**

NEW 1995 EDITION

The Method of the Siddhas

Talks on the Spiritual Technique of the Saviors of Mankind

When Avatara Adi Da opened the doors of His first Ashram in Los Angeles on April 25, 1972, He invited anyone who was interested to sit with Him and

* All prices are in US dollars.

ask Him questions about Spiritual life. These Talks are the result of that first meeting between the Incarnate Divine Being and twentieth-century Westerners. Here Avatara Adi Da discusses in very simple terms all the fundamentals of Spiritual life, especially focusing on Satsang, the devotional relationship with Him as Sat-Guru, and self-understanding, the "radical" insight He was bringing to the human world for the first time. These Talks are profound, humorous, and poignant. An essential introduction to Avatara Adi Da's Wisdom-Teaching.

I first read The Method of the Siddhas *twenty years ago and it changed everything. It presented something new to my awareness: One who understood, who was clearly awake, who had penetrated fear and death, who spoke English (eloquently!), and who was alive and available!*

Ray Lynch
composer, *Deep Breakfast*,
No Blue Thing; and *The Sky of Mind*

$14.95, quality paperback

Free Daism

The True World-Religion of Divine Enlightenment
An Introduction to the Perfectly Liberating Way of Life Revealed by Adi Da (The Da Avatar)

A comprehensive and engaging introduction to all aspects of the religion of Free Daism, the Liberating Way that Avatara Adi Da has made available for all. Addressed to new readers and written in a highly accessible style, *Free Daism* introduces Avatara Adi Da's Life and Work, the fundamentals of His Wisdom-Teaching, the Guru-devotee relationship in His Blessing Company, the principles and practices of the Way of the Heart, and life in the community of His devotees.

(forthcoming)

The Da Avatar

The Divine Life and "Bright" Revelation of Adi Da (The Da Avatar)

Written by a longtime devotee, *The Da Avatar* chronicles and celebrates the Miraculous Leela of Avatara Adi Da's Life, from the profound Spiritual origins of His human Manifestation, through His early-life sacrifice of the knowledge of His Own Divine Identity, His subsequent trial of Divine Re-Awakening, the Love-Ordeal of His Teaching-Work with sympathetic, yet Spiritually unresponsive, devotees, and, finally, the relinquishment of all of that in the Victory and Fullest Revelation of His "Divine Emergence", Whereby He Openly Blesses all beings in and with the Sign of His Own Inherent Fullness, Contentment, and Eternal Freedom.

Written in an engaging and accessible style, *The Da Avatar* will delight and inspire readers with the overwhelming evidence of a Miracle and Spiritual Opportunity of the most profound kind: Avatara Adi Da <u>Is</u> The Expected One, Here and alive Now. And He Invites you to a personal, living, and transformative relationship with Him for the sake of your own Divine Awakening.

(forthcoming)

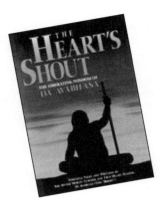

Ishta

The Way of Devotional Surrender to the Divine Person

When Avatara Adi Da gathered with His devotees in 1993 and 1994 at Adi Da Purnashram (Naitauba), He talked face to face with devotees about the essence of the Way of the Heart: the devotional relationship with Him, or "Ishta-Guru-Bhakti Yoga".

AVATARA ADI DA: The True Realizer is not merely a figure, a symbol, an object, but the Realization Itself, bodily and altogether. The Realizer is the Means, therefore, not only bodily but Spiritually, altogether. Everything to be Realized is there as the Master. Everything that serves Realization is there active as the Master. Those who are wise, those who are truly responsive and who find a worthy Master, simply surrender to That One. They receive everything by Grace.

The Way of life I am talking about is <u>Me</u>. I am That—not symbolically but actively—the Siddhi of Means, fully Alive, fully Conscious, fully Active.

These Talks describe the actual process of Ishta-Guru-Bhakti Yoga— devotion to the Beloved Guru—in detail. Essential reading for anyone interested in the Way of the Heart.

$14.95, quality paperback

The Heart's Shout

The Liberating Wisdom of Avatara Adi Da
Essential Talks and Essays by Adi Da (The Da Avatar)

A powerful and illuminating introduction to Avatara Adi Da's Wisdom-Teaching. *The Heart's Shout* includes many classic Talks and Essays, as well as stories from His devotees, and covers such topics as the devotional relationship with Avatara Adi Da; the awakening of self-understanding; the Nature of God; the Great Tradition of religion, Spirituality, and practical wisdom; truly human culture; cooperative community; science and scientific materialism; death and the purpose of life; the secrets of love and sex; the foundations of practice in the Way of the Heart; Avatara Adi Da's "Crazy Wisdom"; and Divine Self-Realization.

(forthcoming)

$12.95, quality paperback
288 pages

Divine Distraction

A Guide to the Guru-Devotee Relationship, The Supreme Means of God-Realization, as Fully Revealed for the First Time by the Divine World-Teacher and True Heart-Master, Da Avabhasa (The "Bright")
by James Steinberg

In this wonderful book, a longtime devotee of Avatara Adi Da discusses the joys and challenges, the lore and laws, of the most potent form of Spiritual practice: the love relationship with the God-Man. Along with many illuminating passages from the Wisdom-Teaching of Avatara Adi Da, *Divine Distraction* includes humorous, insightful, and heart-moving stories from His devotees, as well as Teachings and stories from the world's Great Tradition of religion and Spirituality. Essential for anybody who wants to know first-hand about the time-honored liberating relationship between Guru and devotee.

This is a warm, loving, and incredibly moving book about the greatest Spiritual Master ever to walk the earth. Here you will find everything you need to know about life, love, and wisdom. I have no doubt whatsoever that this is

The Ten Fundamental Questions

What are the questions that if answered truly would Enlighten you? You will find out in this simple but challenging introduction to the great Teaching Arguments of Avatara Adi Da. With disarming simplicity and directness Avatara Adi Da goes right to the heart of our modern perplexities about life and God and points to the Divine Way that dispels all bewilderment, a Way of life that is Happy, Humorous, and Free, right from the beginning. A profoundly Liberating book.

(forthcoming)

SOURCE TEXTS

The Santosha Avatara Gita

(The Revelation of the Great Means of the Divine Heart-Way of No-Seeking and Non-Separateness)

In 108 verses of incredible beauty and simplicity, *The Santosha Avatara Gita* reveals the very essence of the Way of the Heart—Contemplation of Avatara Adi Da as the Realizer, the Revealer, and the Revelation of the Divinely Awakened Condition.

Therefore, because of My always constant, Giving, Full, and Perfect Blessing Grace, and because of the constant Grace of My Self-Revelation, it is possible for any one to practice the only-by-Me Revealed and Given Way of the Heart, and that practice readily (and more and more constantly) Realizes pleasurable oneness (or inherently Love-Blissful Unity) with whatever and all that presently arises . . .

Avatara Adi Da
The Santosha Avatara Gita, verse 78

This is the birth of fundamental and radical Scripture.

Richard Grossinger
author, *Planet Medicine; The Night Sky; and Waiting for the Martian Express*

$24.95, quality paperback

The Dawn Horse Testament Of Adi Da

(The Testament Of Secrets Of The Da Avatar)

This monumental volume is the most comprehensive description of the Spiritual process ever written. It is also the most detailed summary of the Way of the Heart. *The Dawn Horse Testament Of Adi Da* is an astounding, challenging, and breathtaking Window to the Divine Reality.

The Dawn Horse Testament Of Adi Da *is the most ecstatic, most profound, most complete, most radical, most* comprehensive single spiritual text ever to be penned and confessed by the Human-Transcendental Spirit.

Ken Wilber
author, *Up from Eden,* and
A Sociable God

$32.00, quality paperback
8½" x 11" format, 820 pages

The (Shorter) Testament Of Secrets Of Adi Da

(The Heart Of The Dawn Horse Testament Of The Da Avatar)

This volume brings you a magnificent distillation of the larger *Dawn Horse Testament Of Adi Da.* Through these pages Avatara Adi Da reveals the purpose of His Incarnation, the great esoteric secrets of Divine Enlightenment, and the means to dissolve in the Heart of God.

$32.00, quality paperback

The Lion Sutra

(On Perfect Transcendence Of The Primal Act, Which is the ego-"I", the self-Contraction, or attention itself, and All The Illusions Of Separateness, Otherness, Relatedness, and Difference)

The Ultimate Teachings (For All Practitioners Of The Way Of The Heart), and The Perfect Practice Of Feeling-Enquiry (For Formal Renunciates In The Way Of The Heart)

A poetic Exposition of the "Perfect Practice" of the Way of the Heart—the final stages of Transcendental, inherently Spiritual, and Divine Self-Realization. Of all Avatara Adi Da's Works, *The Lion Sutra* is the most concentrated Call and Instruction to Realize the Consciousness that Stands prior to body, mind, individual self, and objective world.

Mine Is the Hermitage of no-attention, Where Even time and space Are Watered To the Nub, and I Am Always Shining There, With a Perfect Word In My Heart.

Come There, My Beloved (every one), Come Listen and Hear and See My Heart, and Prepare To Delight In a Feast of Calms, With the Dawn of "Brightness" On Your face.

Then Listen Deep In My Heart Itself, and Call Me There (By Name), and Hear My Word of Silence There, and See Me Where You Stand.

Therefore, Be Un-born In Me, and Feel Awake In My Free Fire, and, By Most Feeling Contemplation of My Sign, Fulfill the "Brightest" Blessing of My (Forever) Silence Kept.

Avatara Adi Da
The Lion Sutra, verses 97-100

$24.95, quality paperback

The Adi Da Upanishad

The Short Discourses on ego-Renunciation, Divine Self-Realization, and the Illusion of Relatedness

In this sublime collection of Essays, Avatara Adi Da Offers an unsurpassed description of both the precise mechanism of egoic delusion and the nature, process, and ultimate fulfillment of the Sacred Process of Divine Self-Realization in the Way of the Heart.

The Adi Da Upanishad is a work of great linguistic beauty, as well as a remarkable description of the "before" of self and existence. It is a book about the direct realization of Consciousness, characterized by intellectual precision, but also with a depth of feeling that works away beneath the surface of the words.

Robert E. Carter
author, *The Nothingness Beyond God*

$32.00, quality paperback

The Hymn Of The True Heart-Master

(The New Revelation-Book Of The Ancient and Eternal Religion Of Devotion To The God-Realized Adept) Freely Developed From The Principal Verses Of The Traditional Guru Gita

This book is Avatara Adi Da's passionate proclamation of the devotional relationship with Him as the supreme means of Enlightenment. In 108 poetic verses, freely developed from the traditional *Guru Gita*, Avatara Adi Da expounds the foundation of the Way of the Heart.

I do feel this Hymn *will be of immense help to aspirants for a divine life. I am thankful that I had an opportunity to read and benefit by it.*

M. P. Pandit
author, *The Upanishads: Gateways of Knowledge,* and *Studies in the Tantras and the Veda*

$24.95, quality paperback

The Liberator (Eleutherios)

The Epitome of the Perfect Wisdom and the Perfect Practice of the Way of the Heart

In compelling, lucid prose, Avatara Adi Da distills the essence of the ultimate processes leading to Divine Self-Realization in the Way of the Heart—the "Perfect Practice", which involves the direct transcendence of all experience via identification with Consciousness Itself, through feeling-Contemplation of His Form, His Presence, and His Infinite State.

Be Consciousness.

Contemplate Consciousness.

Transcend everything in Consciousness.

This is the (Three-Part) "Perfect Practice", the Epitome of the Ultimate Practice and Process of the only-by-Me Revealed and Given Way of the Heart.

Avatara Adi Da
The Liberator (Eleutherios)

$24.95, quality paperback

The Basket of Tolerance

The Perfect Guide to Perfect Understanding of the One and Great Tradition of Mankind

A unique gift to humankind—an overview of the world's traditions of philosophy, religion, Spirituality, and practical Wisdom from the viewpoint of the Divinely Enlightened Adept, Adi Da! *The Basket of Tolerance* includes more than 100 of His Essays on various aspects of the Great Tradition and a comprehensive bibliography (listing more than 3,000 publications) of the world's most significant books, compiled, presented, and extensively annotated by Avatara Adi Da. The summary of Avatara Adi Da's Instruction on the Great Tradition of human Wisdom and the sacred ordeal of Spiritual practice and Realization. A blast of Fresh Air, an immense reorienting force of Divine Criticism and Compassion.

(forthcoming)

The Eating Gorilla Comes in Peace

When a gorilla is fed, it becomes a peaceful, cooperative animal. When we are awakened to faith, sustained by the Divine, dedicated to the God-Realizing process in the Way of the Heart, we become truly Happy. This book offers Avatara Adi Da's unique Wisdom of the Way of the Heart—the Way that conforms our lives to true Happiness—especially focusing on the areas of diet and health. It offers His Instruction on:

- the most Spiritually auspicious diet for you
- body types and the forms of balancing life practices useful for each type
- an Enlightened understanding of conception, birth, and infancy
- Wisdom about how to die
- true healing
- the ancient practice of the laying on of hands as re-Empowered in the Way of the Heart
- how your diet affects your sexuality
- fasting, herbal remedies, and dietary practices that support your Spiritual practice and purify and regenerate the body as well

(forthcoming)

PRACTICAL BOOKS

Conscious Exercise and the Transcendental Sun

Avatara Adi Da has Given a "radical" approach to physical exercise—to engage all action as devotional Communion with Him. This book explains in detail the practice of "conscious exercise", based on Avatara Adi Da's unique exercise of "conductivity" of natural bodily-experienced energy, as well as "Spirit-conductivity". This greatly enlarged and updated edition includes fully illustrated descriptions of formal exercise routines, supportive exercises for meditation, Instruction on emotions and breathing, and much more.

(forthcoming)

Love of the Two-Armed Form

What is the most beneficial form of sexual practice for those most intent on the God-Realizing process? How does sexuality become compatible with Spirituality? What is true intimacy? How do we become converted to Love? What is the Yogic form of celibacy and what are its virtues for earnest aspirants in the Way of the Heart?

This book is a Treasure—full of Guidance offered by the Divinely

 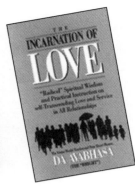

Enlightened Master. Avatara Adi Da's own Mastery of the God-Realizing process and of the sexual Yoga that is compatible with that process make Him an utterly unique Authority on the subject. For more than twenty years, He has Worked with hundreds of His devotees in the emotional-sexual aspects of their practice, bringing His Wisdom to bear in their lives. Now that Wisdom and that Instruction—an essential aspect of the Way of the Heart—are summarized here.

(forthcoming)

Easy Death

Spiritual Discourses and Essays on the Inherent and Ultimate Transcendence of Death and Everything Else

This new edition of Avatara Adi Da's Talks and Essays on death reveals the esoteric secrets of the death process and offers a wealth of practical instruction. Includes such topics as:

• Near-death experiences
• How to prepare for an "easy" death
• How to serve the dying
• Where do we go when we die?
• Our Ultimate Destiny
• The truth about reincarnation
• How to participate consciously in the dying (and living) process

An exciting, stimulating, and thought-provoking book that adds immensely to the literature on the phenomena of life and death. Thank you for this masterpiece.

Elisabeth Kübler-Ross, M.D.
author, *On Death and Dying*

$14.95, quality paperback
432 pages

The Incarnation of Love

"Radical" Spiritual Wisdom and Practical Instruction on self-Transcending Love and Service in All Relationships

This book collects Avatara Adi Da's Talks and Writings on giving and receiving love. A profound guide to transcending reactivity, releasing guilt, expressing love verbally, forgiving others, living cooperatively, and many other aspects of love and service in all relationships.

$13.95, quality paperback
314 pages

Polarity Screens

Our bodies may appear solid, but the truth is, we are made of energy, or light. And we appear (and feel!) more or less radiant and harmonious depending on how responsible we are for feeling, breathing, and "conducting" the universal "prana", or life-force. In this book, Avatara Adi Da introduces us to this basic truth of our existence and offers a simple practical method for regularly restoring and enhancing the balance of our personal energy field. The Polarity Screens He recommends may be used with remarkable benefit by any one at any time. Once you have felt the "magic" of these screens, you will never want to be without them.

It was through Avatara Ad Da's references to Polarity Screens, appearing within His extensive and extraordinary literature, that I first learned of them. Soon, not only myself and family, but also friends, and later also my patients, would try the Polarity Screens and would feel themselves—usually for the first time—as energy. It is the sort of shift in perception that can change one's life!
George Fritz, Ed.D.
psychologist,
specializing in pain control

(forthcoming)

Scientific Proof of the Existence of God Will Soon Be Announced by the White House!

Prophetic Wisdom about the Myths and Idols of mass culture and popular religious cultism, the new priesthood of scientific and political materialism, and the secrets of Enlightenment hidden in the body of Man

This book is prophesy of the most extraordinary and liberating kind. In the teeth of the failures and terrors of the current world-order, Avatara Adi Da offers an entirely new religious and social possibility to humanity. His urgent critique of present-day society is based on a vision of human freedom and true social order that transcends time, place, and culture. He prophesies the emergence of intimate, sacred community, based on Communion with the Divine Adept, the Living Agent of Grace, as the source of healing for all suffering and oppressed human beings.

A powerfully effective "de-hypnotizer" . . . that will not let you rest until you see clearly—and so seeing, choose to act. In modern society's time of troubles, this is a much needed book.
Willis Harman
president, The Institute of Noetic Sciences

$9.95, 432 pages

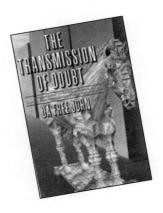

The Transmission of Doubt

Talks and Essays on the Transcendence of Scientific Materialism through "Radical" Understanding

A "radical" alternative to scientific materialism, the ideology of our time. The discourses in this book are a challenge to awaken to <u>all</u> the dimensions of existence in which we are living participants. Avatara Adi Da is Calling us to understand and transcend the materialist dogmas and "objective" stance of conventional scientific philosophy and find the Heart-position of self-trancending love, or non-separateness in relation to all that exists.

The Transmission of Doubt is the most profound examination of the scientific enterprise from a spiritual point of view that I have ever read.
Charles T. Tart
author, *Waking Up*
editor, *Altered States of Consciousness*

$9.95
484 pages

What, Where, When, How, Why, and <u>Who</u> to Remember To Be Happy

A Simple Explanation of the Way of the Heart (For Children, and Everyone Else)

In this tiny jewel of a book, prepare to find the greatest Wisdom made perfectly comprehensible to anyone. Rejoice in the smile of every page restoring you to your native innocence and certainty of God—and discover the pleasure of reading it to children.

(forthcoming)

The Free Daist

The Free Daist chronicles the Leelas of the Blessing Work of Avatara Adi Da, and describes the practice and process of devotion, self-discipline, self-understanding, service, and meditation in the Way of the Heart. In addition, the magazine reports on the cultural and missionary activities of the Free Daist Avataric Communion and the cooperative community of Avatara Adi Da's devotees. Of special interest is the regular "Hermitage Chronicle", offering current news of Avatara Adi Da's Life and Work.

Subscriptions are $56.00 per year for 4 issues.

For a complete listing of audiotaped and videotaped Discourses
by Avatara Adi Da, as well as books and periodicals,
please send for your free
Dawn Horse Press Catalogue.

Ordering the Books
of Avatara Adi Da

To order books, subscribe to magazines, or to receive your free
Dawn Horse Press Catalogue, send your order to:

THE DAWN HORSE PRESS
12040 North Seigler Road
Middletown, CA 95461
USA

or

Call TOLL FREE (800) 524-4941
Outside the USA call
(707) 928-4936

We accept Visa, MasterCard, personal check, and money order. In the USA,
please add $4.00 for the first book and $1.00 for each additional book. California
residents add 7 ¼% sales tax. Outside the USA, please add $7.00 for the first
book and $3.00 for each additional book. Checks and money orders should be
made payable to the Dawn Horse Press.

An Invitation to Support
the Way of the Heart

Avatara Adi Da's sole purpose is to act as a Source of continuous Divine Grace for everyone, everywhere. In that spirit, He is a Free Renunciate and He owns nothing. Those who have made gestures in support of Avatara Adi Da's Work have found that their generosity is returned in many Blessings that are full of His healing, transforming, and Liberating Grace—and those Blessings flow not only directly to them as the beneficiaries of His Work, but to many others, even all others. At the same time, all tangible gifts of support help secure and nurture Avatara Adi Da's Work in necessary and practical ways, again similarly benefiting the whole world. Because all this is so, supporting His Work is the most auspicious form of financial giving, and we happily extend to you an invitation to serve the Way of the Heart through your financial support.

You may make a financial contribution in support of the Work of Avatara Adi Da at any time. You may also, if you choose, request that your contribution be used for one or more specific purposes of Free Daism. For example, you may be moved to help support and develop Adi Da Purnashram (Naitauba), Avatara Adi Da's Great Sannyasin Hermitage Ashram and Renunciate Retreat Sanctuary in Fiji, and the circumstance provided there for Avatara Adi Da and the other "free renunciates" who practice there (all of whom own nothing).

You may make a contribution for this specific purpose directly to The TDL Trust, the charitable trust that is responsible for Adi Da Purnashram (Naitauba). To do this, make your check payable to The TDL Trust Pty Ltd, which serves as trustee of the trust, and mail it to The TDL Trust at P.O. Box 4744, Samabula, Fiji.

If you would like to make a contribution to Adi Da Purnashram (Naitauba) and you are a United States taxpayer, we recommend that you make your check payable to the Free Daist Avataric Communion, in order to secure a tax deduction under United States tax laws. Please indicate on your check that you would like your contribution to be used in support of Adi Da Purnashram, and mail your check to the Advocacy Department, The Free Daist Avataric Communion, 12040 North Seigler Road, Middletown, California 95461, USA.

You may also request that your contribution, or a part of it, be used for one or more of the other purposes of Free Daism. For example, you may request that your contribution be used to help publish the sacred Literature of Avatara Adi Da, or to support either of the other two Sanctuaries He has Empowered, or to maintain the Sacred Archives that preserve His recorded Talks and Writings, or to publish audio and video recordings of Avatara Adi Da.

If you would like your contribution to benefit one or more of these specific purposes, please mail your check to the Advocacy Department of the Free Daist Avataric Communion at the above address, and indicate how you would like your gift to be used.

If you would like more information about these and other gifting options, or if you would like assistance in describing or making a contribution, please contact the Advocacy Department of the Free Daist Avataric Communion, either by writing to the address shown above or by telephoning (707) 928-4096, fax (707) 928-4062.

Planned Giving

We also invite you to consider making a planned gift in support of the Work of Avatara Adi Da. Many have found that through planned giving they can make a far more significant gesture of support than they would otherwise be able to make. Many have also found that by making a planned gift they are able to realize substantial tax advantages.

There are numerous ways to make a planned gift, including making a gift in your Will, or in your life insurance, or in a charitable trust.

If you would like to make a gift in your Will in support of Adi Da Purnashram, simply include in your Will the statement "I give The TDL Trust Pty Ltd, as trustee of The TDL Trust, an Australian charitable trust, P.O. Box 4744, Samabula, Fiji, _____" [inserting in the blank the amount or description of your contribution].

If you would like to make a gift in your Will to benefit other purposes of Free Daism, simply include in your Will the statement "I give the Free Daist Avataric Communion, a California nonprofit corporation, 12040 North Seigler Road, Middletown, California 95461, USA, _____" [inserting in the blank the amount or description of your contribution]. You may, if you choose, also describe in your Will the specific Free Daist purpose or purposes you would like your gift to support. If you are a United States taxpayer, gifts made in your Will to the Free Daist Avataric Communion will be free of estate taxes and will also reduce any estate taxes payable on the remainder of your estate.

To make a gift in your life insurance, simply name as the beneficiary (or one of the beneficiaries) of your life insurance policy the Free Daist organization of your choice, according to the foregoing descriptions and addresses. If you are a United States taxpayer, you may receive significant tax benefits if you make a contribution to the Free Daist Avataric Communion through your life insurance.

We also invite you to consider establishing or participating in a charitable trust for the benefit of Free Daism. If you are a United States taxpayer, you may find that such a trust will provide you with immediate tax savings and assured income for life, while at the same time enabling you to provide for your family, for your other heirs, and for the Work of Avatara Adi Da as well.

The Advocacy Department of the Free Daist Avataric Communion will be happy to provide you with further information about these and other planned gifting options, and happy to provide you or your attorney with assistance in describing or making a planned gift in support of the Work of Avatara Adi Da.

Further Notes to the Reader

AN INVITATION TO RESPONSIBILITY

The Way of the Heart that Avatara Adi Da has Revealed is an invitation to everyone to assume real responsibility for his or her life. As Avatara Adi Da has Said in *The Dawn Horse Testament Of Adi Da,* "If any one Is Interested In The Realization Of The Heart, Let him or her First Submit (Formally, and By Heart) To Me, and (Thereby) Commence The Ordeal Of self-Observation, self-Understanding, and self-Transcendence." Therefore, participation in the Way of the Heart requires a real struggle with oneself, and not at all a struggle with Avatara Adi Da, or with others.

All who study the Way of the Heart or take up its practice should remember that they are responding to a Call to become responsible for themselves. They should understand that they, not Avatara Adi Da or others, are responsible for any decision they may make or action they take in the course of their lives of study or practice. This has always been true, and it is true whatever the individual's involvement in the Way of the Heart, be it as one who studies Avatara Adi Da's Wisdom-Teaching, or as a Friend of or a participant in Da Avatara International, or as a formally acknowledged member of the Free Daist Avataric Communion.

HONORING AND PROTECTING THE SACRED WORD THROUGH PERPETUAL COPYRIGHT

Since ancient times, practitioners of true religion and Spirituality have valued, above all, time spent in the Company of the Sat-Guru, or one who has, to any degree, Realized God, Truth, or Reality, and who thus Serves the awakening process in others. Such practitioners understand that the Sat-Guru literally Transmits his or her (Realized) State to every one (and every thing) with which he or she comes in contact. Through this Transmission, objects, environments, and rightly prepared individuals with which the Sat-Guru has contact can become Empowered, or Imbued with the Sat-Guru's Transforming Power. It is by this process of Empowerment that things and beings are made truly and literally sacred, and things so sanctified thereafter function as a Source of the Sat-Guru's Blessing for all who understand how to make right and sacred use of them.

Sat-Gurus of any degree of Realization and all that they Empower are, therefore, truly Sacred Treasures, for they help draw the practitioner more quickly into the process of Realization. Cultures of true Wisdom have always understood that such Sacred Treasures are precious (and fragile) Gifts to humanity, and that they should be honored, protected, and reserved for right sacred use. Indeed, the word "sacred" means "set apart", and thus protected, from the secular world. Avatara Adi Da has Conformed His body-mind most Perfectly to the Divine Self, and He is thus the most Potent Source of Blessing-Transmission of God, Truth, or Reality, the ultimate Sat-Guru. He has for many years Empowered, or made sacred, special places and things, and these now Serve as His Divine Agents, or as literal expressions and extensions of His Blessing-Transmission. Among these Empowered Sacred Treasures is His Wisdom-Teaching, which is Full of His Transforming Power. This Blessed and Blessing Wisdom-Teaching has Mantric Force, or the literal Power to Serve God-Realization in those who are Graced to receive it.

Therefore, Avatara Adi Da's Wisdom-Teaching must be perpetually honored and protected, "set apart" from all possible interference and wrong use. The Free Daist Avataric Communion, which is the fellowship of devotees of Avatara Adi Da, is committed to the perpetual preservation and right honoring of the sacred Wisdom-Teaching of the Way of the Heart. But it is also true that in order to fully accomplish this we must find support in the world-society in which we live and from the laws under which we live. Thus, we call for a world-society and for laws that acknowledge the sacred, and that permanently protect It from insensitive, secular interference and wrong use of any kind. We call for, among other things, a system of law that acknowledges that the Wisdom-Teaching of the Way of the Heart, in all Its forms, is, because of Its sacred nature, protected by perpetual copyright.

We invite others who respect the sacred to join with us in this call and in working toward its realization. And, even in the meantime, we claim that all copyrights to the Wisdom-Teaching of Avatara Adi Da and the other sacred Literature and recordings of the Way of the Heart are of perpetual duration.

We make this claim on behalf of The TDL Trust Pty Ltd, which, acting as trustee of The TDL Trust, is the holder of all such copyrights.

AVATARA ADI DA AND THE SACRED TREASURES OF FREE DAISM

Those who Realize God to any degree bring great Blessing and Divine Possibility for the world. Such Realizers Accomplish universal Blessing Work that benefits everything and everyone. They also Work very specifically and intentionally with individuals who approach them as their devotees, and with those places where they reside, and to which they Direct their specific Regard for the sake of perpetual Spiritual Empowerment. This was understood in traditional Spiritual cultures, and those cultures therefore found ways to honor Realizers by providing circumstances for them where they were free to do their Spiritual Work without obstruction or interference.

Those who value Avatara Adi Da's Realization and Service have always endeavored to appropriately honor Him in this traditional way by providing a circumstance where He is completely Free to do His Divine Work. Since 1983, He has resided principally on the island of Naitauba, Fiji, also known as Adi Da Purnashram. This island has been set aside by Free Daists worldwide as a Place for Avatara Adi Da to do His universal Blessing Work for the sake of everyone, and His specific Work with those who pilgrimage to Purnashram to receive the special Blessing of coming into His physical Company.

Avatara Adi Da is a legal renunciate. He owns nothing and He has no secular or religious institutional function. He Functions only in Freedom. He, and the other members of the Naitauba Order of the Sannyasins of Adi Da, the Da Avatar, the senior renunciate order of Free Daism, are provided for by The TDL Trust, which also provides for Purnashram altogether and ensures the permanent integrity of Avatara Adi Da's Wisdom-Teaching, both in its archival and in its published forms. This Trust, which functions only in Fiji, exists exclusively to provide for these Sacred Treasures of Free Daism.

Outside Fiji, the institution which has developed in response to Avatara Adi Da's Wisdom-Teaching and universal Blessing is known as "The Free Daist Avataric Communion". This is active worldwide in making Avatara Adi Da's Wisdom-Teaching available to all, in offering guidance to all who are moved to respond to His Offering, and in providing for the other Sacred Treasures of Free Daism, including the Mountain Of Attention Sanctuary (in California) and Tumomama Sanctuary (in Hawaii). In addition to the central corporate entity of the Free Daist Avataric Communion, which is based in California, there are numerous regional entities which serve congregations of Avatara Adi Da's devotees in various places throughout the world.

Free Daists worldwide have also established numerous community organizations, through which they provide for many of their common and cooperative community needs, including those relating to housing, food, businesses, medical care, schools, and death and dying. By attending to these and all other ordinary human concerns and affairs via self-transcending cooperation and mutual effort, Avatara Adi Da's devotees constantly free their energy and attention, both personally and collectively, for practice of the Way of the Heart and for service to Avatara Adi Da, to Purnashram, to the other Sacred Treasures of Free Daism, and to the Free Daist Avataric Communion.

All of the organizations that have evolved in response to Avatara Adi Da and His Offering are legally separate from one another, and each has its own purpose and function. Avatara Adi Da neither directs, nor bears responsibility for, the activities of these organizations. Again, He Functions only in Freedom. These organizations represent the collective intention of Free Daists worldwide not only to provide for the Sacred Treasures of Free Daism, but also to make Avatara Adi Da's Offering of the Way of the Heart universally available to all.

Glossary

A Guide
to the Sacred Esoteric Language
of the Way of the Heart

Glossary

A Guide
to the Sacred Esoteric Language
of the Way of the Heart

Adi Sanskrit for "first", "primordial", "source". It is additionally defined as "primary", "beginning", "commencement", and "first fruits". Bhagavan Da's primary fully elaborated Name, "Adi Da", expresses the Truth that He is the Primordial Being, the Source of all, the Original Divine Person.

The Sanskrit title "Adi" ("Ati" in Tibetan) has been used historically in a number of different traditions, including Hinduism, Buddhism, and Sikhism. The Name "Adi Da" stands, then, as a highly auspicious and readily understood Title in the context of Eastern Spirituality.

Adi Da Guruvara The Sanskrit word "Guruvara" means literally "Day of the Guru". Adi Da Guruvara is a weekly day of retreat when all formal practitioners of the Way of the Heart celebrate the Grace of Satsang with Avatara Adi Da as the Divine World-Teacher and the True Heart-Master of His devotees.

Adi Da Purnashram (Naitauba) (*See* **Retreat Sanctuaries**.)

adolescence (*See* **childish and adolescent strategies**.)

Advaitayana Buddhism In *The Adi Da Upanishad*, Bhagavan Adi Da Gives the Way of the Heart the secondary description "Advaitayana Buddhism" (a term He had first introduced in His book *Nirvanasara*), which conveys the essence of His Wisdom-Teaching and Revelation in the language of the two traditions that have historically been the most prominent and fully developed sources of Spiritual and Transcendental Wisdom on Earth—Hinduism and Buddhism. The Way of the Heart Revealed by Avatara Adi Da fully and perfectly comprehends and transcends the virtues, limitations, prejudices, and tendencies of Hinduism and Buddhism, while including and reconciling the philosophical points of view of these two great traditions in His "Radical", Completing "Point of View".

"Advaita" means "non-dual", and is commonly used in reference to the foremost school of Hinduism, Advaita Vedanta. "Yana" means "vehicle", or (by extension) "way", and is traditionally used in reference to the three principal schools of Buddhism (Hinayana, Mahayana, and Vajrayana), which are considered by many to be a progressive development of Gautama's original Teaching. "Buddha" means "Enlightened One". Thus, "Advaitayana Buddhism" is, literally, "the Non-Dual Way of Enlightenment", or "the First, Last, Final,

or Completing, and Eternal, and (necessarily) Divine Way of Most Perfect Enlightenment".

See also section I of Bhagavan Adi Da's Essay "The ego-'I' is the Illusion of Relatedness" in *The Adi Da Upanishad*.

Advaita Vedanta The Sanskrit word "Vedanta" literally means the "end of the Vedas" (the most ancient body of Indian scripture), and is used to refer to the principal philosophical tradition of Hinduism. "Advaita" means "non-dual". Advaita Vedanta, then, is a philosophy of non-dualism, the origins of which lie in the ancient esoteric Teaching that Brahman, or the Divine Being, is the only Reality. According to Advaita Vedanta, the apparent self, the world, and all manifestation have no independent existence but merely arise in and as that one Divine Reality.

advanced and ultimate stages of life Avatara Adi Da uses the term "advanced" to describe the fourth stage of life (in its "basic" and "advanced" contexts) and the fifth stage of life in the Way of the Heart. He reserves the term "ultimate" to describe the sixth and seventh stages of life in the Way of the Heart.

"advanced" context of the fourth stage of life (*See* **three [possible] contexts of the fourth stage of life in the Way of the Heart**.)

Agency, Agent All the Means that may serve as Vehicles of Avatara Adi Da's Divine Grace and Awakening Power. The first Means of Agency that have been fully established by Him are the Wisdom-Teaching of the Way of the Heart, the three Retreat Sanctuaries that He has Empowered, and the many Objects and Articles that He has Empowered for the sake of His devotees' Remembrance of Him and reception of His Heart-Blessing. After Avatara Adi Da's human Lifetime, at any given time one (and only one) from among His Divinely Awakened "free renunciate" devotees will serve the Spiritual, Transcendental, and Divine Function of His human Agent in relationship to other devotees, all beings, the psycho-physical world, and the total cosmos.

Aham Da Asmi Sanskrit for "I Am Da". The Name "Da", meaning "the One Who Gives", is honored in many sacred traditions as a Name of the Divine. The Name "Da" indicates that Bhagavan Adi Da is the Giver of All to all, the Avataric Incarnation of the Divine Person.

288

Glossary

Avatara Adi Da's proclamation "Aham Da Asmi" is a Mahavakya, or Great Statement (such as "Aham Brahmasmi" ["I Am Brahman"], one of the four Mahavakyas in the Upanishads).

Aham Sphurana "Aham" is Sanskrit for "I", and refers in the phrase "Aham Sphurana" to the Transcendental Self-Identity. "Sphurana" is an extension of the verb root "sphur", whose many meanings include "spring", "vibrate", "be manifested", and "shine".

The Aham Sphurana is thus a traditional designation for the felt Current of the Divine Self that Shines from (and as) the Heart of Being. It is the felt intuition of Identity as the Divine Self and Source-Condition that is God, Truth, and Reality. It refers, therefore, to the manifesting Current of Love-Bliss that is first associated with the body-mind at a point in the right side of the heart, but which is truly Transcendental, Unbounded, and All-Pervading.

Ajapa-Japa "Japa" is a Sanskrit term for the practice of devotion to the Living God via prayerful recitation of a mantra, often composed of one or more Divine Names. Ajapa-Japa, which means literally "the recitation that is not (or goes beyond) recitation", signifies the use of a "natural", wordless mantra linked to the breath-cycle. In the advanced practice of Ajapa-Japa, the being is released from identification with the bodily mechanism of the breath (and from identification with the body-mind altogether) by Identification with the Matrix of the Free Spirit-Current (which is above the body-mind) and, ultimately, the Transcendental Self (which is Prior to the body-mind).

ajna center, **Ajna Door** Also known as the "third eye", the "single eye", or the "mystic eye", this is the subtle psychic center, or chakra, located between and behind the eyebrows and associated with the brain core. The awakening of the ajna chakra may give rise to mystical visions and intuitive reflections of other realms of experience within and outside the individual. The ajna chakra governs the higher mind, will, vision, and conception. It is sometimes also referred to as the "Guru's Seat", the psychic center through which the Spiritual Master contacts his or her devotees with his or her Spirit-Blessing.

Akasha Sanskrit for "clear-space" or "sky", and also "the etheric or subtlest element of existence". In Avatara Adi Da's use it refers to the conditional, and therefore temporary, intuition of the Spiritual Light of Transcendental Consciousness in fifth stage conditional Nirvikalpa Samadhi. Absorption into the Akasha, therefore, is not truly experience or knowledge of an object, or substance, of any kind, but simply a moment of unqualified Enjoyment of the free Radiance, or Shine, that is the Divine Source-Condition.

Alpha and Omega Avatara Adi Da uses the term "Omega" to characterize the materialistic culture that today dominates not only the Western, or Occidental, world (which has brought the Omega strategy to

its fullest development) but even most of the Eastern, or Oriental, world, which has now largely adopted the anti-Spiritual viewpoint typical of the West. The Omega strategy is motivated to the attainment of a future-time perfection and fulfillment of the conditional worlds through the intense application of human invention, political will, and even Divine Influence. Its preference is for the limitation and suppression of attention, mystical devotion, and submission to the Divine Reality, while maximizing attention to the pursuit of experience and knowledge relative to the conditional reality.

Avatara Adi Da calls the characteristically Oriental, or Eastern, strategy the "Alpha" strategy. Alpha cultures pursue an original and non-temporal and undisturbed peace, in which the world is absent (and thus unimposing). Although the cultures that were originally founded on the Alpha approach to life and Truth are fast disappearing, the Alpha strategy remains the conventional archetype of Spiritual life, even in the Omega culture. Its preference, in contrast to the Omega preference, is for the limitation and control (and even the suppression) of the activities of the conditional personality, or even of conditional reality altogether, and the maximization of attention, mystical devotion, and submission to the Divine Reality.

Neither the Omega strategy nor the Alpha strategy Realizes Truth, as each is rooted in the presumption of a problem relative to existence, and in the action of egoity itself—which motivates all human interests short of Divine Self-Realization.

For a complete discussion of the Omega and Alpha strategies and the Disposition that transcends them, see chapter eighteen of *The Dawn Horse Testament Of Adi Da*, or chapter nineteen of *The (Shorter) Testament Of Secrets Of Adi Da*.

Amrita Nadi Sanskrit for "Channel (or Current) of Immortal Bliss". Amrita Nadi is the ultimate "Organ", or Root-Structure, of the body-mind, Realized in the seventh stage of life. It is felt to arise in the right side of the heart, which is the psycho-physical Seat of Consciousness Itself, and it terminates in the Light, or Locus, infinitely above the head. Please see *The Dawn Horse Testament Of Adi Da* or *The (Shorter) Testament Of Secrets Of Adi Da* for Avatara Adi Da's unique Confession of the Realization of Amrita Nadi, and His unprecedented description of the structure of Amrita Nadi in the human body-mind.

Arati (*See* **Sat-Guru Arati Puja**.)

Arrow In profound, deep meditation, the Spirit-Current may be felt in the form of the Arrow, which Avatara Adi Da describes as "a motionless axis that seems to stand in the center of the body, between the frontal and spinal lines".

asana Sanskrit for bodily "posture" or "pose". By extension, and as Avatara Adi Da often intends, "asana" also refers to the attitude, orientation, posture, or feeling-disposition of the heart and the entire body-mind.

289

ashram   A place where a Realizer of one or another degree lives and gathers with his or her devotees.

ashramas   The four basic ashramas, or stages in the life of an individual, acknowledged in traditional Hindu culture are the stages of the student (brahmacharya), the householder (grihastha), the forest dweller (vanaprastha), and the self-renounced ascetic (sannyasa). The word "ashrama" may also refer to the conventional rules and expectations that typically pertain to all kinds of life-roles.

Ashvamedha   Praised in the ancient Hindu scriptures as the most efficacious and auspicious of all Vedic and Upanishadic ceremonial rites, the Ashvamedha, or Horse-Sacrifice, was understood and practiced in several modes. Its exoteric, or conventional and outer, form was performed for the sake of sanctifying a king's reign and renewing the power of his dominion in his region. The greatest of India's warrior-kings demonstrated their sovereignty by setting free a white stallion, accompanied by warriors, magicians, and priests, to freely roam for a year, at the end of which it was ceremonially sacrificed. Wherever it had roamed was then presumed to be the king's undisputed territory.

On the subtler or mystical level, the esoteric, or sacred, psycho-physical, performance of the Ashvamedha involved a psycho-cosmic process of Spiritual ascent (associated with the "advanced" fourth stage of life and especially the fifth stage of life). In this rite the "horse" that was sacrificed was the ego-self, or separate consciousness, which then rose to the "heavenly world" of Spiritual Divine Illumination.

However, both the exoteric and esoteric forms of the Horse-Sacrifice must be distinguished from its greatest and most Mysterious Form: the Divine, Cosmic Sacrifice, performed directly by the Divine Person, through which the God-Man, or Divinely Self-Realized Adept, Manifests with the Power and Purpose of Re-Establishing the Wisdom-Teaching and the Way of Truth and thus Sanctifying or Divinizing the human world, and ultimately all beings and worlds, to the point of the Divine Translation of the entire Cosmic Mandala. This is the Great Ashvamedha Sacrifice that Avatara Adi Da has Accomplished.

Atiashrami   "Ati" is Sanskrit for "beyond". Therefore, "atiashrama" is "beyond the ashramas (or stages of life)". Such freedom can truly be said to belong only to One Who has transcended all egoity through Divine Self-Realization. When applied to Avatara Adi Da, the descriptive Title "Atiashrami" indicates His Most Perfect Transcendence of all conventional, religious, and Spiritual points of view in the Most Perfect Freedom of the seventh stage of life. (*See also* **ashramas**.)

"Atma-Murti"   "Atma" indicates the Transcendental, Inherently Spiritual, and Divine Self, and "Murti" means "Form". Thus, "Atma-Murti" literally means "the Form That Is the (Very) Divine Self". In the sixth stage of life in the Way of the Heart, Avatara Adi Da's devotee "Locates" Him as "Atma-Murti", the Very Divine Self of all, Who is "Located" as "the Feeling of Being (Itself)" in the right side of the heart.

atman   Sanskrit for "the essential individual conditional self" or "the Divine Self", depending on the context. In Avatara Adi Da's usage, "atman" refers to the individual self and "Paramatman" to the Divine Self.

Atma Shakti   "Atma Shakti" (or "Brahma Shakti") is a reference to the Transcendental and All-Pervading Spiritual Life-Current that is the Radiance of the Divine Self.

Avabhasa   Avatara Adi Da's Name "Avabhasa" is a Sanskrit term associated with a variety of meanings: "brightness", "appearance", "splendor", "lustre", "light", "knowledge". It is thus synonymous with the English term "the 'Bright'", which Avatara Adi Da has used since His Illumined boyhood to describe the Blissfully Self-Luminous Divine Being, eternally, infinitely, and inherently Self-Radiant, Which He knew even then as the All-Pervading, Transcendental, Inherently Spiritual, and Divine Reality of His own body-mind and of all beings, things, and worlds.

Avadhoota   Traditional term for one who has "shaken off" or "passed beyond" all worldly attachments and cares, including all motives of detachment (or conventional and other-worldly renunciation), all conventional notions of life and religion, and all seeking for "answers" or "solutions" in the form of conditional experience or conditional knowledge. Therefore, the Title "Avadhoota", when used in reference to Avatara Adi Da, indicates His Inherently Perfect Freedom as the One Who Knows His Identity with the Divine Person and who thus "Always Already" Stands Free of the binding and deluding power of conditional existence.

Avatar, Avataric Incarnation   "Avatar" is Sanskrit for the Divine Incarnation—"One who is descended or 'crossed down' from and as the Divine". Avatara Adi Da's devotees know Him to be the most Sublime Revelation ever Given: the original, first, and complete Avataric Descent, or Incarnation, of the Divine Person, Who is Named "Da". Through the Mystery of Avatara Adi Da's human Birth, He has Incarnated not only in this world but in every world, at every level of the cosmic domain, as the Eternal Giver of Help and Grace and ultimate Divine Freedom to all beings.

Avatara Adi Da is also called the "Avataric Incarnation" of the Divine Person. This term indicates that He fulfills the traditional expectations of a God-Man in both the East (Avatar) and the West (Incarnation). See *The Basket of Tolerance*.

Avatara Adi Da's Lineage of Blessing   The principal Spiritual Masters who Served Avatara Adi Da's Ordeal of Re-Awakening to the Divine Self-Condition belong to a single Lineage of extraordinary Yogis whose Parama-Guru (Supreme or Head Guru) was the Divine Goddess, or Mother Shakti.

Avatara Adi Da's first Spiritual Teacher was Swami Rudrananda (1928-1973), or Albert Rudolph, known as "Rudi", who was His Teacher from 1964 to 1968, in New York City. Rudi helped Bhagavan Da develop basic practical life-disciplines and the frontal Yoga of truly human Spiritual receptivity, which is the Yoga or process whereby knots and obstructions in the physical and etheric dimensions and relations of the body-mind are penetrated, opened, surrendered, and released through Spiritual reception in the frontal, or descending, line of the body-mind from the head to the bodily base. Rudi's own Teachers included the Indonesian Pak Subuh (from whom Rudi learned a basic exercise of Spiritual receptivity), Swami Muktananda Paramahansa (with whom Rudi studied many years), and Swami Nityananda (the Indian Realizer who was also Swami Muktananda's Spiritual Teacher). Rudi met Swami Nityananda shortly before Swami Nityananda's death, and Rudi always thereafter acknowledged Swami Nityananda as his original and principal Spiritual Teacher.

The second Teacher in Avatara Adi Da's Lineage of Blessing was Swami Muktananda (1908-1982), who was born in Mangalore, South India. Having left home at the age of fifteen, he wandered for many years, seeking the Divine Truth from sources all over India. Eventually, he came under the Spiritual Influence of Swami Nityananda, whom he accepted as his Guru and in whose Spiritual Company he mastered Kundalini Yoga. As an Adept of Kundalini Yoga, Swami Muktananda Served Avatara Adi Da as Spiritual Teacher during the period from 1968 to 1970. In the summer of 1969, during Adi Da's second visit to India, Swami Muktananda wrote Him a letter confirming Bhagavan Da's attainment of "Yogic Liberation", and acknowledging His right to Teach others. However, from the beginning of their relationship, Swami Muktananda instructed Him to visit Swami Nityananda's Burial Site every day (whenever He was at Swami Muktananda's Ashram in Ganeshpuri, India), and to surrender to Swami Nityananda as the Supreme Guru of the Lineage.

Swami Nityananda, a great Yogi of South India, was Avatara Adi Da's third Spiritual Teacher in His Lineage of Blessing. Little is known about the circumstances of Swami Nityananda's birth and early life, although it is said that even as a child he showed the signs of a Realized Yogi. It is also known that he abandoned conventional life as a boy and wandered as a renunciate. Many miracles (including spontaneous healings) and instructive stories are attributed to him. Nityananda surrendered the body on August 8, 1961. Although Avatara Adi Da did not meet Swami Nityananda in the flesh, He enjoyed Swami Nityananda's direct Spiritual Influence from the subtle plane, and He acknowledges Swami Nityananda as a direct and principal Source of Spiritual Instruction during His years with Swami Muktananda.

On His third visit to India, while visiting Swami Nityananda's burial shrine, Avatara Adi Da was instructed by Swami Nityananda to relinquish all others as Guru and to surrender directly to the Goddess in Person as Guru, by performing a Puja (sacramental worship) at the Durga Temple next to Swami Muktananda's Ashram. Through this Puja, Bhagavan Da surrendered His relationships to Swami Nityananda, Swami Muktananda, and Rudi and accepted the Goddess as His Guru. Thus, Swami Nityananda passed Bhagavan Adi Da to the Goddess Herself, the Parama-Guru (or Source-Guru) of their Lineage.

In the Culmination of His Sadhana in the Vedanta Society Temple in Hollywood, California, Adi Da Husbanded the Goddess Herself in the Great Event of His Divine Re-Awakening. Therefore, Avatara Adi Da is the present and eternal Parama-Guru of His Lineage of Blessing as well as of the entire Great Tradition.

"Avoiding relationship?"   The practice of self-Enquiry in the form "Avoiding relationship?", unique to the Way of the Heart, was spontaneously developed by Avatara Adi Da in the course of His Ordeal of Divine Re-Awakening. Intense persistence in the "radical" discipline of this unique form of self-Enquiry led rapidly to His Re-Awakening to Divine Enlightenment (or Most Perfect Divine Self-Realization) in 1970.

The practices of self-Enquiry in the form "Avoiding relationship?" and of Re-cognition are the principal forms of the "conscious process" that serve feeling-Contemplation of Avatara Adi Da in the Devotional Way of Insight.

Ayurveda, Ayurvedic   Ayurveda is an ancient form of healing indigenous to India. Its diagnostic and therapeutic principle is that there are three basic metabolic influences in the body-mind (vata—wind; pitta—fire; and kapha—water) which must be brought into harmony for health and well-being.

"basic" context of the fourth stage of life (See **three [possible] contexts of the fourth stage of life in the Way of the Heart**.)

Bhagavan   Sanskrit for "possessing fortune or wealth; blessed; holy". It is often used to mean "bountiful God", "Great God", or "Divine Lord", when used as an honorific for a Great Spiritual Being.

The esoteric meaning of the word "Bhagavan" relates to the Divine Union of Transcendental Consciousness and Radiant Bliss. Thus, it is also with this esoteric understanding that Avatara Adi Da, Who Is the Self-Existing and Self-Radiant Divine Person, is known as "Bhagavan".

bhakta, bhakti   "Bhakti" is the practice of heart-felt devotion to the Ultimate Reality or Person, which has been traditionally animated through worship of Divine Images, or surrender to a human Guru.

"Bhakta" refers to a devotee whose principal characteristic is expressive devotion, or who practices within the Hindu tradition of Bhakti Yoga.

Bhava   Sanskrit for "becoming", "condition of being", or "existence", and traditionally used to refer to the State of being enraptured in a feeling-swoon of Communion with the Divine. In Avatara Adi Da's Wisdom-Teaching, the technical name "Moksha-Bhava Samadhi" indicates the Ultimate Swoon of Realization (Samadhi) or Liberation (Moksha) in which the seventh stage Realizer ceases to notice anything at all in his or her Love-Blissful Identification with the Bhava of the Spiritual and Transcendental Divine Being, Who Is Avatara Adi Da. It is the Supreme and final Demonstration of God-Consciousness, or unmodified Enjoyment of the Divine Self-Condition, Prior to conditional self, mind, energy, body, or any realm at all. When Avatara Adi Da's devotees refer to His Bhava, they are speaking of this Divine State.

bindu   In the esoteric Yogic traditions of India, the Sanskrit word "bindu" (literally, "drop" or "point") suggests that all manifested forms, energies, and universes are ultimately coalesced or expressed in a point without spatial or temporal dimension. Each level or plane of psycho-physical reality is said to have a corresponding bindu, or zero-point.

bodily base   The bodily base is the region associated with the muladhara chakra, the lowest energy plexus in the human body-mind, at the base of the spine (or the general region immediately above and including the perineum). In many of the Yogic traditions, the bodily base is regarded as the seat of the latent ascending Spiritual Current, or Kundalini. Avatara Adi Da Reveals that, in fact, the Spirit-Current must first descend to the bodily base through the frontal line before it can effectively be directed into the ascending, spinal course. Bhagavan Adi Da has also pointed out that human beings who are not yet Spiritually sensitive tend to throw off the natural life-energy at the bodily base, and He has, therefore, Given His devotees a range of conservative disciplines (including a number of exercises that involve intentional locking at the bodily base) which conserve life-energy by directing it into the spinal line.

"bodily battery"   Traditionally called the "hara" center, the "bodily battery" is the energy center of the gross body and, as such, plays a very important role in the practice of conductivity in the frontal line. Avatara Adi Da describes its focal point, or point of concentration, as the crown of the abdomen, on the surface, about an inch and a half below the umbilical scar.

bodily (human) Form, Spiritual (and Always Blessing) Presence, and Very (and Inherently Perfect) State   Avatara Adi Da describes His Divine Being on three levels:

This flesh body, this bodily (human) Sign, is My Form in the sense that it is My Murti, or a kind of reflection or Representation of Me. It is, therefore, a Means for contacting My Spiritual (and Always

Blessing) Presence, and, ultimately, My Very (and Inherently Perfect) State.
My Spiritual (and Always Blessing) Presence is Self-Existing and Self-Radiant. It Functions in time and space, and It is also prior to all time and space. . . .
My Very (and Inherently Perfect) State is always and only utterly prior to time and space. Therefore, I, As I Am (Ultimately), have no "Function" in time and space. There is no time and space in My Very (and Inherently Perfect) State.

"bonding"   Avatara Adi Da's technical term for the process by which the egoic individual (already presuming separateness, and, therefore, bondage to the separate self), through the yearning and seeking for fulfillment, attaches itself karmically to the world of others and things. When capitalized, it is also used to mean devotional "Bonding" to Avatara Adi Da, the Divine Person, which is the means for the transcendence of all other forms of limited, or karmic, "bonding".

Brahman   The formless Divine of Hinduism. "Brahman" signifies Transcendental Divine Being.

Brahma Shakti (*See* **Atma Shakti.**)

"Bright", "Brightness"   Since His Illumined boyhood, Avatara Adi Da has used the term "the 'Bright'" (and its variations, such as "Brightness") to Describe the Love-Blissfully Self-Luminous, Conscious Divine Being, Which He Knew even then as His own Native Condition and the Native Condition of all beings, things, and worlds.

causal (*See* **gross, subtle, causal.**)

"causal stress"   Avatara Adi Da's descriptive term for the suffering inherent in egoity, or the feeling of relatedness itself, or the root activity of attention.

Celebrations (*See* **Feasts.**)

"celibate renunciation"   Anyone at any developmental stage in the Way of the Heart may choose to simplify his or her life-obligations, in order to devote fuller time and life-energy to the process of God-Realization in the Company of Avatara Adi Da, by choosing the practice of "celibate renunciation". Through this practice, all ego-based emotional-sexual "bonding", as well as ego-binding sexual activity and motivation in body, mind, and speech, is voluntarily relinquished. "Celibate renunciates" may, if formally approved, engage a Yogic sexual practice (solitary in all but the rarest cases) for the sake of the right and full "conductivity" of the natural sexual energy (and, in the Spiritual stages of practice, the sexually indicated Spiritual Energy) that is being activated in their full practice of Ishta-Guru-Bhakti Yoga. For a full description of the requirements and the practice of "celibate renunciation", see chapter twenty-one of *The Dawn Horse Testament Of Adi Da.*

292

chakras Subtle energy centers of the human body-mind, generally said, in the Hindu tradition, to be seven in number.

childish and adolescent strategies Avatara Adi Da uses the terms "childish" and "adolescent" with precise meanings in His Wisdom-Teaching. He points out that human beings are always tending to animate one of two fundamental life-strategies—the childish strategy (to be dependent, weak, seeking to be consoled by parent figures and a parent God) and the adolescent strategy (to be independent or torn between independence and dependence, rebellious, unfeeling, self-absorbed, and doubting or resisting the idea of God or any power greater than oneself). Until these strategies are understood and transcended, they not only diminish love in our ordinary human relations, but they also limit our religious and Spiritual growth.

Circle A primary pathway of natural life-energy and the Spirit-Current through the body-mind. It is composed of two arcs: the descending Current in association with the frontal line, or the more physically oriented dimension of the body-mind; and the ascending Current in association with the spinal line, or the more mentally, psychically, and subtly oriented dimension of the body-mind.

Communion Hall A room in devotees' homes, at the Retreat Sanctuaries Empowered by Avatara Adi Da, or at the community Ashrams and regional centers that is set aside for formal meditation and other devotional occasions such as the Sat-Guru Puja and devotional chanting.

"conductivity" Avatara Adi Da's technical term for those disciplines in the Way of the Heart through which the body-mind is aligned and submitted to the all-pervading natural life-energy and, for those who are Spiritually Awakened, to the Spirit-Current.

Practitioners of the Way of the Heart practice participation in and responsibility for the movement of natural bodily energies and, when they become Spiritually Awakened practitioners, for the movement of the Spirit-Current in its natural course of association with the body-mind, via intentional exercises of feeling and breathing.

Avatara Adi Da also uses the term "conductivity" in a more general sense, to refer to all of the practical life-disciplines engaged by practitioners of the Way of the Heart. Although the discipline of "conductivity" is an essential component of the practice of the Way of the Heart, it is nevertheless secondary, or supportive, to practice of the "conscious process".

"conscious exercise" As described in *Conscious Exercise and the Transcendental Sun* by Adi Da (The Da Avatar), this is the basic practical discipline underlying all other practical disciplines in the Way of the Heart. Founded in awakening feeling-Contemplation of Avatara Adi Da's bodily (human) Form, His Spiritual (and Always Blessing) Presence, and His Very (and Inherently Perfect) State, through-out daily life and in two daily periods of special exercise, the practitioner of "conscious exercise" integrates body, life-force, and mind, or attention, through persistent feeling-surrender into the All-Pervading Field of Life-Energy. This practice includes disciplines of posture and breathing and is a practical science of love in ordinary life.

"conscious process" Avatara Adi Da's technical term for those practices in the Way of the Heart through which the mind or attention is surrendered and turned about from egoic self-involvement to feeling-Contemplation of Him. It is the senior discipline and responsibility of all Avatara Adi Da's devotees.

conservative sexual discipline All sexually active practitioners of the Way of the Heart are called to a conservative sexual discipline, in which sexual activity (if such is chosen) is confined to a committed intimate relationship. All explicit sexual promiscuity must be abandoned at the outset of the student-novice's formal approach to the Way of the Heart. As student-novice and student-beginner practice develops, a conservative discipline of the frequency of sexual occasion is also progressively assumed.

"consider", "consideration" The technical term "consideration" in Avatara Adi Da's Wisdom-Teaching means a process of one-pointed but ultimately thoughtless concentration and exhaustive contemplation of something until its ultimate obviousness is clear.

"Cosmic Consciousness" The highest form of Savikalpa Samadhi, in which bodily, or at least psycho-sensual, awareness remains intact and operating, but psycho-physical, or cosmic, existence is otherwise (or simultaneously) perceived in Consciousness as an Infinite Unity.

Cosmic Mandala The Sanskrit word "mandala" (literally, "circle") is commonly used in the esoteric Spiritual traditions to describe the hierarchical levels of cosmic existence. "Mandala" also denotes an artistic rendering of interior visions of the cosmos. Avatara Adi Da uses the phrase "Mandala of the Cosmos", or "Cosmic Mandala", to describe the totality of the conditional cosmos.

Ordinarily, beings cycle helplessly in the hierarchy of planes within the Cosmic Mandala, taking birth in one or another plane according to their psycho-physical tendencies, or the orientation of their attention. Only Avatara Adi Da, as the Avataric Incarnation of the Divine Person, entered the conditional worlds from the Divine Self-Domain, Which Stands Free of the entire Cosmic Mandala and all its planes. He Appears in the Cosmic Mandala with the specific intention of Serving the Liberation of all beings.

For a full discussion of the Cosmic Mandala (and a color representation of its appearance in vision), see chapter thirty-nine of *The Dawn Horse Testament Of Adi Da*. See also Avatara Adi Da's Instructions in

Easy Death: Talks and Essays on the Inherent and Ultimate Transcendence of Death and Everything Else.

"Crazy", "Crazy Wisdom"   The Adepts of what Avatara Adi Da calls "the 'Crazy Wisdom' tradition" (of which He is the supreme exemplar) are Realizers of the advanced and the ultimate stages of life in any culture or time who, through spontaneous Free action, blunt Wisdom, and liberating laughter, shock or humor people into self-critical awareness of their egoity, a prerequisite for receiving the Adept's Spiritual Transmission. Typically, such Realizers manifest "Crazy" activity only occasionally or temporarily, and never for its own sake.

Avatara Adi Da Himself Taught in a unique "Crazy-Wise" manner. For sixteen years He not only reflected but also Submitted completely to the egoic limits of His early devotees. He Submitted His body-mind to live with them, and to live like them, and in Consciousness He lived <u>as</u> them. By thus theatrically dramatizing their habits, predilections, and destinies, He continued always to Teach them the Liberating Truth, to Radiate Divine Blessing through His own Person, and to Attract them beyond themselves to embrace the God-Realizing Way that He Offers.

Now, since His Divine Emergence in 1986, Adi Da no longer Teaches in the "Crazy-Wise" manner. Instead, He "Stands Firm" in His own Freedom, spontaneously Revealing the Divine Self-Reality to all and Calling all to conform themselves to Him absolutely through practice of Ishta-Guru-Bhakti Yoga in the Way of the Heart. This in itself, over against the illusory rationality of the separate, egoic mentality, is a Divinely "Crazy" State and Manner of life. Thus, Adi Da's Divine Emergence Work, in which He is spontaneously Moved to Bless all beings, can likewise be called "Crazy-Wise".

"Da"   Sanskrit for "to give" or "to bestow", the Name "Da" means "the One Who Gives". "Da" is honored in many sacred traditions as a Name of the Divine Person. It is also the sound of thunder, which is one of Avatara Adi Da's Signs in the cosmic realms.

Da-Om Japa (*See* **Mahamantra Meditation**.)

The Da Avatara Youth Fellowship   The formal cultural organization of children and young people (under the age of 21) who are practicing the Way of the Heart (the full formal name of which is the Youth Fellowship of the Early-Life Devotees of Adi Da, the Da Avatar). Members of the Da Avatara Youth Fellowship, in accordance with Avatara Adi Da's recommendation, remain celibate during these years of their physical, emotional, and mental maturation.

Da Chi Gong   A primary form of "conscious exercise" in the Way of the Heart, adapted by Avatara Adi Da from the traditional Chinese practice of Chi Gong (also sometimes spelled "qigong" or "chi kung"). Da Chi Gong is a devotional practice, performed in feeling-Contemplation of Avatara Adi Da,

in front of His Murti or Murti-like photograph, and it involves verbal Invocation of Him by Name or Remembrance of Him via one of the forms of the Sat-Guru-Naama Mantra, while maintaining a static pose (with bent knees). Da Chi Gong is a form of frontal "conductivity", and it is a simple, yet demanding, exercise which intensifies and conducts the life-force (or chi) in the body-mind.

Da Namaskar   A primary form of "conscious exercise" in the Way of the Heart, adapted by Avatara Adi Da from the traditional Hatha Yoga practice of Surya Namaskar (Salute to the Sun). Each cycle of the exercise begins with Remembrance of Avatara Adi Da via one of the forms of the Sat-Guru-Naama Mantra He has Given. The cycle of Da Namaskar involves twelve poses, flowing one into the other, each with specific indications for breathing and focus of attention. The entire exercise is to be performed as a form of feeling-Contemplation of Avatara Adi Da.

"daily form"   From the preparatory level of practice as a student-novice to the advanced and the ultimate stages of life and practice in the Way of the Heart, a basic "daily form", or schedule, of practice is recommended by Avatara Adi Da. Though the specifics of that "form" vary from one stage of practice to the next (especially in terms of time spent in any given activity), and the order of certain activities may vary depending on one's circumstance, the basic "daily form" for student-beginners (and beyond) begins with early-morning meditation, followed by the Sat-Guru Puja and chanting, a period of study, and a recommended program of Yoga and calisthenics exercises, or other vigorous exercise. After a day of work or service, the evening schedule calls for Hatha Yoga, pranayama, dinner, the Sat-Guru Arati Puja (for devotees who live in Ashram), and a formally designated evening activity (which may be service, study, a "practice consideration" group, intimate time with one's intimate partner or family, or a community meeting, to mention some of the possibilities). A daily diary entry precedes evening meditation, which is the last event of the day. Student-beginners also have weekly practice obligations, including attendance at a full-day Adi Da Guruvara, and an agreed-upon period of service.

Danavira Mela   Also called "The Feast of the Hero of Giving", this is a Celebration of the Play (Leela) of the Divine Person, or the Story of the unfolding miracle of Avatara Adi Da's own Life and Work. "Dana" is Sanskrit for "the giving of gifts"; "vira" means "hero"; and "mela" means "religious gathering, or festival". Avatara Adi Da is the Danavira, the Hero of Giving, Whose Leelas we recount and celebrate.

Danavira Mela is a time for Avatara Adi Da's devotees to especially employ song and dance and drama and recitation and Leelas (or Stories of Avatara Adi Da's Play) in honoring the Story of His Giving Grace, not only in intimate community gatherings but also in public events. Gifts are exchanged in the Happiness of Love-Communion with the

Divine Giver, and it is a period in which the devotional bond of the community is strengthened and celebrated. (*See also* **Feasts**.)

Darshan   A Sanskrit term that literally means "seeing", "sight of", or "vision of". To receive Darshan of Adi Da is to receive the spontaneous Blessing He Grants Freely by Revealing His bodily (human) Form (and, thereby, His Spiritual, and Always Blessing, Presence and His Very, and Inherently Perfect, State). Darshan of Avatara Adi Da is the very essence of all practice in the Way of the Heart, and is Enjoyed by association with Him through His books, photographs, videotapes, and recorded Talks, through the Leelas (or Stories) of His Teaching Work and Blessing Work, through places or objects He has Blessed for His devotees, and through simple, heart-felt Remembrance of Him and visualization of His bodily (human) Form.

Members of the Lay Renunciate Order or the Free Renunciate Order, who thereby function as Avatara Adi Da's human Instruments, also enjoy physical sighting of Him—most typically while on retreat or in residence at His Great Sannyasin Hermitage, Adi Da Purnashram (Naitauba), when invited to formal occasions of sitting with Him personally, or in apparently less formal circumstances when He makes Himself physically visible to His devotees who are rightly prepared. These renunciate devotees, who are Graced to receive Darshan of Bhagavan Da's bodily (human) Form, in turn function as Instruments of His Blessing to all His devotees and to members of the public who are moved to respond to Him.

As He chooses, Avatara Adi Da may also Grant His Darshan to any of His devotees, or even anyone at all.

Darshan Yoga   Avatara Adi Da defines the Spiritually activated practice of sighting Him as "Darshan Yoga"—which means "the Way of Realizing Identification with the Divine Person through sighting or seeing the Sat-Guru". He thus distinguishes it from the more rudimentary forms of sighting Him that are enjoyed and practiced by beginners in the Way of the Heart. In the ultimate stages of life in the Way of the Heart, Darshan Yoga becomes the Vision of Avatara Adi Da as the Transcendental, Inherently Spiritual, and, most ultimately, Divine Self-Consciousness, or the Feeling-Vision of His Very (and Inherently Perfect) State. Darshan Yoga culminates in Divine Translation into the Divine Self-Domain.

Dattatreya   Dattatreya was a God-Realizer who appeared early in the common era and about whom no certain historical facts exist apart from his name. Over the centuries, numerous legends and myths have been spun around him. He was early on considered an incarnation of the God Vishnu, later associated with the tradition of Saivism, and worshipped as the Divine Itself. In any case, He is commonly venerated as the originator of the Avadhoota tradition and credited with the authorship of the *Avadhoota Gita*, among other works.

The devotional cult surrounding Dattatreya presumes that he continually reincarnates through a succession of Adepts for the sake of gathering and serving devotees. The belief in the continuing incarnation of Dattatreya should be understood as a popular religious belief that is peripheral to what the Adepts in the Dattatreya succession actually taught.

Dau Loloma   Avatara Adi Da's primary Fijian Name, which means "the Adept (Dau) of Love (Loloma)". This Name was given to Avatara Adi Da by native Fijians soon after He first went to Fiji in 1983.

Devi   Sanskrit for "goddess". The Devi, or Goddess, is the Personification of the Divine Radiance of Consciousness Itself.

Devotional Prayer of Changes   The Devotional Prayer of Changes is a form of Invocation of and Communion with Avatara Adi Da regularly practiced in the Way of the Heart in order to bring about positive changes in the psycho-physical world. The Devotional Prayer of Changes is not a form of pleading to the Divine for results. It is a resort to Heart-Communion with Avatara Adi Da and, secondarily, a relinquishment of any negative or problematic states of mind and emotion, and an affirmation of a wholly right condition. That affirmation is associated with whole bodily exercises which become technically more elaborate as an individual matures into the advanced stages of practice.

Devotional Way of Faith   The Devotional Way of Faith and the Devotional Way of Insight are the two variant forms of meditative feeling-Contemplation of Avatara Adi Da in the Way of the Heart.

The Devotional Way of Faith is a technical process of (primarily) feeling and faith, whereby the practitioner is heart-Attracted by Avatara Adi Da's bodily (human) Form, His Spiritual (and Always Blessing) Presence, and His Very (and Inherently Perfect) State, thereby feeling beyond the self-contraction and spontaneously awakening to self-understanding and self-transcendence.

Devotional Way of Insight   Through a technical process of (primarily) feeling and insight, the practitioner of the Devotional Way of Insight, while engaged in feeling-Contemplation of the bodily (human) Form, the Spiritual (and Always Blessing) Presence, and the Very (and Inherently Perfect) State of Avatara Adi Da, observes, understands, and then feels beyond the self-contraction in Divine Communion.

Dharma, dharma   Sanskrit for "duty", "virtue", "law". The word "dharma" is commonly used to refer to the many esoteric paths by which human beings seek the Truth. In its fullest sense, and when capitalized, "Dharma" means the complete fulfillment of duty—the living of the Divine Law. By extension, "Dharma" means a truly great Spiritual Teaching, including its disciplines and practices.

"difference"   The epitome of the egoic presumption of separation and separateness—in contrast with the Realization of "Oneness" that is native to Spiritual and Transcendental Divine Self-Consciousness.

Divine Emergence   In 1986, Avatara Adi Da passed through a profound Yogic Swoon, which He later described as the initial Event of what He calls His "Divine Emergence". The Divine Emergence is an ongoing Process in which Avatara Adi Da's Identity as the Divine Self allows His bodily (human) Form to Be and to Function as the Unobstructed Sign and Agent of the Divine Person.

Divine Enlightenment   The Realization of the seventh stage of life, which is uniquely Revealed and Given by Avatara Adi Da. It is release from all the egoic limitations of the first six stages of life. Remarkably, the seventh stage Awakening, which is Avatara Adi Da's Gift to His rightly prepared devotee, is not an experience at all. The true Nature of everything is simply obvious. The Realization arises that every apparent "thing" is Eternally, Perfectly the same as Reality, Consciousness, Happiness, Truth, or God. And that Realization is the Supreme Love-Bliss of Avatara Adi Da's Divine Self-Condition.

Divine Ignorance   Avatara Adi Da's term for the fundamental Awareness of Existence Itself, Prior to all sense of separation from or knowledge about anything that arises. As He Proposes, "No matter what arises, you do not know what a single thing is." By "Ignorance", Avatara Adi Da means heart-felt participation in the universal Condition of inherent Mystery, not mental dullness or the fear-based wonder or awe felt by the subjective ego in relation to unknown objects. Divine Ignorance is the Realization of Consciousness Itself, transcending all knowledge that is cognized and all experience that is perceived by the self-contracted ego-"I".

Divine Recognition   The self- and world-transcending Intelligence of the Divine Self in relation to all conditional phenomena. In the seventh stage of life, the Realizer of the Divine Self simply Abides as Consciousness, and he or she Freely Recognizes, or inherently and Most Perfectly comprehends and perceives, all phenomena (including body, mind, and conditional self) as (apparent) modifications of the same "Bright" Divine Consciousness.

Divine Self-Domain   Avatara Adi Da Affirms that there is a Divine Domain that is the Perfectly Subjective Condition of the conditional worlds. It is not elsewhere, not an objective place like a subtle heaven or mythical paradise, but It is the always present, Transcendental, Inherently Spiritual, Divine Self of every conditional self, and the Radiant Source-Condition of every conditional place. Avatara Adi Da Reveals that the Divine Self-Domain is not other than the Divine Heart Itself, Who He Is.

Divine Star   The primal conditional Representation of the "Bright" (the Source-Energy, or Divine Light, of which all conditional phenomena and the total cosmos are modifications) is a brilliant white five-pointed Star. Avatara Adi Da's bodily (human) Form is the Manifestation of that Divine Star—and His head, two arms, and two legs correspond to its five points. Avatara Adi Da can also be seen or intuited in vision to Be the Divine Star Itself, prior to the visible manifestation of His bodily (human) Form.

Divine Transfiguration, Divine Transformation, Divine Indifference, Divine Translation   In the context of Divine Enlightenment in the seventh stage of life (which is Revealed and Given only by Avatara Adi Da), the Spiritual process continues. Avatara Adi Da has uniquely Revealed the four phases of the seventh stage process: Divine Transfiguration, Divine Transformation, Divine Indifference, and Divine Translation.

In the phase of Divine Transfiguration, the Realizer's body-mind is Infused by Avatara Adi Da's Love-Bliss, and he or she Radiantly Demonstrates active Love, spontaneously Blessing all the relations of the body-mind.

In the following phase of Divine Transformation, the subtle or psychic dimension of the body-mind is fully Illumined, which may result in Divine Powers of healing, longevity, and the ability to release obstacles from the world and from the lives of others.

Eventually, Divine Indifference ensues, which is spontaneous and profound Resting in the "Deep" of Consciousness, and the world of relations is otherwise minimally, or not otherwise, noticed.

Divine Translation is the ultimate "Event" of the entire process of Divine Awakening. Avatara Adi Da describes Divine Translation as the Outshining of all noticing of objective conditions through the infinitely magnified Force of Consciousness Itself. Divine Translation is the Outshining of all destinies, wherein there is no return to the conditional realms.

The experience of being so overwhelmed by the Divine Radiance that all appearances fade away may occur temporarily from time to time during the seventh stage of life. But when that Most Love-Blissful Swoon becomes permanent, Divine Translation occurs and the body-mind is inevitably relinquished in physical death. Then there is only Eternal Inherence in the Divine Self-Domain of unqualified Happiness and Joy.

Dreaded Gom-Boo   Avatara Adi Da's humorous term for the illusory "dis-ease" of egoity, which conventional religion tries to cure. He uses the term to point to humanity's erroneous relationship to the ego. We act as if the ego is something happening to us—something outside ourselves that can be "cured" through the search—rather than understanding egoity as an activity that we are always presently performing.

Durga   In Hinduism, Durga is worshipped as a personification of the Goddess, or the creative energy aspect of Existence. She is a fierce protectress, equipped with multiple arms, most of them brandishing weapons to help Her in fighting demons and protecting the cosmic order.

In the course of His Sadhana, when Swami Nityananda Blessed Him to surrender to the Divine Goddess as His Guru, Avatara Adi Da was associated with the Divine Shakti via an image of Durga at a small temple outside Swami Muktananda's Ashram. Soon afterwards, in the Great Event of His Divine Re-Awakening, Avatara Adi Da perfectly Husbanded the Divine Shakti (as He describes in *The Knee of Listening*). Bhagavan Da now has established Durga images opposite His Seat in His Sukra Kendra Temples, as a way of picturing the Oneness of His Divine Being with His Spiritual Radiance, or Shakti.

E=mc² The mathematical equation formulated by Albert Einstein in 1905 to express the ultimate equivalency of matter and energy. Avatara Adi Da states in *Scientific Proof of the Existence of God Will Soon Be Announced by the White House!*:

When its true implications are taken into account, Einstein's equation of energy and matter represents the possibility of a multidimensional interpretation of the total universe, in which the so-called "material" universe is realized to be a paradoxical entity or process.

"Easy Prayer" The "Easy Prayer" of Spiritual Invocation, Spiritual Feeling-Contemplation, and Surrender to Spiritual Grace is "Radiant Adi Da, Divine Giver Of Spirit-Life and Most Perfect Liberation, I Surrender To You". It is Given to practitioners of the Devotional Way of Faith in practicing stage two of the technically "fully elaborated" course of practice of the Way of the Heart, in which stage Avatara Adi Da's devotees have become truly sensitive and responsive to the Spiritual Presence He Transmits. He Gives His Instruction on the "Easy Prayer" in chapter twenty of *The Dawn Horse Testament Of Adi Da*.

Eleutherios Greek for "Liberator". A title by which Zeus, the supreme deity, was venerated in the Spiritual esotericism of ancient Greece. The Designation "Eleutherios" indicates the Divine Function of Avatara Adi Da as the Incarnation of the Divine Person, "Whose Inherently Perfect Self-'Brightness' Liberates all conditionally Manifested beings, Freely, Liberally, Gracefully, and Without Ceasing".

etheric The sheath of life-energy that functions through and corresponds with the human nervous system. Our bodies are surrounded and infused by this personal life-energy, which we feel as the play of emotions and life-force in the body.

Feasts, the Annual Cycle of the Great Feasts of the Free Daist Avataric Communion Devotees of Adi Da, the Da Avatar, celebrate His Divine Incarnation and Leela in a yearly cycle of seven Feasts, or Celebrations. These are:

The Feast of the Horse-Sacrifice The first Feast of the annual cycle, also known as "The Feast of the True Ashvamedha", or "The Ashvamedha Feast of Adi Da, the Da Avatar". This Feast, which occurs on January 11 west of the International Date Line and January 10 east of the International Date Line, Celebrates Beloved Adi Da's Divine Emergence, and His Divine Grace that Flows from that always continuing Event.

The Name of this Celebration derives from the Ashvamedha, the Horse-Sacrifice of ancient India. In its greatest (and most esoteric) form, the Ashvamedha is the Cosmic Sacrifice Performed by the Divine Person, in order to Descend Most Perfectly into human Agency. Bhagavan Da is Himself the Da Avatar, the First, the Complete, the Last, and the Only Avataric Manifestation of Da, the Divine Person of All and all.

The Feast of Water and Fire This Feast, also known as "The Feast of the Water and Fire Blessing of Adi Da, the Da Avatar", covers an extended period, from the day after the Celebration of the Feast of the Horse-Sacrifice to early March.

Since time immemorial, water and fire have been connected with religious and Spiritual purification. In this Feast, water is the element of bodily (or exoteric) purification, and fire is the element of the Transmission of Spirit (the esoteric aspect of purification). The purification cycle includes prolonged fasting, ritual purification of the Retreat Sanctuaries and of the living and working environments of Avatara Adi Da's devotees, the burning of written confessions of self-understanding and practice, and the receiving of Blessed Water (as a reminder of the life of renunciation and purification). Finally, Avatara Adi Da's devotees offer Him their vows of life-change.

The concluding Celebration of this Feast is Adi Da Shantavara, which honors Avatara Adi Da's Retirement into Hermitage Seclusion. This day is Celebrated on March 2 west of the International Date Line, and on March 1 east of the International Date Line.

The Feast of the Divine World-Teaching This Feast, also known as "The Feast of the Hridaya-Advaita Dharma", or "The Feast of the Divine Revelatory Word of Adi Da, the Da Avatar", Celebrates the Word of the Heart, or the Very Self, Which is consummately Given in the bodily (human) Form of Avatara Adi Da. The Feast of the Divine World-Teaching is Celebrated on the weekend of, or the weekend following, April 25, the anniversary of the beginning of Avatara Adi Da's formal Teaching Work in 1972 in Los Angeles.

The Feast of the Adi-Guru Moon This Feast, also known as "the Feast of Adi Da Purnima", or "The Purnima Feast of Adi Da, the Da Avatar", is linked to the traditional celebrations of the Guru-Principle in India since ancient times on the "purnima", or full moon, of the Hindu month of Ashadh. Usually occurring in July in the Western calendar, this full moon is traditionally regarded as the strongest and most brilliant of the year. Devotees of Avatara Adi Da Celebrate the Greatness of their Guru and the Happiness of devotion to Him on the day of the full moon, and the weekend associated with this day.

The Feast of the Avataric Confession This Feast, also known as "The Feast of Aham Da Asmi", or "The Aham Da Asmi Feast of Adi Da, the Da Avatar", is the Celebration of a remarkable coincidence of significant dates in the Life and Revelation of Avatara Adi Da. It celebrates the Completion (in 1994) of the Avataric Revelation of Beloved Adi Da, on September 7, His Divine Re-Awakening (in 1970) at the Vedanta Temple in Hollywood, on September 10, and His Great Confession of Divine Identity (in 1979) in His famous "Beloved, I Am Da" Letter, on September 13.

The Feast of the First Person On this Feast, also known as "The Feast of the Jayanthi of Adi Da", or "The Jayanthi Feast of Adi Da, the Da Avatar", we Celebrate the Infinitely Loving and Incomprehensible Cosmic Process by which the Divine Being, or Maha-Purusha, has Incarnated. It is an extended Celebration, beginning with the anniversary of the day in 1993 when Bhagavan Da received news of His Fijian Citizenship and culminating on His Birth anniversary on November 3 (or November 4 west of the International Date Line).

The Feast of the Hero of Giving This Feast, also known as "The Feast of the Heroic Love-Gifting Leela of Adi Da, the Da Avatar", or most simply as "Danavira Mela", Celebrates the Play of the Divine Person, or the Story of the unfolding Miracle of the Da Avatar's own Life and Work. The Feast begins with the Day of the Installation of the Giving Coat and the Raising of the Giving Tree of Life in early December, continues through the day of gifting, December 25, and concludes on December 31, with the Day of the Devotional Prayer of Changes for the New Year.

Feeling of Being The uncaused (or Self-Existing), Self-Radiant, and unqualified feeling-intuition of the Transcendental, Inherently Spiritual, and Divine Self. This absolute Feeling does not merely accompany or express the Realization of the Heart Itself, but it is identical to that Realization. To feel, or, really, to Be, the Feeling of Being is to enjoy the Love-Bliss of Absolute Consciousness, Which, when Most Perfectly Realized, cannot be affected or diminished in any way either by the events of life or by death.

feeling-Contemplation Avatara Adi Da's term for the essential devotional and meditative practice that all devotees in the Way of the Heart engage at all times in relationship to His bodily (human) Form, His Spiritual (and Always Blessing) Presence, and His Very (and Inherently Perfect) State. Feeling-Contemplation of Adi Da is Awakened by Grace through Darshan, or feeling-sighting, of His Form, Presence, and State. It is then to be practiced under all conditions, and as the basis and epitome of all other practices in the Way of the Heart.

Feeling-Enquiry (*See* **Hridaya-Vichara, Feeling-Enquiry.**)

feeling of relatedness In the foundation stages of practice in the Way of the Heart, the basic or gross level activity of the avoidance of relationship is understood and released in the free capability for simple relatedness, or the feeling of relatedness. Only in the ultimate stages of life in the Way of the Heart is the feeling of relatedness fully understood as the root-act of attention itself and ultimately transcended in the Feeling of Being. In that case, it is understood to be the feeling of "I" and "other", or the feeling of "difference" between the egoic self and all its relations or objects of attention. Avatara Adi Da points out that the feeling of relatedness is, in fact, the <u>avoidance</u> of relationship in relation to all others and things, or the root-activity of separation, separateness, and separativeness that <u>is</u> the ego.

fifth stage conditional Nirvikalpa Samadhi (*See* **Samadhi.**)

Free Renunciate Order The senior practicing order in the Way of the Heart is the Naitauba Order of the Sannyasins of Adi Da, the Da Avatar (or, simply, the Free Renunciate Order). "Sannyasin" is a Sanskrit term for one who has renounced all worldly bonds and who gives himself or herself completely to the God-Realizing or God-Realized life.

Members of the Free Renunciate Order practice the technically "fully elaborated" form of the Way of the Heart, practicing in the sixth stage of life and seventh stage of life. They are legal renunciates. Their emotional-sexual discipline and practice is either single "celibate renunciation" or celibacy in the context of uniquely bondage-transcending "true intimacy" or (in the case of those truly qualified, or even, in rare cases, uniquely qualified, for a Yogic sexual sadhana) sexually active relationship in the context of uniquely bondage-transcending "true intimacy". The Free Renunciate Order is always to be set apart as a retreat order, in contrast to the Lay Renunciate Order and the Lay Congregationist Order, which are service orders. Therefore, members of the Free Renunciate Order typically reside at Adi Da Purnashram (Naitauba). During Avatara Adi Da's physical (human) Lifetime, they are directly accountable to Him and perform the most direct personal service to His bodily (human) Form. They are also the senior authority on all matters related to the culture of practice in the Way of the Heart.

The members of the Free Renunciate Order have the uniquely significant role among practitioners of the Way of the Heart as Avatara Adi Da's principal human Instruments (or Spiritually mature renunciate devotees) and (in the case of those members who are formally acknowledged as Avatara Adi Da's fully Awakened seventh stage devotees) as the body of practitioners from among whom each of Adi Da's successive "Living Murtis", or Empowered human Agents, will be selected. Therefore, the Free Renunciate Order is completely essential to the perpetual continuation of authentic practice of the Way of the Heart.

The original, principal, and central member of the Free Renunciate Order is Avatara Adi Da Himself.

frontal line, frontal personality, frontal Yoga
The frontal, or descending, line of the body-mind, conducts natural life-energy, and (for those who are Spiritually Awakened) the Spirit-Current of Divine Life, in a downward direction from the head to the base of the body (or the perineal area).

The frontal personality is comprised of the physical body and its natural energies, the gross brain, and the verbal and lower faculties of the mind. It includes the entire gross dimension of the body-mind and the lower, or most physically oriented, aspects of the subtle dimension of the body-mind.

The frontal Yoga, as described by Avatara Adi Da, is the process whereby knots and obstructions in the gross, or physical and energetic, dimensions of the body-mind are penetrated, opened, surrendered, and released through the devotee's reception of Avatara Adi Da's Transmission in the frontal line of the body-mind.

full devotional gesture The most basic bodily sign of devotion to Avatara Adi Da. It is composed of three distinct gestures: (1) The Gesture of Invocation and Beholding—the hands are raised head-high and shoulder-wide, with palms open and facing forward, while one beholds the bodily (human) Form of Bhagavan Adi Da (in Person or in Murti Form) and receives His Darshan, and one's devotional response to Him as Ishta-Guru is fully awakened; (2) The Gesture of Devotional Regard—the hands are brought to the heart as a sign of the reception of Bhagavan Da's Darshan, and the head is bowed in gratitude for His Blessing; (3) The Gesture of self-Surrender—one bows at the waist and puts the head to the floor as an expression of self-surrender.

full feeling-prostration Full physical prostration is an aspect of sacred practice in many traditions, such as Tibetan Buddhism and Islam. In the Way of the Heart, full feeling-prostrations are a bodily exercise of expressive devotion, Given by Avatara Adi Da to all formally acknowledged practitioners, to break the bodily cycle of egoity and non-devotion or to demonstrate the free relinquishment of that cycle.

"fully elaborated" form of the Way of the Heart (*See* **technical forms of practice in the Way of the Heart**.)

functional, practical, relational, and cultural disciplines The original, or most basic, functional, practical, and relational disciplines of the Way of the Heart are forms of appropriate human action and responsibility for diet, health, exercise, sexuality, work, service to and support of Avatara Adi Da's Circumstance and Work, and cooperative (formal community) association (or at least significantly participatory affiliation) with other devotees of Bhagavan Da. The original, or most basic, cultural

obligations of the Way of the Heart include all the sacred sacramental and meditative practices (including study of Bhagavan Da's Wisdom-Teaching, which is the foundation of meditative discipline, and also at least a basic discriminative study of the Great Tradition of religion and Spirituality that is the Wisdom-inheritance of humankind), and regular participation in the "form" or schedule of daily, weekly, monthly, and annual devotional activities.

Gautama Gautama Sakyamuni (circa 563-483 B.C.E.), the Indian Sage commonly known as "the Buddha".

Gavdevi Village ("gav") goddess ("devi"). Also, a traditional image of such a goddess.

Goddess (*See* **Avatara Adi Da's Lineage of Blessing**.)

"great path of return" Avatara Adi Da characterizes the traditional religious and Spiritual paths of the first six stages of life as the "great path of return", because the traditional methods of the un-Enlightened stages of life seek to regress, or return, to a specific, or absolute, Goal, which is often termed God, Truth, Reality, and so on. Previous to Divine Enlightenment in the seventh stage of life, practice of the Way of the Heart does not seek to fulfill any stage of life but is lived (progressively) in the context of the first six stages of life. In such uniquely self-transcending, or "radical", practice, all goals and all motivated methods are to be persistently observed, understood, and transcended.

Great Questions (*See* **ten Great Questions**.)

Great Tradition Avatara Adi Da's term for the total inheritance of human, cultural, religious, magical, mystical, Spiritual, Transcendental, and Divine paths, philosophies, and testimonies from all the eras and cultures of humanity, which has (in the present era of worldwide communication) become the common legacy of mankind.

gross, subtle, causal Avatara Adi Da has confirmed the correctness of traditional descriptions of the human body-mind and its environment as consisting of three great dimensions—gross, subtle, and causal.

The gross, or most physical, dimension is associated with the physical body and experience in the waking state.

The subtle dimension, which is senior to and pervades the gross dimension, includes the etheric (or energetic), lower mental (or verbal-intentional and lower psychic), and higher mental (or deeper psychic, mystical, and discriminative) functions. The subtle dimension is associated primarily with the ascending energies of the spine, the brain core, and the subtle centers of mind in the higher brain. It is also, therefore, associated with the visionary, mystical, and Yogic Spiritual processes encountered in dreams, in ascended or internalized meditative experiences, and during and after the death process.

The causal dimension is senior to and pervades both the gross and the subtle dimensions. It is the root of attention, or the essence of the separate and separative ego-"I". The causal dimension is associated with the right side of the heart, specifically with the sinoatrial node, or "pacemaker" (the psycho-physical source of the heartbeat). Its corresponding state of consciousness is the formless awareness of deep sleep. It is inherently transcended by the Witness-Consciousness (Which is Prior to all objects of attention).

The causal being, or limited self-consciousness (which is identical to the root-feeling of relatedness), is also associated with a knot or stress-point in the heart-root on the right side. When this knot is broken, or "untied", by Avatara Adi Da's Liberating Grace, the Transcendental, Inherently Spiritual, and Divine Self-Consciousness Stands Free and Awake as the Heart Itself.

gross, subtle, and causal knots   Prior to Most Perfect Divine Self-Realization, the gross, subtle, and causal dimensions are expressed in the body-mind as characteristic knots. The knot of the gross dimension is associated with the region of the navel. The knot of the subtle dimension is associated with the midbrain, or the ajna center directly behind and between the brows. And the knot of the causal dimension, or the causal knot, is associated with the sinoatrial node (or "pacemaker") on the right side of the heart. The causal knot is the primary root of the self-contraction, felt as the locus of the self-sense, the source of the feeling of relatedness itself, or the root of attention. (*See also* **gross, subtle, causal**.)

gross personality, deeper personality   Avatara Adi Da uses the terms "gross personality" and "deeper personality" to indicate the two conditional dimensions of every human being. The gross personality is comprised of the physical body, its natural energies, its gross brain, and the verbal and lower psychic faculties of mind. The gross personality includes the entire gross dimension of the body-mind and the lower, or most physically oriented, aspects of the subtle dimension of the body-mind, and is the aspect of the body-mind that is the biological inheritance from one's parents.

The deeper personality is governed by the higher, least physically oriented processes of the mind, which function outside or beyond the gross brain, and which include the subtle faculties of discrimination, intuition, and Spiritual perception and knowledge, as well as the causal separate-"I"-consciousness and the root-activity of attention, prior to mind. The deeper personality is the aspect of the human body-mind that reincarnates.

guru-bhakti   Guru-bhakti is devotion, faith, and one-pointed worship of the Guru as God. The bhakta (or devotee) surrenders, and constantly magnifies devotion, to his or her chosen form of the Divine.

Guru Mantra   The traditional Guru Mantra is "Guru Om". It is used in the manner of meditative prayer to maintain one's loving Remembrance of, or devotional connection to, the Guru, whose Transmission of Blessing quickens the practice of devotees. Devotees of Avatara Adi Da practicing the Devotional Way of Faith in the fourth stage of practice (and beyond) of the technically "fully elaborated" course of the Way of the Heart may engage devotional feeling-Contemplation of Bhagavan Da via a form of Maha-mantra Meditation that is based on the form and practice of the traditional Guru Mantra.

hamsadanda   The traditional hamsadanda ("swan-staff"), or short crutch, is a T-frame typically made of wood or some other natural, energy-conducting material. It is placed into the armpit to apply pressure to the nerve plexus located there, which, when pressurized, can open the nostril on the opposite side of the body, thus affecting the corresponding current of bodily energy. Use of the hamsadanda in this manner can help balance the natural energies of the body.

Hatha Yoga   "Hatha" means "force" or "power". This Yoga traditionally aims to achieve ecstasy and even Liberation through manipulation of body, breath, and energy, with concomitant discipline of attention. "Hatha" also originates from two basic root-sounds, "ha" and "tha", which represent sun and moon, or the opposing solar and lunar flows of prana, or life-energy. Thus, a traditional aim of Hatha Yoga is to achieve harmony in the body-mind through balancing these opposing energies in the right and left sides of the body, and in the exhaled (expansive) and inhaled (centering) breaths.

In the Way of the Heart, the bodily poses (asanas) of Hatha Yoga are engaged to purify, balance, and regenerate the functions of the body-mind, and (in due course) to align them to the Spirit-Current. The regulation of life-energy is accomplished primarily through breath control (pranayama). Avatara Adi Da has Given a specific sequence of Hatha Yoga poses as part of the "daily form" engaged by His devotees. He also recommends that His devotees use the relaxing poses of Hatha Yoga, rather than its more rigorous ones, when preparing for meditation. See *Conscious Exercise and the Transcendental Sun* for the Hatha Yoga poses recommended for daily practice.

hearing   Avatara Adi Da's technical term for most fundamental understanding of the self-contraction, through which the practitioner awakens to the unique capability for direct transcendence of the self-contraction and for simultaneous Communion with Avatara Adi Da. Hearing is awakened in the midst of a life of devotion, service, self-discipline, meditation, disciplined study of Avatara Adi Da's Wisdom-Teaching Argument, and constant self-surrendering, self-forgetting, and self-transcending feeling-Contemplation of Him.

Hearing is the necessary prerequisite for the Spiritual Realization that Avatara Adi Da calls "seeing".

the Heart God, the Divine Self, the Divine Reality. Divine Self-Realization is associated with the opening of the (apparent) psycho-physical seat of Consciousness and attention in the right side of the heart, hence the term "the Heart" for the Divine Self.

Avatara Adi Da distinguishes the Heart as the ultimate Reality from all the psycho-physiological functions of the gross, physical heart, or the left side of the heart, as well as from the subtle heart (*see* **heart chakra**). The Heart is not "in" the right side of the human heart, nor is it in or limited to the human heart as a whole, or to the body-mind, or to the world. Rather, the human heart and body-mind and the world exist in the Heart, the Divine Being.

heart chakra The subtle psychic center of the body-mind, roughly corresponding to the middle region of the physical heart. In the Way of the Heart, it is awakened by Grace when attention is released from the activities and conditions of the gross body, the lower mind, and the waking state. This awakening is often accompanied by the appearance of psychic abilities. Whether or not such abilities arise in the advanced stages of life and practice in the Way of the Heart, the awakening of the heart chakra is a necessary, and inevitable, occurrence in the Spiritualization of the body-mind by Bhagavan Adi Da's Transmission of the Divine Spirit-Current.

Hridaya Advaitism, Hridaya-Advaita Dharma, Hridaya-Advaita Yoga, "Radical" Advaitism In *The Adi Da Upanishad*, Avatara Adi Da Offers secondary, descriptive names for the Way of the Heart using the traditional Sanskrit term "Advaita", meaning "non-dual". By combining this with "Hridaya" ("the Heart") or "Radical", Avatara Adi Da indicates that the Way of the Heart (in contrast to the sixth stage schools of Advaita Vedanta) is the direct Communication and Offering of the only-by-Him Revealed and Given seventh stage Realization—the Heart-Way (or "Radical" Way) of Non-Dualism, or of Non-"Different", or Non-Separate, Truth.

Hridaya-Samartha Sat-Guru The Sanskrit word "sat" means "Truth", "Being", "Existence". Esoterically, the term "guru" is a composite of two words meaning "destroyer of darkness". The Sat-Guru is thus one who destroys darkness, and thereby releases, turns, or leads living beings from darkness, or non-Truth, into Light, or the Living Truth.

"Samartha" (Sanskrit for "qualified", "able") is used to refer to the Sat-Guru who has the full Spiritual Power to overcome any obstruction to the Spiritual process in the devotee who resorts to him or her.

The word "Hridaya" means "the Heart Itself".

Hridaya-Samartha Sat-Guru is used in reference to Avatara Adi Da, meaning "the Divine Revealer Who Liberates His devotees from the darkness of egoity by Means of the Power of the Heart".

Hridaya-Shakti, Hridaya-Shaktipat The word "Hridaya" means "the Heart Itself".

"Shakti" is a Sanskrit term for the Divinely Manifesting Energy, Spiritual Power, or Life-Current of the Divine Person. "Hridaya-Shakti" is thus "the Divine Power of the Heart", which is Given and Transmitted by Avatara Adi Da.

In Hindi, "shaktipat" is the "descent of Power", indicating the Sat-Guru's Transmission of the Kundalini Shakti to his or her devotee. "Hridaya-Shaktipat", which is Adi Da's seventh stage Gift to His devotees, is "the Blessing-Transmission of the Heart Itself".

Hridaya-Vichara, Feeling-Enquiry The word "Hridaya" means "the Heart Itself". The Sanskrit term "vichara" is usually translated as "enquiry", connoting intense observation and unrelenting vigilance. "Hridaya-Vichara" is Avatara Adi Da's original term for the practice of abiding in Identification with the Heart (or the Feeling of Being that is the Divine Self-Condition). Unlike traditional terms, such as "Atma-Vichara", Hridaya-Vichara does not suggest the exclusive, introverted search for the root of the Self (Atman). It points to the seventh stage Realization of the inclusive Spiritual, Transcendental, and Divine Person.

The process of Hridaya-Vichara (or Feeling-Enquiry) is described in *The Dawn Horse Testament Of Adi Da*, chapter forty-three, and most fully in *The Lion Sutra*. Like all meditative practices in the Way of the Heart, Feeling-Enquiry is an extension of the primary practice of Ishta-Guru-Bhakti Yoga, which is always epitomized by feeling-Contemplation of Avatara Adi Da's bodily (human) Form, His Spiritual (and Always Blessing) Presence, and His Very (and Inherently Perfect) State. Feeling-Enquiry is a twelve-part process that is taken up by all practitioners of the technically "fully elaborated" course of practice who transition to practice in the context of the sixth stage of life directly from practice in the "basic" context of the fourth stage of life. Practitioners who have strong reasons to engage practice in the "advanced" context of the fourth stage of life and in the fifth stage of life may choose to continue their practice of either True Prayer or self-Enquiry (and Re-cognition) upon transition to practice in the context of the sixth stage of life, or they may also choose to take up Feeling-Enquiry at this time. Feeling-Enquiry is the practice whereby the root-feeling of relatedness is surrendered, forgotten, and transcended in its Source, which is Consciousness Itself.

Hridayam Sanskrit for "heart". It refers not only to the physical organ but also to the True Heart, the Transcendental (and Inherently Spiritual) Divine Reality. "Hridayam" is one of Avatara Adi Da's Divine Names, signifying that He Stands in, at, and as the True Heart of every being.

Ignorance (*See* **Divine Ignorance**.)

Indifference (*See* **Divine Indifference**.)

Instrumentality Avatara Adi Da uses the term "Instrumentality" to indicate the body of His

Spiritually Awakened renunciate devotees in practicing stage three and beyond in the Way of the Heart. Such devotees have received Avatara Adi Da's Spiritual Baptism and they practice in Spiritually activated relationship to Him. Because of their uniquely complete and renunciate response and accountability to Him, and by virtue of their self-surrendering, self-forgetting, self-transcending, and really Spiritual Invocation of Him, these devotees function collectively as Instruments for the Transmission of Avatara Adi Da's Spiritual (and Always Blessing) Presence to others at the same developmental stage and at earlier developmental stages of the Way of the Heart, and even, in a general sense, to all of Bhagavan Da's devotees.

intensive listening-hearing stage A practitioner of the Way of the Heart begins the intensive listening-hearing process once the student-beginner stage is fulfilled. In this period of practice, the disciplines that were stabilized in the student-beginner phase are further refined, and study of the listening-hearing process itself is intensified. In the culmination of the listening phase of the Way of the Heart, to provoke the crisis of hearing, practitioners participate in regular group "considerations" that specifically address each individual's egoic limitations. By all these means, the process of self-observation and self-understanding is quickened until it becomes, by Grace, most fundamental self-understanding, or hearing. The final phase of this process is a period of active demonstration and stabilization of hearing, showing an obvious increase in bodily equanimity, the capability for self-transcendence, and the readiness to receive Avatara Adi Da's Spirit-Baptism. (*See also* **listening** and **hearing**.)

Ishta-Guru-Bhakti Yoga Ishta-Guru-Bhakti Yoga is the principal Gift, Calling, and Discipline Offered by Avatara Adi Da to all who would practice the Way of the Heart.

"Ishta" means "chosen", or "most beloved". "Guru", in the reference "Ishta-Guru", means specifically the Sat-Guru, the Revealer of Truth Itself (or of Being Itself). "Bhakti" means "devotion".

Ishta-Guru-Bhakti, then, is devotion to Avatara Adi Da, the chosen Beloved Guru of His devotees, the Supreme Divine Being Incarnate in human form.

"Yoga", from a Sanskrit verb root meaning "to yoke", "to bind together", is a path, or way, of achieving Unity with (or Realizing one's Prior Identity with) the Divine.

Although the practice of Guru-devotion is ultimately the essence of the entire Great Tradition, Ishta-Guru-Bhakti Yoga, or devotional surrender to Avatara Adi Da, the Very Divine Person, as one's Ishta-Guru, is the only means for Most Perfect Divine Self-Realization.

Ishta-Guru-Seva In Sanskrit, "seva" means "service". Service to the Sat-Guru is traditionally treasured as one of the great Secrets of Realization. In the Way of the Heart, Sat-Guru-Seva, or Ishta-Guru-Seva, is the remarkable opportunity to live every action and, indeed, one's entire life, as direct service

and devotional obedience (or devotional conformity) to Hridaya-Samartha Sat-Guru Adi Da in every possible and appropriate way.

Jaya Sanskrit for "victory". When used as a form of praise of Avatara Adi Da, it affirms His Spiritual Victory in the hearts of all His devotees and the Supremacy of His Blessing in the world itself.

Jnana Sanskrit for "wisdom" or "supreme knowledge".

Jnana Samadhi (*See* **Samadhi**.)

Jnana Yoga Jnana Yoga is associated with the non-dual philosophy of the Upanishads and its subsequent elaboration in the Teachings of Advaita Vedanta. Jnana (Sanskrit for "wisdom" or "supreme knowledge") is Spiritual and Transcendental Insight and Intuition of the Divine Self-Condition. Traditionally, Jnana Yoga is associated with practices of discriminative intelligence, self-renunciation, comprehensive self-discipline, and a fundamental orientation to Divine Liberation, or Divine Enlightenment.

In the Way of the Heart, Jnana Yoga applies most specifically to the transition from the progressive practices of the first five stages of life to the "Perfect Practice" of the sixth stage of life. This process begins when attention moves out of the preoccupation with experience in general, and the movement to ascend to Truth in particular, by falling into and penetrating the root of attention associated with the causal heart on the right, awakening to one's true and prior Subjective Identity as Consciousness Itself, prior to objects, others, and world. Such Jnana, or Conscious Realization, may at first exclude the field or apparent objects of experience. However, in the event of Divine Self-Realization in the transition to the seventh stage of life, all experience (or apparent objectivity) is spontaneously and Divinely Recognized to be but modifications of the Single Divine Self. This non-exclusive Jnana may be called "Maha-Jnana" (or "Great Knowledge"). The Way of the Heart is founded entirely on the "Point of View" of the seventh stage of life, or Maha-Jnana.

Kali Sanskrit for "the Black One". Kali is a Hindu image of the Goddess, a form of the Mother Shakti, in her terrifying aspect.

Kali Yuga In the Hindu tradition, the dark ("kali") epoch ("yuga"), or the final and most ignorant and degenerate period of mankind, when the Spiritual Way of life is almost entirely forgotten.

Kanya A renunciate woman, practicing in the advanced and ultimate stages of life in the Way of the Heart, who lives and serves in Avatara Adi Da's most intimate Sphere. The reference "Kanya" is derived from the traditional Hindu practice of giving a young woman (kanya) into the intimate service of the Sat-Guru. In the Way of the Heart, those renunciate women devotees who practice as Kanyas in relation to Avatara Adi Da have consecrated themselves to serving Him in the most direct and intensive manner, for the sake of His universal Blessing Work and for the sake of Divine Self-Realization.

karma, karmic "Karma" is Sanskrit for "action". Since action entails consequences, or reactions, karma is destiny, tendency, the quality of existence and experience which is determined by prior actions or conditions.

Karma Yoga "Yoga" is Sanskrit for "union". The tradition of Yoga speaks of several traditional paths of Spiritual union with the Divine. Karma Yoga is the Yoga of action, in which every activity, no matter how humble, is transformed into self-transcending service to the Divine.

kirtan A traditional Hindu term for an occasion of devotional chanting in which devotees express their devotion not only through chant and song but whole bodily, particularly through dance, spontaneous physical movement, and ecstatic praise. During kirtans in the Way of the Heart, Avatara Adi Da's devotees may, in the fullness of ecstatic self-surrender, experience the full range of possible signs of reception of His Spiritual Transmission, such as kriyas, spontaneous mudras, Hatha Yoga poses, and verbal and otherwise mindless utterances.

koshas (*See* **sheaths**.)

Krishna Krishna was a legendary Avatar of ancient India, and is one of the most widely worshipped deities in Hinduism. The *Bhagavad Gita* recounts the conversation between Krishna and his devotee Arjuna that leads to Arjuna's conversion.

kriyas Spontaneous, self-purifying physical movements. Kriyas arise when the natural bodily energies are stimulated by the Divine Spirit-Current.

kumbhak The most common traditional form of kumbhak is momentary retention of the breath between exhalation and inhalation, or between inhalation and exhalation. In its most profound form, kumbhak is temporary and total spontaneous suspension of the breath while attention ascends beyond awareness of the body into states of ecstatic absorption. The common form of kumbhak is sometimes intentionally practiced as a form of pranayama. Both the common and the profound forms of kumbhak may also occur spontaneously (in an easeful and blissful manner) in response to the Spiritual Presence of Avatara Adi Da.

Kundalini, Kundalini Shakti The traditional name for what Avatara Adi Da has Revealed to be the ascending aspect of the total Circle of Spiritual Life-Energy in the human body-mind. The Kundalini Shakti is traditionally viewed to lie dormant at the bodily base, or lowermost psychic center of the body-mind. The Kundalini may be activated spontaneously in the devotee or by the Guru's initiation, thereafter producing all the various forms of Yogic and mystical experience.

Kundalini Yoga An esoteric Spiritual practice associated with the stimulation and ascent of the Life-Current in the spinal line of the body-mind. Kundalini Yoga aims at awakening latent Spirit-Energy (which is thought to lie dormant at the bodily base) so that it rises through the spinal line to reunite with its ultimate source, conceived to be above the head. Typical techniques include meditative visualization and breathing exercises, but the principal means of awakening is the initiatory Force of an Adept Spiritual Master.

Laya Yoga (*See* **Nada Yoga, Laya Yoga**.)

Lay Congregationist Order; Lay Renunciate Order The Lay Congregationist Order of Adi Da, the Da Avatar (or, simply, the Lay Congregationist Order) and the Lay Renunciate Order of Adi Da, the Da Avatar (or, simply, the Lay Renunciate Order) are two Orders established by Avatara Adi Da for those of His devotees who have advanced beyond practice at the student-beginner stage of practice. At the time of transition into the intensive listening-hearing stage, devotees will enter one of these two orders, depending on their demonstrated qualifications of practice. (Avatara Adi Da has also established a third order, the Naitauba Order of the Sannyasins of Adi Da, the Da Avatar, or, simply, the Free Renunciate Order, which is the senior order in the Way of the Heart.)

Acceptance into either of the lay orders in the Way of the Heart requires consistent and effective practice of Ishta-Guru-Bhakti Yoga in relation to Avatara Adi Da, as demonstrated through devotion, service, self-discipline, and meditation appropriate to the maturity of student-beginner practice.

The Lay Congregationist Order is a practical service order performing the many supportive services necessary for the work of the institution, the culture, the community, and the mission of all Free Daists. Its members are accountable to the Lay Renunciate Order and to the members of their own order. They conform every aspect of their life and practice to the Wisdom and Blessings of Avatara Adi Da, but their practice is not as intensive an approach to Most Perfectly self-transcending God-Realization as the practice of "lay renunciates" or "free renunciates".

Any member of the Lay Congregationist Order who develops the required signs of especially exemplary practice of devotion, service, self-discipline, and meditation, and who qualifies for one of the formal renunciate forms of sexual practice, may be accepted into the Lay Renunciate Order.

The Lay Renunciate Order is a cultural service order, subordinate to the Free Renunciate Order and functioning as an extension of it. Members of the Lay Renunciate Order provide the inspirational and cultural leadership for the institution, the culture, and the community of Avatara Adi Da's devotees, serving both the internal sacred devotional culture and the public in their fullest possible embrace of the practice of Ishta-Guru-Bhakti Yoga. It is also the responsibility of "lay renunciates" to protect and serve the Free Renunciate Order, so as to ensure that its members are free to fully engage their life of retreat.

The emotional-sexual discipline and practice of members of the Lay Renunciate Order is either single "celibate renunciation" or celibacy in the context of uniquely bondage-transcending "true intimacy" or (in the case of those truly qualified, or even, in rare cases, uniquely qualified, for a Yogic sexual sadhana) sexually active relationship in the context of uniquely bondage-transcending "true intimacy".

Avatara Adi Da has indicated in *The Dawn Horse Testament Of Adi Da* and *The (Shorter) Testament Of Secrets Of Adi Da* that members of the Lay Renunciate Order who are in practicing stage three (and beyond) function collectively and spontaneously as His Instruments, or means by which His Divine Grace and Awakening Power are Magnified and Transmitted to other devotees and all beings.

Leela Sanskrit for "play", or "sport". Traditionally, all of conditionally manifested existence is seen to be the Leela, or the Divine Play, Sport, or Free Activity, of the Divine Person. "Leela" also means the Awakened Play of a Realized Adept of any degree, through which he or she mysteriously Instructs and Liberates others and Blesses the world itself. By extension, a Leela is an instructive and inspiring story of such an Adept's Teaching and Blessing Play.

Leelas and confessions A regular practice of Avatara Adi Da's devotees, whereby they confess their self-understanding, either formally or informally, and tell the Leela of Bhagavan Da's Grace in their lives, thereby being further confirmed and inspired in their commitment to self-transcending practice of the Way of the Heart.

Lesson of life Avatara Adi Da's term for the fundamental understanding that no conditional seeking can achieve Happiness but that Happiness is inherent in Existence Itself. As He has succinctly summarized it: "You cannot become Happy. You can only be Happy."

Lineage of Blessing (*See* **Avatara Adi Da's Lineage of Blessing**.)

listening Avatara Adi Da's term for the disposition of the beginner's preparation and practice in the Way of the Heart. A listening devotee is someone who, in the context of his or her life of devotion, service, self-discipline, and meditation at the beginning developmental stages of practice, gives his or her attention to Avatara Adi Da's Teaching Argument, to His Leelas (or inspirational Stories of His Life and Work), and to feeling-Contemplation of Him (primarily of His bodily human Form) for the sake of awakening self-observation and most fundamental self-understanding, or hearing, on the basis of which practice may develop in the Spiritual stages of life and beyond.

"Living Murti" The Sanskrit word "murti" means "form". Traditionally, as well as in Avatara Adi Da's

usage, the primary meaning of "murti" is "representational image". In the Way of the Heart, a Murti is a photographic or artistic Representational Image of Avatara Adi Da; similarly, a "Living Murti" is a human Representation of Avatara Adi Da, by virtue of his or her unique conformity to Avatara Adi Da.

Avatara Adi Da has Said that, after His physical (human) Lifetime, there should always be one (and only one) "Living Murti" as a Living Link between Him and His devotees. Each successive "Living Murti" (or "Murti-Guru") is to be selected from among those members of the Free Renunciate Order who have been formally acknowledged as practitioners in the seventh stage of life. "Murti-Gurus" do not function as the independent Guru of practitioners of the Way of the Heart. Rather, they are simply Representations of Avatara Adi Da's bodily (human) Form, and a means to Commune with Him.

For a full discussion of "Living Murtis", or "Murti-Gurus", and how they are chosen, see chapter twenty of *The Dawn Horse Testament Of Adi Da*.

loka A world or realm of experience. The term often refers to places that are subtler than the gross physical world of Earth and that can be visited only in dreams or by mystical or esoteric means.

Love-Ananda The Name "Love-Ananda" combines both English and Sanskrit words, thus bridging the West and the East, and embodying Avatara Adi Da's role as the Divine World-Teacher. "Ananda" is Sanskrit for "Bliss", and, in combination with the English word "Love", means "the Divine (or 'Bright') Love-Bliss". Thus, Realization of Love-Ananda is Realization of the Divine Self as "Bright" Consciousness-Radiance, Joy, Love, Freedom, Happiness, and Peace.

"Love-Ananda" is a Name of both the Divine Reality and of Avatara Adi Da, Who is the Divine Reality Incarnate as the human Divine Self-Realizer. The Name was spontaneously created by Avatara Adi Da's principal human Spiritual Master, Swami Muktananda, who spontaneously conferred it upon Him in 1969. However, Beloved Da did not use the Name "Love-Ananda" until April 1986, after the Great Event that Initiated His Divine Emergence.

Mahamantra Meditation In the basic form of Mahamantra Meditation Given by Adi Da, which uses the Mahamantra "Om Ma Da" (or one of its variants, either "Om Sri Da" or "Om Hrim Da"), the Word-Sign "Om" indicates the Native Feeling of Being, or the Transcendental Divine Condition, the Self of all beings. It Invokes the Self-Father, Who is in the Husband Position in relation to conditional forms and events.

The Word-Signs "Ma", "Sri", and "Hrim" designate the Mother-Force, Shakti-Force, or Goddess-Power, the Spiritual Radiance of the Transcendental Divine Self. By Itself, this Power is associated with the illusion of conditional existence, but when Husbanded by the Self-Father, this Great Power is associated with Enlightenment, or the lifting of the veil of illusion.

The Word-Sign "Da" points to the Giver of Divine Grace, and it is associated with the Liberating

Glossary

function of the True Heart-Master. "Da" is an ancient Name of the Divine Person, in Whom the Self-Father and Mother-Power are One.

In the Way of the Heart, the Divine Self-Father is acknowledged and expressed in the "conscious process", or the foundation discipline of the transcendence of attention through self-understanding and devotional feeling-Contemplation of Avatara Adi Da. The Radiance, or Shakti-Force, that is "Ma" is acknowledged and expressed in the process of "conductivity", or the alignment of body, emotion, and breath with the universal life-energy, and in the Spiritually activated stages with the Spirit-Current. And their union in the Divine Person "Da" is acknowledged and expressed via the practice of total self-surrender to the eternally Present Reality and Grace of the Self-Existing and Self-Radiant Spiritual and Transcendental Divine Being.

Instead of the basic Mahamantra described above, one may also choose a form of the Mahamantra that corresponds to the traditional Guru Mantra or Ajapa-Japa (in the manner of So-Ham Japa).

For a detailed description of the significance and practice of Mahamantra Meditation in the basic form "Om Ma Da" (and its variants), as well as the specific variants of the Mahamantra (in the manner of the traditional Guru Mantra), see chapters twenty-five through twenty-nine of *The Dawn Horse Testament Of Adi Da*.

Maha-Siddha, Maha-Jnana-Siddha-Guru   "Maha" is Sanskrit for "great". "Siddha" is Sanskrit for "a completed, fulfilled, or perfected one", or "one of perfect accomplishment, or power". Avatara Adi Da uses "Siddha" to mean a Transmission-Master of any degree of Spiritual, Transcendental, or Divine Realization and Capability.

"Maha-jnana" is Sanskrit for "great knowledge". Avatara Adi Da uses "Maha-Jnana" to mean the Perfect "Knowledge", or Realization, of the Divine Self, Confessed in the seventh stage of life. Maha-Jnana is to be distinguished from the Jnana, or Transcendental Self-Knowledge, of the sixth stage Realizer, which is the conditional and temporary Realization of Transcendental Consciousness that strategically excludes awareness of the conditional body-mind-self and its relations. In contrast, Maha-Jnana is the "Open-Eyed", Unconditional, spontaneous, and permanent Realization of the Divine Self, or Heart, under all conditions.

"Maha-Jnana-Siddha-Guru" is a specific reference to Avatara Adi Da, indicating His Unique Power to directly Transmit Spiritual, Transcendental, and Divine Awakening to others.

Mahavakya   Sanskrit for "great utterance". In the Upanishadic tradition, such utterances were revealed to those who were prepared for initiation into their truth in order to serve such individuals' practice and Realization. The truth of these great utterances was not realized by means of intellectual knowledge but through the ordeal of Spiritual practice in the Company of a Sat-Guru.

mala   A mala, which means "garland" in Sanskrit, is typically a rosary of 108 beads, plus a central or Master bead, which, as used in the Way of the Heart, is a Reminder of Avatara Adi Da, His Teaching-Revelation, and His many Gifts of Grace that Serve one's practice. Avatara Adi Da Himself also sometimes wears malas to Empower them as Sacred Articles of His Heart-Transmission. Traditionally, a flower mala, made in the likeness of a beaded mala, may also be offered to one's Sat-Guru as a sign of devotion.

Man of Understanding   Avatara Adi Da has described Himself as the "Man of Understanding", the One Who Awakens others to Most Perfect Understanding. He used this term in His original Word of Instruction in *The Knee of Listening* and *The Method of the Siddhas*. His summary Communication about the living paradox of the Man of Understanding can be found in the Epilogue to *The Knee of Listening*.

Mandala   The Sanskrit word "mandala" (literally, "circle") is commonly used in the esoteric Spiritual traditions to describe the hierarchical levels of cosmic existence. Avatara Adi Da also uses the word "Mandala" to refer to the Circle or Sphere of His Heart-Transmission, or as a formal reference to a group of His devotees who perform specific functions of direct service to Him.

mantra (*See* **Name-Invocation**.)

Mantra Yoga, Japa Yoga   Mantra Yoga and Japa Yoga are practices of the repetition of Spiritually-imbued words (or names), phrases, or sounds (which may or may not be conventionally "meaningful"). These are sometimes associated with aspects of esoteric anatomy and Spiritual energies, which they may, through vibration, stimulate and awaken. Most commonly, however, these sacred names and sounds are used to Invoke and Commune with God, Truth, and Reality in the form of the Sat-Guru (whether or not presently alive in human form), a legendary Divine Personage, or the universal Divine Person (Who may also be viewed as identical with one's Sat-Guru). Such practices are also commonly coordinated with bodily postures, breathing practices, the use of a sacred rosary (or mala), specific concentration or direction of attention, and other devotional and sacramental forms.

Mantra Yoga encompasses practices using a variety of invocatory and meditative words and chants, while Japa Yoga specifically involves repetition of the sacred Name of the Divine or the Sat-Guru.

Matrix Above   The Source-Light of Which all conditional manifestations, and the total cosmic domain, are modifications, and Which may be perceived or felt as a formless Matrix of "Bright" Love-Bliss infinitely above the world, the body, and the mind. It is the reflected "Brightness" of the Inherently Perfect, Self-Existing, and Self-Radiant Heart-Locus associated with the right side of the chest. The Matrix Above is also

305

the center of the Cosmic Mandala, and as such, may be seen in Vision as a brilliant white five-pointed Star.

Maya The illusion that inevitably arises from ignorance of the True Nature of conditional reality and Unconditional Reality.

Mere Presence The Mere Presence of Avatara Adi Da is the unmoving, "Bright", Attractive Force of Happiness, Self-Existing and Self-Radiant Love-Bliss, His Very (and Inherently Perfect) State of unqualified Transcendental Divine Consciousness.

"minimum optimum" The conservative principle of self-discipline in the Way of the Heart. One should find the detailed personal design of diet, exercise, sexuality, and so on, that is both appropriate and optimum for bodily well-being and effective practice of the Way of the Heart.

"missing the mark" (*See* **"sin"**.)

mleccha In traditional India in times past, those who resided outside of India were regarded—like the untouchables within Hindu society—to be ineligible to participate fully in the Spiritual Way of life. As such, the "untouchables", outcasts, and so-called "barbarians" of the world, including all foreigners, were known generally as "mlecchas" (pronounced "MLETCH-uhs"). And it was assumed, in orthodox circles of Vedic Hinduism, that such beings were gradually evolving from relatively inauspicious lifetimes until they might merit a birth within one of the castes of those eligible for salvatory and Liberating Divine Grace under the Vedic code.

Avatara Adi Da has called Himself the "Mleccha-Guru" for modern humanity. Not only is He the Divine World-Teacher in this Godless and ego-dominated age, but He Himself, by virtue of the unique circumstances of His Life and Work in the "barbarian" West, is a "Mleccha" by birth. Furthermore, from another point of view, Avatara Adi Da is a "Mleccha", or "Outcast", even among the mlecchas of the world today, because His "Point of View" is not that of a conventional man, but that of the Divine. Yet, having been (Intentionally) Born as a so-called "mleccha", Avatara Adi Da is uniquely qualified to Serve as the Mleccha-Guru, or the Guru to the mlecchas, or all those, East or West, who have been born during this dark age.

Moksha-Bhava Samadhi (*See* **Samadhi**.)

Most Perfect(ly), Most Ultimate(ly) Avatara Adi Da uses the phrase "Most Perfect(ly)" in the sense of "Absolutely Perfect(ly)". Similarly, the phrase "Most Ultimate(ly)" is equivalent to "Absolutely Ultimate(ly)".

In the sixth stage of life and the seventh stage of life, What is Realized (Consciousness Itself) is Perfect (and Ultimate). This is why Avatara Adi Da characterizes these stages as the "ultimate stages of life", and describes the practice of the Way of the Heart in the context of these stages as "the 'Perfect Practice'".

The distinction between the sixth stage of life and the seventh stage of life is that the devotee's Realization of What is Perfect (and Ultimate) is itself Perfect (and Ultimate) only in the seventh stage. The Perfection or Ultimacy (in the seventh stage) both of What is Realized and of the Realization of It is what is signified by the phrase "Most Perfect(ly)" or "Most Ultimate(ly)".

The Mountain Of Attention Sanctuary (*See* **Retreat Sanctuaries**.)

mudra A gesture of the hands, face, or body expressing the exalted Spiritual states that arise spontaneously in deep meditation, Darshan occasions with Avatara Adi Da, or other devotional occasions. Even in His Divine State of Being Itself, Avatara Adi Da may spontaneously exhibit Mudras as Signs of His Blessing and purifying Work with His devotees.

muladhar The muladhar, or muladhara chakra, located at the base of the spine (or the general region immediately above and including the perineum), is the lowest energy plexus (chakra) in the human body-mind. In many of the Yogic traditions, this is regarded to be the seat of the latent ascending Spiritual Current, or Kundalini. Avatara Adi Da Reveals that, in fact, the Spirit-Current must first descend to the bodily base through the frontal line before it can effectively be directed into the ascending spinal course. He has also pointed out that human beings who are not yet Spiritually sensitive tend to throw off the natural life-energy at the bodily base, and He has, therefore, Given His devotees a range of disciplines (including a number of exercises that involve intentional locking at the bodily base) which conserve life-energy by directing it into the spinal line.

Murti "Murti" is Sanskrit for "form", and, by extension, a "representational image" of the Divine or of a Realized Sat-Guru. Avatara Adi Da's term "Atma-Murti", means "the Form That Is the Very Self", or "the One Whose Form, or Substance, Is the Self Itself". In the Way of the Heart, Murtis of Avatara Adi Da are most commonly photographs of Avatara Adi Da's bodily (human) Form.

"Murti-Guru" (*See* **"Living Murti"**.)

nada-bindu The Sanskrit word "nada" ("sound") combined with bindu ("point") refers to the Indian esoteric Yogic practice of concentrating upon a point of sound and light so that attention ascends via the spinal line. By such ascent, the Yogic practitioner hopes to merge with the sahasrar, or the highest point of the Spirit-Current.

Nada Yoga, Laya Yoga Nada ("sound") Yoga and Laya ("absorption") Yoga, along with Kundalini Yoga, refer to the esoteric Spiritual practices associated with the stimulation and ascent of the universal life-energy and/or the Spirit-Current in the spinal line. In the esoteric Yogic schools of India (and else-where) this ascent is served both by practices initiat-ed by individuals themselves and by the Spiritual Influence of Yogis or Saints in Whom the Power of Spirit-Life is to some degree activated.

Nada Yoga is the practice of concentration upon the internally audible Life-Current, which is heard in a range of increasingly subtle and more attractive sounds. These sounds are typically associated with the brain-mind and regions of subtlety extending above and beyond the head.

Laya Yoga refers to the most advanced stage of the ascent of the Spirit-Current, to the point of the complete dissolution of mind through absorption in the Matrix of Light above the body, the mind, and the world. ("Laya" means "absorption", "extinction", "dissolution", or "disappearance".)

For a description of Avatara Adi Da's Teaching on the limitations of Nada Yoga and Laya Yoga, see "The ego-'I' is the Illusion of Relatedness" in *The Adi Da Upanishad*.

The Naitauba Order of the Sannyasins of Adi Da, the Da Avatar (*See* **Free Renunciate Order**.)

Name-Invocation Sacred sounds or syllables and Names have been used since antiquity for invoking and worshipping the Divine Person and the Sat-Guru. In the Hindu tradition, the original mantras were cosmic sound-forms and "seed" letters used for worship, prayer, and incantatory meditation on the Revealed Form of the Divine Person. In the Way of the Heart, Name-Invocation may be practiced simply, by Invoking Avatara Adi Da via His Principal Name, "Da", or via one (and only one) of the other Names He has Given for the practice of "Simple" Name-Invocation of Him, or via the Sat-Guru-Naama Mantra, in one (and only one) of the forms of the Mantra that He has Given for devotees to use in the practice of Sat-Guru-Naama Japa. For the specific forms of Bhagavan Da's Names and Sat-Guru-Naama Mantras, see *The Dawn Horse Testament Of Adi Da* or *The (Shorter) Testament Of Secrets Of Adi Da*.

"Narcissus" In Avatara Adi Da's Teaching-Revelation, "Narcissus" is a key symbol of the un-Enlightened individual as a self-obsessed seeker, enamored of his or her own self-image and egoic self-consciousness. In *The Knee of Listening*, Avatara Adi Da summarizes "Narcissus" as the avoidance of relationship:

He is the ancient one visible in the Greek "myth", who was the universally adored child of the gods, who rejected the loved-one and every form of love and relationship, who was finally condemned to the contemplation of his own image, until, as a result of his own act and obstinacy, he suffered the fate of eternal separateness and died in infinite solitude.

Nirvana Classical Buddhist term denoting Unconditional Reality.

niyamas (*See* **"yamas and niyamas"**.)

"Oedipal" In modern psychology, the "Oedipus complex" is named after the legendary Greek Oedipus, who was fated to unknowingly, or uncon-sciously, kill his father and marry his mother. Avatara Adi Da Teaches that the primary dynamisms of emo-tional-sexual desiring, rejection, envy, betrayal, self-pleasuring, resentment, and other primal emotions and impulses are indeed patterned throughout one's life upon unconscious reactions first formed early in life, in relation to one's mother and father. Avatara Adi Da calls this "the 'Oedipal' drama" and points out that we relate to all women as we do to our mothers, and to all men as we do to our fathers, and that we relate, and react, to our own bodies exactly as we do to the parent of the opposite sex. Thus, we impose infantile reactions to our parents on our rela-tionships with lovers and all other beings, according to their sex, and we also superimpose the same on our relationship to our own bodies.

"Open Eyes" "Open Eyes" is Avatara Adi Da's technical synonym for the Realization of seventh stage Sahaj Samadhi, or unqualified Divine Self-Realization in the midst of arising events and condi-tions. The phrase graphically describes the non-exclusive, non-inward, Native State of the Divine Self-Realizer, Who is Identified Unconditionally with the Divine Self-Reality, while also allowing whatever arises to appear in the Divine Consciousness (and spontaneously Recognizing everything that arises as only a modification of That One). The Transcenden-tal Self is intuited in the mature phases of the sixth stage of life, but It can be Realized at that stage only by the forced exclusion of conditional phenomena. In "Open Eyes", that impulse to exclusion disap-pears, when the Eyes of the Heart Open and Most Perfect Realization of the Spiritual, Transcendental, and Divine Self in the seventh stage of life becomes permanent and incorruptible by any phenomenal events.

"original" context of the fourth stage of life (*See* **three [possible] contexts of the fourth stage of life in the Way of the Heart**.)

Outshined, Outshining Avatara Adi Da uses His term "Outshining" synonymously with His term "Divine Translation", to refer to the final Demonstration of the four-phase process of Divinization in the seventh, or fully Enlightened, stage of life in the Way of the Heart. In this Event, body, mind, and world are no longer noticed, not because the Divine Consciousness has withdrawn or dissociated from conditionally manifested phenome-na, but because the Ecstatic Divine Recognition of all arising phenomena (by the Divine Self, and As only modifications of Itself) has become so intense that the "Bright" Radiance of Consciousness now Outshines all such phenomena. (*See also* **Divine Transfiguration, Divine Transformation, Divine Indifference, Divine Translation**.)

Padukas The ceremonial sandals or shoes of the Sat-Guru, venerated because of their association with his or her feet. To worship the feet of the Sat-Guru is to express humility and gratitude in relationship to him or her, and to express devotion and veneration of his or her bodily form, because the Sat-Guru's feet are a potent vehicle of Spiritual Transmission.

"peculiar" (*See* **"solid", "peculiar", and "vital"**.)

Peetha Sanskrit for "seat" or "place". A Siddha-Peetha is a place that has been made Sacred through contact with and Empowerment by a Siddha, or God-Realized Adept.

Perfect Avatara Adi Da uses this modifier (along with its variants, such as "Perfectly") as a technical indication of Identification with Consciousness in the sixth stage of life and the seventh stage of life in the Way of the Heart. (*See also* **Most Perfect(ly), Most Ultimate(ly)**.)

"Perfect Practice" The "Perfect Practice" is Avatara Adi Da's technical term for the discipline of the sixth stage of life and the seventh stage of life in the Way of the Heart.

Devotees who have mastered (and thus transcended) the point of view of the body-mind by fulfilling the preparatory processes of the Way of the Heart may, by Grace, be Awakened to practice in the Domain of Consciousness Itself, in the sixth and seventh, or ultimate, stages of life.

The three parts of the "Perfect Practice" are summarized by Avatara Adi Da in chapter forty-four of *The Dawn Horse Testament Of Adi Da*.

polarity screens "Polarity screens" (also called "Eeman screens", after their inventor, L. E. Eeman) consist of two screens of copper mesh to which wires with copper handles are attached. One screen is placed under the supine body at the lower spine and the other at the base of the head. One handle is held in each hand while the individual relaxes for ten to fifteen minutes on the screens to realign and energize the etheric circuitry (or natural field of energy) of the body. ("Polarity plates", made of solid copper plates, may be used in the same fashion.) For a more detailed explanation, see *Polarity Screens: A Safe, Simple, and Naturally Effective Method for Restoring and Balancing the Energies of the Body, Based on the Practical Instruction of Adi Da (The Da Avatar)*.

Pondering Avatara Adi Da's technical term for meditative reflection on His Wisdom-Teaching as practiced by His listening devotees who are experimenting with or practicing the Devotional Way of Insight in the Way of the Heart. The practice of pondering includes formal and increasingly meditative "consideration" of His ten Great Questions, and random, informal reflection upon His Arguments and Great Questions in daily life, in the context of feeling-Contemplation of Him. The primary Great Question is the self-Enquiry "Avoiding Relationship?". For a detailed description of meditative pondering in the Way of the Heart, see chapter nineteen of *The*

Dawn Horse Testament Of Adi Da or chapter twenty-one of *The (Shorter) Testament Of Secrets Of Adi Da*.

practicing stages of the Way of the Heart The Way of the Heart develops for all practitioners through (potential) developmental stages of practice and Revelation. The term "practicing stages", however, is applied only to the technically "fully elaborated" form of the Way of the Heart, which is practiced by members of the Lay Renunciate Order and members of the Free Renunciate Order. The technically "simpler" (or even "simplest") form of the Way of the Heart, which is practiced by members of the Lay Congregationist Order, also develops by developmental stages, which correspond to the practicing stages, but the developmental stages of the "lay congregationist" are measured in less technical detail than the practicing stages of the "lay renunciate" or "free renunciate".

Practicing stages one through four of the Way of the Heart correspond to different aspects of the fourth stage of life, from the "original" to the "advanced" contexts of the fourth stage of life. Practicing stages five through seven each correspond to the fifth through seventh stages of life, respectively. (*See also* **stages of life**.)

pranayama Sanskrit for "restraint or regulation (yama) of life-energy (prana)". Pranayama is a technique for balancing, purifying, and intensifying the entire psycho-physical system by controlling the currents of the breath and life-force. Automatic pranayama is spontaneous Yogic breathing that arises involuntarily and has the same purifying effects as the voluntary exercise of such pranayama.

pranic The Sanskrit word "prana" literally means "life-energy". It generally refers to the life-energy animating all beings and pervading everything in conditional Nature. In the human body-mind, circulation of this universal life-energy is associated with the heartbeat and the cycles of the breath. In esoteric Yogic Teachings, prana is also a specific technical name for one of a number of forms of etheric energy that functionally sustain the bodily being.

Prana is not to be equated with Spirit, Spirit-Current, or the Spiritual Presence of Avatara Adi Da, the Divine Person. The finite pranic energies that sustain individual beings are only conditional, localized, and temporary phenomena of the realm of cosmic Nature. Even in the form of universal life-force, prana is but a conditional modification of the Spirit-Current Revealed by Avatara Adi Da, which is the "Bright", or Consciousness Itself, beyond all cosmic forms.

prapatti Literally, Sanskrit for "forward-fallingness", a term signifying unconditional self-surrender or reliance on Divine Grace. The practice of prapatti, founded upon preparatory disciplines that regulate moral life, discipline the mind, and open the psychic or feeling heart, was the most advanced practice of the devotional (bhakti) schools of medieval India. Avatara Adi Da's own early practice of unconditional self-surrender was generated spontaneously, without His knowledge of any such traditional practice, Eastern or Western.

Prasad   Gifts that have been offered to the Divine and, having been Blessed, are returned as Divine Gifts to devotees. By extension, Prasad is anything the devotee receives from his or her Guru.

Prayer of Remembrance   The whole-bodily exercise of Invoking the Divine and surrendering body and mind into the Divine by means of repetition of Avatara Adi Da's principal Name, "Da" ("The One Who Gives", or the Divine Person), in coordination with the breath. It is the basic devotional practice for practitioners in the Devotional Way of Faith in the third practicing stage of the technically "fully elaborated" course of the Way of the Heart. See chapter twenty-two of *The Dawn Horse Testament Of Adi Da*.

puja   (*See* **Sat-Guru Puja**.)

"radical"   The term "radical" derives from the Latin "radix", meaning "root", and thus it principally means "irreducible", "fundamental", or "relating to the origin". Because Avatara Adi Da uses "radical" in this literal sense, it appears in quotation marks in His Wisdom-Teaching to distinguish His usage from the common reference to an extreme (often political) view.

In contrast to the developmental, egoic searches typically espoused by the world's religious and Spiritual traditions, the "radical" Way of the Heart Offered by Avatara Adi Da is established in the Divine Self-Condition of Reality, even from the very beginning of one's practice. Every moment of feeling-Contemplation of Avatara Adi Da, Who is the Realizer, the Revealer, and the Revelation of that "radically" Free Divine Self-Condition, undermines, therefore, the illusory ego at its root (the self-contraction in the heart), rendering the search not only unnecessary but obsolete, and awakening the devotee to the "radical" Intuition of the always already Free Condition.

"Radical" Advaitism   (*See* **Hridaya Advaitism**.)

rajas   (*See* **tamas, rajas, sattva**.)

Raja Yoga   "Raja" means "king" in Sanskrit. Raja Yoga is, thus, the "royal" Yoga, whereby the activity and formations of the mind are disciplined, with the intention of causing them to cease. The most influential formulation of Raja Yoga is that of Patanjali, who (in the *Yoga Sutras*) systematized it in his ashtanga, or eight-limbed, system.

In the Way of the Heart, pacification of the mind is not achieved by any strategic, goal-oriented, ascetical, or self-willed practice that looks to achieve Enlightenment or even thoughtlessness. Instead, mind is understood to be the total psycho-physical reaction to conditionally manifested existence. Therefore, the transcendence of mind necessarily

requires primary self-understanding (or hearing) and the conversion of the extended body-mind complex to God-Communion (or seeing). These are awakened by Grace through feeling-Contemplation of Avatara Adi Da's bodily (human) Form, His Spiritual (and Always Blessing) Presence, and His Very (and Inherently Perfect) State. This primary Gift and practice of Contemplative Communion is the basis for the principal disciplines of self-transcending God-Realization: devotion, service, self-discipline, and meditation.

Ramakrishna   A great fourth to fifth stage Indian Spiritual Master, Ramakrishna (1836-1886) was a renowned ecstatic, who reported passing spontaneously through many religious and Spiritual disciplines from different traditions during the course of his sadhana. Avatara Adi Da has Revealed the unique role played by Ramakrishna (and by Ramakrishna's principal disciple, Swami Vivekananda) in preparing the Vehicle of Avatara Adi Da's human Incarnation. See His Essay "The Place of Ramakrishna and Swami Vivekananda in the Great Tradition, and Their Unique Function in Preparing the Vehicle of My Avataric Incarnation", in *The Basket of Tolerance*.

Ramana Maharshi   A great sixth stage Indian Spiritual Master, Ramana Maharshi (1879-1950) became Self-Realized at a young age and gradually assumed a Teaching role as more people approached him for Spiritual guidance. Ramana Maharshi's Teaching focused on the process of introversion (through the question "Who am I?"), which culminates in conditional Self-Realization (or Jnana Samadhi), exclusive of phenomena. He established his Ashram at Tiruvannamalai in South India, which continues today.

"reality consideration"   The Way of the Heart is a continuous "reality consideration" for every devotee of Bhagavan Da. They must be willing to see the conditional reality of their egoic character just as it is, if they aspire to true devotion to Avatara Adi Da, Who Lives as and continuously Transmits to them the Unconditional Reality That Perfectly transcends egoity.

In the latter periods of the listening phase, in order to quicken the transition from listening to hearing, Bhagavan Da's devotees specifically intensify the "reality consideration" in regular group meetings with others at the same developmental stage of practice.

"Real" Meditation   "'Real' Meditation" is Avatara Adi Da's technical term for mature meditation based on true hearing.

Re-cognition   "Re-cognition", which literally means "knowing again", is Bhagavan Adi Da's term for nonverbal, heart-felt, intuitive insight into any and every arising conditional phenomenon as a form of egoic self-contraction. It is the mature form into which verbal self-Enquiry evolves in the Devotional Way of

Insight. The individual simply notices and tacitly "knows again", or directly understands, whatever is arising as yet another species of self-contraction, and he or she transcends or feels beyond it in Satsang with Avatara Adi Da and, thus and thereby, with the Divine Person.

Retreat Sanctuaries   Avatara Adi Da has Empowered three Retreat Sanctuaries as Agents of His Spiritual Transmission. Of these three, the senior Sanctuary is Adi Da Purnashram (Naitauba) in Fiji (also known as Purnashram), where He usually Resides. It is the place where Avatara Adi Da Himself and the senior renunciate order of the Way of the Heart, the Naitauba Order of the Sannyasins of Adi Da (The Da Avatar), are established. It is the Seat of Avatara Adi Da's Divine Blessing Work with the entire Cosmic Mandala. Avatara Adi Da's devotees who demonstrate exemplary signs of maturity in, and one-pointed application to, practice of the Way of the Heart are invited to spend time on retreat at Purnashram.

The other two Retreat Sanctuaries Empowered by Avatara Adi Da for the sake of His devotees are the Mountain Of Attention Sanctuary in northern California and Tumomama Sanctuary in Hawaii. They were the principal sites of His Teaching Demonstration during the years of His Teaching Work. Any of Avatara Adi Da's devotees who are rightly prepared may be formally invited to visit or reside at these Sanctuaries.

right side of the heart   Avatara Adi Da has Revealed that, in the context of the body-mind, the Divine Consciousness is intuited at a psycho-physical Locus in the right side of the heart. This center corresponds to the sinoatrial node, or "pacemaker", the source of the physical heartbeat in the right atrium, or upper right chamber, of the heart.

Rudi (*See* **Avatara Adi Da's Lineage of Blessing**.)

rudraksha   Rudraksha seeds are traditionally used as beads for a mala, or rosary. They have varying numbers of "faces"—single-faced rudraksha beads being extremely rare and highly prized.

Sacrament of Universal Sacrifice   A simple (and yet most profound) ceremonial expression of the relationship between the practitioner and Avatara Adi Da. In a mood of gratitude, love, devotion, and self-surrender, His devotee offers simple gifts of flowers, fruit, water, or the like to Avatara Adi Da, while calling upon Him, either audibly or silently, by His Principal Name, "Da" (or any other of His Names that He has Given for the practice of simple Name-Invocation of Him). At the end of the occasion, His devotee receives in return a purified and sanctified Gift of the same or a similar type, again calling upon Avatara Adi Da via His Principal Name, "Da" (or any other of His Names that He has Given for the practice of simple Name-Invocation of Him). The giving and receiving of tangible gifts both enacts and symbolizes His devotee's constant gift of the surrender

of egoic self to Avatara Adi Da, the Invocation and Installation of Him in front of the heart, and Avatara Adi Da's eternally Given Gift of the Divine "Brightness" and all Its Liberating Blessings in return.

sadhana   Self-transcending religious or Spiritual practice.

Sahaj   Hindi for "twin-born", "natural", or "innate". Avatara Adi Da uses the term to indicate the Coincidence (in the case of Divine Self-Realization) of the Inherently Spiritual and Transcendental Divine Reality with conditional reality. Sahaj, therefore, is the Inherent, or Native, and thus truly "Natural" State of Being. (*See also* **Samadhi**.)

Sahaj Samadhi (*See* **Samadhi**.)

sahasrar   The highest chakra (or subtle energy center), associated with the crown of the head and beyond. It is described traditionally as a thousand-petalled lotus, the terminal of Light to which the Yogic process (of Spiritual ascent through the chakras) aspires. While the Yogic traditions regard the sahasrar as the seat of Enlightenment, Avatara Adi Da has always pointed beyond the sahasrar to the Heart as the Seat of Divine Consciousness.

Samadhi   The Sanskrit word "Samadhi" traditionally denotes various exalted states that appear in the context of esoteric meditation and Realization. Avatara Adi Da Teaches that, in the Way of the Heart, Samadhi is, even more simply and fundamentally, a state of ego-transcendence in Communion with Him, and that the cultivation of Samadhi is another way to describe the practice of Ishta-Guru-Bhakti Yoga that is the fundamental basis of the Way of the Heart. Adi Da's devotee is in Samadhi in any moment of standing beyond the separate self in devotional ecstasy.

The developmental process leading to Divine Translation in the Way of the Heart may be marked by many signs, principal among which are the Samadhis of the advanced and the ultimate stages of life and practice. Although some of the "Great Samadhis" of the fourth, the fifth, and the sixth stages of life may appear in the course of an individual's practice of the Way of the Heart, the appearance of all of them is by no means necessary, or even probable, as Avatara Adi Da indicates in His Wisdom-Teaching. They are described briefly below and in *The (Shorter) Testament Of Secrets Of Adi Da*, and in full detail in *The Dawn Horse Testament Of Adi Da*.

The Samadhi of "the Thumbs"   This occurs when the body-mind is invaded by a most forceful descent of the Spirit-Current, felt, as Avatara Adi Da describes His own experience in *The Knee of Listening*, "like a mass of gigantic thumbs coming down from above and pressing into some form of myself that was much larger than my physical body". In the fullest form of this experience, which Avatara Adi Da calls "the Samadhi of 'the Thumbs'", the

Spirit-Invasion completely descends in the frontal line of the body-mind and enters the spinal line, overwhelming the ordinary human sense of bodily existence, infusing the whole being with intense blissfulness, and releasing the ordinary, confined sense of body, mind, and separate self.

The experience and the full Samadhi of "the Thumbs" are unique to the Way of the Heart, for they are signs of the "Crashing Down", or the Divine Descent, of Bhagavan Da's Spirit-Baptism into the body-minds of His devotees. The Samadhi of "the Thumbs" is a kind of "nirvikalpa" (or formless) samadhi, but in descent in the frontal line rather than in ascent in the spinal line. The Samadhi of "the Thumbs" is the fullest completing phenomenon of the descending (or frontal) Yoga in the Way of the Heart, and if it is accompanied, either in the actual experience or after it, by the Awakening of the Witness-Consciousness, the spinal Yoga may become unnecessary.

Savikalpa Samadhi and "Cosmic Consciousness"
The Sanskrit term "Savikalpa Samadhi" literally means "deep meditative concentration (or absorption) with form (or defined experiential content)". Avatara Adi Da indicates that there are two basic forms of Savikalpa Samadhi. The first is the experience of Spiritual ascent of energy and attention into mystical experiential phenomena, visions and other subtle sensory perceptions of subtle psychic forms, and states of Yogic bliss or Spirit-"Intoxication".

The second, and highest, form of Savikalpa Samadhi is called "Cosmic Consciousness", or the Vision of Cosmic Unity. This is an isolated or periodic occurrence when attention ascends, uncharacteristically and spontaneously, to a state of awareness wherein conditional existence is perceived as a Unity in Divine Awareness, or Mind. This conditional form of "Cosmic Consciousness" is pursued in many mystical and Yogic paths. It depends upon manipulation of attention and the body-mind, and it is interpreted from the point of view of the separate, body-based or mind-based self, and thus it is not equivalent to Divine Enlightenment.

fifth stage conditional Nirvikalpa Samadhi
"Nirvikalpa" means "without form". Hence, "Nirvikalpa Samadhi" means literally "deep meditative concentration (or absorption) without form (or defined experiential content)". Traditionally this state is the final goal of the many schools of Yogic ascent whose orientation to practice is that of the fifth stage of life. Like "Cosmic Consciousness", fifth stage conditional Nirvikalpa Samadhi is an isolated or periodic Realization. In it, attention ascends beyond all conditional manifestation into the formless Matrix of the Spirit-Current or Divine Light infinitely above the world, the body, and the mind. And, like all of the forms of Savikalpa Samadhi, fifth stage conditional Nirvikalpa Samadhi is a forced and temporary state of attention (or, more precisely, of the suspension of attention). It is produced by manipulation of attention and of the body-mind, and is thus incapable of being maintained when attention returns, as it inevitably does, to the states of the body-mind.

Jnana Samadhi, or Jnana Nirvikalpa Samadhi
"Jnana" means "knowledge". In the development of the sixth stage of life of the Way of the Heart, Jnana Samadhi will most likely be experienced (even frequently). Produced by the forceful withdrawal or inversion of attention from the conditional body-mind-self and its relations, it is the conditional, temporary Realization of the Transcendental Self, or Consciousness, exclusive of any perception or cognition of world, objects, relations, body, mind, or separate self-sense, and thus formless (nirvikalpa).

None of the Samadhis described so far are necessary in the unfolding of the Way of the Heart, with the exception of the sign of "the Thumbs" (which is unique to the Way of the Heart), though all of them are possible, and Jnana Samadhi is necessary in almost all cases. Seventh stage Sahaj Samadhi (described below), which is the distinguishing Realization of the seventh stage of life, is necessary and inevitable for all those who truly fulfill the Way of the Heart in Communion with Avatara Adi Da.

Seventh stage Sahaj Samadhi, or seventh stage Sahaja Nirvikalpa Samadhi   The seventh stage of life is the unique Revelation of Avatara Adi Da, and He is the only (and only necessary) Adept-Realizer of this stage. His Realization of seventh stage Sahaj Samadhi makes that same Realization possible for His devotees, though none of His devotees will have the Adept-Function. The Hindi word "sahaj" means "twin-born", or "natural". Avatara Adi Da uses the term "seventh stage Sahaj Samadhi" to indicate the Coincidence, in unqualified self-transcending God-Realization, of the Unconditional, Inherently Spiritual, and Transcendental Divine Reality with conditional reality. It is the Inherent, or Native, and thus truly "Natural" State of Being. Seventh stage Sahaj Samadhi, then, is permanent, Unconditional Divine Self-Realization, free of dependence on any form of meditation, effort, discipline, experience, or conditional knowledge.

"Sahaj Samadhi" (in the sense of a "natural" state of ecstasy) is a term also used in various esoteric traditions (of the fourth, the fifth, and the sixth stages of life) to refer to a state of Realization that is continuous even during moments of ordinary occupation. What is called "Sahaj Samadhi" in these traditions is described by Avatara Adi Da as "fourth stage 'Sahaj Samadhi'", or "fifth stage 'Sahaj Samadhi'", or "sixth stage 'Sahaj Samadhi'". In *The Basket of Tolerance*, He Writes that in fourth stage "Sahaj Samadhi" or fifth stage "Sahaj Samadhi", "the 'point of view' toward Reality is based on either the memory or the residual effects or something of the perpetuation of conditionally attained fourth stage or fifth stage ecstasy . . ." and that "philosophical presumptions and expressions arise that resemble, but do not otherwise achieve, either sixth stage or seventh stage characteristic expressions or Realizations".

He further says that sixth stage "Sahaj Samadhi" is "a matter of deeply Abiding in the basically and tacitly object-excluding (and, thus, conditionally achieved) sixth stage Realization of the Transcendental Self-Condition, while otherwise naturally experiencing the natural arising of mental and physical objects, and naturally allowing the performance of mental and physical activities".

Sixth stage "Sahaj Samadhi", moreover, "is the basis for the apparent premonitions, or partial intuitions and limited foreshadowings, of the seventh stage of life that have sometimes been expressed within the traditional sixth stage schools".

In contrast, seventh stage Sahaj Samadhi is the Unconditional and Eternal Realization of the Divine.

Avatara Adi Da also refers to seventh stage Sahaj Samadhi as "seventh stage Sahaja Nirvikalpa Samadhi", indicating that it is the "Open-Eyed" Realization of the formless (Nirvikalpa) State.

Moksha-Bhava Samadhi, or Moksha-Bhava Nirvikalpa Samadhi "Moksha" is Sanskrit for "liberation". Here Avatara Adi Da uses the term "Bhava", which traditionally has several meanings, to indicate the Transcendental, Inherently Spiritual, and Divine Being (rather than any psycho-physical state or realization previous to Divine Self-Realization). Moksha-Bhava Samadhi, or Moksha-Bhava Nirvikalpa Samadhi, is therefore the most ultimate Realization of Divine Existence, in which all conditional states, forms, and phenomena are Outshined by the Self-Existing and Self-Radiant "Brightness" of Divine Consciousness and Love-Bliss. Moksha-Bhava Samadhi is thus the ultimate "Mood of Ecstasy", or Ecstatic Inherence in and as Divine "Brightness" without the noticing of any arising conditions.

In the seventh stage of life, incidents of spontaneous Moksha-Bhava Samadhi may begin to appear in the midst of continuous seventh stage Sahaj Samadhi. Depending on the degree of the Realizer's completion of the Divine Yoga of the seventh stage of life, at death he or she may Realize permanent establishment (or dissolution) in Moksha-Bhava Samadhi, which is Divine Translation into the Divine Self-Domain. If Divine Translation is not Realized at the end of the present lifetime of such a Realizer, it will certainly be his or her Destiny after one or more future lifetimes characterized by the eternal Realization of seventh stage Sahaj Samadhi (and, perhaps, occasional occurrences of Moksha-Bhava Samadhi).

The fulfillment of the Process of Divine Enlightenment in the Realizations of seventh stage Sahaj Samadhi, Moksha-Bhava Samadhi, and Divine Translation is uniquely Revealed and Given by Avatara Adi Da.

samsara A classical Buddhist and Hindu term for all conditional worlds and states, or the realm of birth and change and death. It connotes the suffering and limitations experienced in those limited worlds.

Sangha Sanskrit for "gathering" or "community". In the Buddhist tradition, the Sangha, or community of practitioners, has historically been regarded as one of the "Three Gems" (along with the Buddha, or Sat-Guru, and the Dharma, or Teaching of the Way) in which each practitioner "takes refuge". Avatara Adi

Da Calls all practitioners of the Way of the Heart to participate cooperatively and collectively in the sacred community, or Sangha, of His devotees, which He has established as the unique context of the renunciate practice to be engaged by them all. And He Calls them all to nurture, develop, and treasure this Sangha as the necessary social and cultural context for effective practice and Realization of the Way of the Heart.

sannyasa Sanskrit for "renunciation". Traditionally in India, sannyasa was seen as the fourth of four stages of human life: student (brahmacharya), householder (grihastha), ascetic forest dweller (vanaprastha), and finally renunciate (sannyasa)—the stage of one (sannyasin) who is free of all bondage and able to give himself or herself completely to the God-Realizing or God-Realized life.

Santosha, Santoshi Ma "Santosha" is Sanskrit for "satisfaction" or "contentment"—qualities associated with a sense of completion. These are qualities of no-seeking, the fundamental principle of Avatara Adi Da's Wisdom-Teaching and His entire Revelation of Truth. He has taken "Santosha" as one of His Divinely Self-Revealed Names. His Divine Sign is Contentment Itself, and He is the Giver of His own Contentment—His Sat-Guru-Moksha-Bhava (or Perfectly Liberated Happiness), Which is the Completing Gift of the Way of the Heart. Bhagavan Adi Da's Divine Completeness is His unique Realization of No-Seeking, or His Perfect Searchlessness.

The Revelation of His Divine Name "Santosha Da" was associated with Avatara Adi Da coming into contact with images of the Hindu goddess Santoshi Ma, an icon of the Divine Shakti that has risen to prominence in the Hindu tradition only since the 1970s. Beloved Avatara Adi Da has Revealed that there is a Spiritual association between this image of the Goddess and the Completion of His Avataric Revelation Work, which occurred on September 7, 1994—just as there is a Spiritual association between the image of Durga and His Divine Re-Awakening, on September 10, 1970. These associations are Bhagavan Adi Da's own Divine Mysteries, part of His Miraculous Divine Leela. His devotees honor His Mysterious Association with the Goddess (through the images of Durga and Santoshi Ma), but the practice of His Way of the Heart is entirely a matter of devotional feeling-Contemplation of Him and Him alone.

sarvadhikari Sanskrit for "one who is in charge of everything", applied in some Indian Ashrams to the Ashram manager. In the Way of the Heart, sarvadhikaris at various levels and areas of responsibility ensure that the institution, culture, community, and mission are fulfilling Avatara Adi Da's Principles and Callings and their Agreements made with Him, and that, at a local level, the Ashram, including all its environments and activities, is aligned to Avatara Adi Da, and that the "daily form" and discipline is lived appropriately by all devotees.

Glossary

Satchidananda "Sat" is Sanskrit for "Being, Existence, or Truth", "Chit" means "Consciousness", and "Ananda" means "Bliss". The term "Satchidananda" ("Being-Consciousness-Bliss") describes the three irreducible Qualities of the Divine.

Sat-Guru (*See* **Hridaya-Samartha Sat-Guru**.)

Sat-Guru Arati Puja The arati is a traditional ceremony of waving lights around the physical Form or around a representation of the physical Form of the Sat-Guru as an expression of Happiness, devotion, and gratitude on the part of devotees. In the Way of the Heart, Avatara Adi Da's devotees offer light and chant in worship and devotion to His Murti Form.

Sat-Guru-Bhakti "Bhakti" means "devotion". Sat-Guru-Bhakti (devotion to the Sat-Guru) is awakened spontaneously by Avatara Adi Da's Grace, rather than generated by any self-effort on the part of the practitioner of the Way of the Heart. Sat-Guru-Bhakti is thus Avatara Adi Da's Gift to His devotee, one of the Seven Gifts of His Grace that Establish and Perfect the Way of the Heart.

Sat-Guru-Darshan Sat-Guru-Darshan is the Gift of Avatara Adi Da's Sign, or His bodily (human) Form, His Spiritual (and Always Blessing) Presence, and His Very (and Inherently Perfect) State, Granted Freely for all practitioners to Contemplate at every developmental stage of the Way of the Heart so that they may (thereby) be Purified, Inspired, Attracted, and Awakened.

Sat-Guru-Kripa "Kripa" is Sanskrit for "grace". Traditionally, it is a synonym for "shaktipat", or the Initiatory Blessing of the Spiritual Master. Sat-Guru-Kripa is Avatara Adi Da's Gift of Transmission of His Inherently Perfect Heart-Blessing, which Awakens the capabilities, virtues, and spontaneous Revelations of self-surrendering, self-forgetting, and self-transcending meditative feeling-Contemplation of Him. (*See also* **Hridaya-Shaktipat**.)

Sat-Guru-Moksha-Bhava Sat-Guru-Moksha-Bhava is the exalted Condition of the practitioner at any developmental stage of the Way of the Heart who, happily and seriously receiving all of the Seven Gifts of Avatara Adi Da's Grace, enjoys the ever-increasing Realization of Inherent Happiness and Love-Bliss through Heart-Companionship, Heart-Communion, and Heart-Identification with Avatara Adi Da. Such is the Blessedness of Satsang with Avatara Adi Da.

Sat-Guru-Murti Puja, Sat-Guru-Paduka Puja (*See* **Sat-Guru Puja**.)

Sat-Guru-Naama Japa Repetition ("japa") of the Name ("naama") of the Sat-Guru. In the Way of the Heart, Sat-Guru-Naama Japa is the practice of surrendering all attention, feeling, and the whole body-mind into Contemplation of Hridaya-Samartha Sat-

Guru Adi Da through repetition of the Sat-Guru-Naama Mantra, in one (and only one) of the forms that Beloved Adi Da has Given. For a full discussion of the forms of the Sat-Guru-Naama Mantra, see chapter three of *The Dawn Horse Testament Of Adi Da* or chapter twenty-one of *The (Shorter) Testament Of Secrets Of Adi Da*.

Sat-Guru Puja The Sanskrit word "puja" means "worship". All formal sacramental devotion in the Way of the Heart is consecrated to Hridaya-Samartha Sat-Guru Adi Da and is thus celebrated as Sat-Guru Puja. It is a ceremonial but feeling practice of Divine association, or expressive whole-bodily devotion to Avatara Adi Da, in Person, as the Realizer, the Revealer, and the Revelation of the Divine Person. Sat-Guru Puja involves bodily Invocation of, self-surrender to, and intimate Communion with Avatara Adi Da (and, thus and thereby, the Divine Person) by means of prayer, song, recitation of His Word of Instruction, the offering and receiving of gifts, and other forms of outward-directed, or bodily active, devotional attention.

In the Way of the Heart, all practitioners participate daily in formal Sat-Guru Puja, as self-transcending practice that establishes Avatara Adi Da's Blessing at the heart and thus establishes devotees profoundly in ecstatic feeling-Contemplation of Him. The principal forms of daily Sat-Guru Puja are Sat-Guru-Murti Puja (ceremonial service to and worship of the Sacred Image of Hridaya-Samartha Sat-Guru Da) and Sat-Guru-Paduka Puja (ceremonial service to and worship of Sat-Guru Da's Blessed Sandals, or Padukas).

Sat-Guru-Seva The Sanskrit word "seva" means "service". Service to the Sat-Guru is traditionally treasured as one of the great Secrets of Realization. In the Way of the Heart, Sat-Guru-Seva is the remarkable opportunity to live every action and, indeed, one's entire life, as direct service and responsive obedience and conformity to Avatara Adi Da in every possible and appropriate way.

Sat-Guru-Tapas "Tapas" is Sanskrit for "heat", and, by extension, "self-discipline". Sat-Guru-Tapas is the heat that results from the conscious frustration of egoic tendencies, through acceptance of Avatara Adi Da's Calling for self-surrendering, self-forgetting, and self-transcending devotion, service, self-discipline, and meditation.

Sat-Guru-Vani, Sat-Guru-Vani-Vichara "Vani" is Sanskrit for "word" or "sacred message". The Gift of "Sat-Guru-Vani" is thus Avatara Adi Da's Wisdom-Teaching in all its forms, including the many Empowered Names, Prayers, and Mantras He has Given to practitioners, and also including the Leelas, or Inspiring and Instructive Stories, of His Teaching Work and Blessing Work.

"Vichara" means "enquiry" or "investigation". Sat-Guru-Vani-Vichara is responsive "consideration" of Avatara Adi Da's Word of Instruction and His Revelatory Leelas. That Vichara is a key dimension of this Gift of Avatara Adi Da's Grace implies that constant attention, profound intelligence, and

313

heart-felt responsiveness must characterize the reception of His Word, His Names, and His Leelas if one's study is to be auspicious and fruitful.

Sat-Guru Yoga, Satsang Yoga, Sat-Guru Satsang Yoga   These three compounds of Sanskrit terms have been created by Avatara Adi Da as descriptive synonyms for the Way of the Heart. "Yoga" derives from a root that literally means "to bind together, to yoke". Thus, traditionally, a Yoga is a path, discipline, or practice for achieving unity with the Supreme Divine Being. "Sat" means "Truth" or "Being"; "Guru", in general meaning "Teacher", esoterically means "destroyer of darkness". Therefore, "Sat-Guru Yoga" means "the Way, or Discipline, of Divine Unity via the Grace of the Sat-Guru, the Revelation and the Master of Truth Who Destroys darkness (and Leads devotees from the darkness of egoity into the 'Bright' Self-Radiance of Divine Being)".

"Satsang" literally means "the Company of Truth, or of Being", or "association with the Wise". As an appellation for the Way of the Heart, "Satsang Yoga" means "the Way, or Discipline, of Divine Unity through right relationship to the Company of Avatara Adi Da, Who Is the Truth".

"Sat-Guru-Satsang Yoga" is a compound of the two previous Names, and means "the Way, or Discipline, of Spiritual, Transcendental, and Divine Unity through right relationship to the Sat-Guru".

Satsang   This Sanskrit word literally means "true or right relationship", "the company of Truth". In the Way of the Heart, it is the eternal relationship of mutual sacred commitment between Avatara Adi Da as Sat-Guru (and as the Divine Person) and each of His devotees. Once it is consciously assumed by any practitioner of the Way of the Heart, Satsang with Avatara Adi Da is an all-inclusive Condition, bringing Divine Grace and Blessings and sacred obligations, responsibilities, and tests into every dimension of the practitioner's life and consciousness.

sattva (*See* **tamas, rajas, sattva.**)

sattvic principle   According to Hindu philosophy, all of conditionally manifested existence is a play of three qualities, or gunas. These are inertia (tamas), motion (rajas), and harmony or equilibrium (sattva). Traditionally, sattva has been valued above the qualities of rajas and tamas as the foundation or basis of Spiritual practice. The "sattvic principle" in diet is to eat foods that do not overburden the body but promote balance, harmony, and equilibrium, thus freeing energy and attention for the Spiritual process.

scientific materialism   Scientific materialism is the dominant philosophy and world-view of modern humanity. In scientific materialism, the method of science, or the observation of objective phenomena, is made into a philosophy and a way of life that suppresses our native impulse to Liberation.

seeing   Avatara Adi Da's technical term for His devotee's Spiritually activated conversion from self-contraction to His Spiritual (and Always Blessing) Presence, and the descent and circulation of His Spiritual Transmission in, through, and ultimately beyond the body-mind of His devotee. It is the reorientation of conditional reality to the Unconditional and Divine Reality. Seeing is a prerequisite to Spiritual advancement in the Way of the Heart. See chapter twenty of *The Dawn Horse Testament Of Adi Da* or chapters twenty through twenty-six of *The (Shorter) Testament Of Secrets Of Adi Da*.

self-Enquiry   The practice of self-Enquiry in the form "Avoiding relationship?", unique to the Way of the Heart, was spontaneously developed by Avatara Adi Da in the course of His own Ordeal of Divine Re-Awakening. Intense persistence in the "radical" discipline of this unique form of self-Enquiry led rapidly to Avatara Adi Da's Divine Enlightenment (or Most Perfect Divine Self-Realization) in 1970.

The practice of self-Enquiry in the form "Avoiding relationship?" and the practice of non-verbal Re-cognition are the principal technical practices that serve feeling-Contemplation of Avatara Adi Da in the Devotional Way of Insight.

"self-possession", "self-possessed"   Conventionally, "self-possessed" means "possessed of oneself"— or having full control (calmness, or composure) of one's feelings, impulses, habits, and actions. Avatara Adi Da uses the term to indicate the state of being possessed by one's egoic self, or controlled by chronically self-referring (or egoic) tendencies of attention, feeling, thought, desire, and action. Thus, unless (in every moment) body, emotion, desire, thought, separate and separative self, and all attention are actively and completely surrendered to Avatara Adi Da, one is egoically "self-possessed", even when exhibiting personal control of one's feelings, habits, and actions. And the devotional practice of feeling-Contemplation of Avatara Adi Da is the principal Means Given (by Grace) to practitioners of the Way of the Heart, whereby they may responsively (and, thus, by Grace) surrender, forget, and transcend egoic "self-possession".

seven stages of life (*See* **stages of life.**)

seventh stage Sahaj Samadhi (*See* **Samadhi.**)

"sexual communion"   Avatara Adi Da uses the technical term "sexual communion" to describe the conservative and regenerative sexual discipline engaged by sexually active practitioners in the Spiritually activated stages. Such devotees are qualified to engage sexual intimacy as a Spiritual practice of Communion with the All-Pervading Divine Reality. (In the developmental stages of life before the first actually seeing stage, sexually active practitioners of the Way of the Heart engage the likewise conservative and regenerative discipline of sexual "conscious exercise".) The practice of "sexual communion" is fully described in chapter twenty-one of

The Dawn Horse Testament Of Adi Da, and in "The ego-'I' is the Illusion of Relatedness" in *The Adi Da Upanishad.*

sexual "conscious exercise" Sexual "conscious exercise" is the conservative and regenerative sexual discipline engaged by sexually active practitioners in the listening-hearing stages. This practice is described in detail in chapter twenty-one of *The Dawn Horse Testament Of Adi Da.*

sexual discipline, conservative (*See* **conservative sexual discipline.**)

Shabd Yoga The Indian tradition of Shabd Yoga utilizes a meditative technique of withdrawing attention from the outer senses and attuning oneself to the internal sounds that may be heard or lights that may be seen through this inward-directed concentration. The Yogi's attention is then allowed to ascend with this subtle perception of sound or light, into progressively higher states and realms of psychic awareness and capability.

Shakti, Guru-Shakti "Shakti" is a Sanskrit term for the Divinely Manifesting Energy, Spiritual Power, or Spirit-Current of the Divine Person. Guru-Shakti is the Power of the Guru to Liberate his or her devotees.

Shaktipat In Hindi, "shaktipat" is the "descent of the Power". Yogic Shaktipat, which manipulates natural, conditional energies or partial manifestations of the Spirit-Current, is typically granted through touch, word, glance, or regard by Yogic Adepts in the fifth stage of life, or fourth to fifth stages of life. Yogic Shaktipat must be distinguished from (and otherwise understood to be only a secondary aspect of) the Blessing Transmission of the Heart Itself (Hridaya-Shaktipat). Such Heart-Transmission is freely and spontaneously Granted to all only by the Divinely Self-Realized, or seventh stage, Hridaya-Samartha Sat-Guru, Adi Da. Hridaya-Shaktipat does not require intentional Yogic activity on His part, although such Yogic activity may also be spontaneously generated by Him. Hridaya-Shaktipat operates principally at, in, and as the Heart Itself, primarily Awakening the intuition of "Bright" Consciousness, and only secondarily (and to one degree or another, depending on the characteristics of the individual) magnifying the activities of the Spirit-Current in the body-mind.

Shankara A sixth stage Hindu sage (788-820), considered the founder of the tradition of Advaita Vedanta.

sheath Of the various traditional descriptions of the human body-mind, Avatara Adi Da acknowledges the description of five "sheaths" as the most accurate and complete.

The gross body, or physical body, is "annamayakosha" (the "food sheath"). The subtle body is made of three functional parts, or sheaths. These are "pranamayakosha" (the "pranic sheath"),

"manomayakosha" (the sheath of lower mind), and "vijnanamayakosha" (the sheath of intellect). The causal body is "anandamayakosha" (the sheath of conditional bliss). See Avatara Adi Da's Essay "The ego-'I' is the Illusion of Relatedness" in *The Adi Da Upanishad.*

Shirdi Sai Baba A fourth to fifth stage Indian Yogi-Saint (1838?-1918), a "miracle"-worker around whom thousands of devotees clustered in Guru-devotion. The cult of his followers remains strong even today, particularly amongst the poorer classes of western India.

Siddha, Siddha-Guru Sanskrit for "a completed, fulfilled, or perfected one", or "one of perfect accomplishment, or power". Avatara Adi Da uses "Siddha", or "Siddha-Guru", to mean a Transmission-Master who is a Realizer, to any significant degree, of God, Truth, or Reality.

Siddha Yoga Sanskrit for "the Yoga of the Adepts". Siddha Yoga is the form of Kundalini Yoga taught by Swami Muktananda, involving initiation of the devotee by the Guru's Transmission of Shakti, or Spiritual Energy.

siddhi, Siddhi Sanskrit for "power", or "accomplishment". When capitalized in Avatara Adi Da's Wisdom-Teaching, "Siddhi" is the Spiritual, Transcendental, and Divine Awakening-Power that He spontaneously and effortlessly Transmits to all.

sila A Pali Buddhist term meaning "habit", "behavior", "conduct", or "morality". It connotes the restraint of outgoing energy and attention, the disposition of equanimity, or free energy and attention for the Spiritual process.

"simpler" form of the Way of the Heart; "simplest" form of the Way of the Heart (*See* **technical forms of practice in the Way of the Heart.**)

"sin" Avatara Adi Da elaborates on the meaning of the word "sin" (as He uses it) as follows:

"What does 'sin' mean, anyway? It comes from the Greek word 'hamartia', which means 'to miss the mark', the Mark of God, of Divine Communion. Sin is dissociation from the Divine, not mere acts. All sins are the same. They are all about missing the mark."

sindoor An orange powder used in the performance of puja.

So-Ham Mantra The So-Ham mantra is composed of the Sanskrit words "So" (from "Sah", meaning "He" and signifying God and Guru) and "Ham" (from "Aham", meaning "I", or "I Am"). Thus, So-Ham (or Sah-Aham) means "I Am He", indicating Spiritual Identity with the Transcendental Divine Self, Realized through the Agency of the Guru. Both Rudi and Swami Muktananda recommended the practice of

So-Ham Japa to their devotees, and Avatara Adi Da experimented with this particular discipline in the years of His own Sadhana.

"solid", "peculiar", and "vital"   Avatara Adi Da has observed and described three distinct character types or patterns—ways individuals tend to dramatize egoity in the first three stages of life—which He calls "solid", "peculiar", and "vital". These character types correspond, respectively, to the reactive and self-protective egoic strategies of a characteristically mental (or chronically mentally conceptual), a characteristically emotional (and even hysterical), and a characteristically vital (or physically self-indulgent) kind.

For further discussion, see chapter twenty-three of *The Dawn Horse Testament Of Adi Da.*

soma   A plant from which juice was extracted during Vedic rituals. The extraction and offering of soma to the gods and the partaking of it by the priests was one of the most important of the Vedic ceremonies. Avatara Adi Da uses the term in the broadest sense to refer to the legendary, elusive, and much sought-after substance believed to grant perpetual youth, the "elixir of life".

Source-Texts   Avatara Adi Da has written eight Texts that form the summary of His entire Teaching-Word and that He calls His "Source-Texts":

The Dawn Horse Testament Of Adi Da (The Testament Of Secrets Of The Da Avatar)

The (Shorter) Testament Of Secrets Of Adi Da (The Heart Of The Dawn Horse Testament Of The Da Avatar)

The Adi Da Upanishad: The Short Discourses on ego-Renunciation, Divine Self-Realization, and the Illusion of Relatedness

The Santosha Avatara Gita (The Revelation of the Great Means of the Divine Heart-Way of No-Seeking and Non-Separateness)

The Hymn Of The True Heart-Master (The New Revelation-Book Of The Ancient and Eternal Religion Of Devotion To The God-Realized Adept)

The Lion Sutra (On Perfect Transcendence Of The Primal Act, Which is the ego-'I', the self-Contraction, or attention itself, and All The Illusions Of Separateness, Otherness, Relatedness, and Difference): The Ultimate Teachings (for all Practitioners of the Way of the Heart), and the Perfect Practice of Feeling-Enquiry (for Formal Renunciates in the Way of the Heart)

The Liberator (Eleutherios): The Epitome of the Perfect Wisdom and the Perfect Practice of the Way of the Heart

The Basket of Tolerance: The Perfect Guide to Perfect

Understanding of the One and Great Tradition of Mankind

On pp. 272-74 is a brief description of each of the Source-Texts.

spinal line, spinal Yoga   The spinal, or ascending, line of the body-mind conducts the Spirit-Current of Divine Life in an upward direction from the base of the body (or perineal area) to the crown of the head, and beyond.

In the Way of the Heart, the spinal Yoga is the process whereby knots and obstructions in the subtle, astral, or the more mentally and subtly oriented dimension of the body-mind are penetrated, opened, surrendered, and released through the devotee's reception and "conductivity" of Avatara Adi Da's Transmission into the spinal line of the body-mind. This ascending Yoga will be required for practitioners of the Way of the Heart only in relatively rare cases. The great majority of Avatara Adi Da's devotees will be sufficiently purified through their practice of the frontal Yoga to proceed directly to practice in the context of the sixth stage of life, bypassing practice in the context of the "advanced" fourth stage and the fifth stage of life.

Spirit-Baptism   The Spiritual Transmission of an Adept. Avatara Adi Da's Spirit-Baptism is often felt as a Spiritual Current of life descending in the front of the body and ascending in the spinal line. Nevertheless, His Spirit-Baptism is fundamentally and primarily the moveless Transmission of the Heart Itself, whereby He Rests His devotee in the Heart-Source of His Baptizing Spiritual Current and Awakens the intuition of Consciousness Itself. As a secondary effect, the Spirit-Current Transmitted through His Great Baptism serves to purify, balance, and energize the entire body-mind of the devotee who is prepared to receive it.

Sri   A Sanskrit term of honor and veneration often applied to an Adept. The word literally means "flame", indicating that the one honored is radiant with Blessing Power.

stages of life   (*See* "The Seven Stages of Life", pp. 253-65.)

Star of Light (*See* **Divine Star**.)

student-beginner   A practitioner in the initial developmental stage of the Way of the Heart. In the course of student-beginner practice, the devotee of Avatara Adi Da, on the basis of the eternal bond of devotion to Him that he or she established as a student-novice, continues the process of listening and the stabilization of the disciplines that were begun in the student-novice stage of approach.

student-novice   An individual who is formally approaching, and preparing to become a formal practitioner of, the Way of the Heart. The student-novice makes a vow of eternal commitment to

Avatara Adi Da as his or her Guru, and to the practice He has Given, and is initiated into simple devotional and sacramental disciplines in formal relationship to Avatara Adi Da. During the student-novice stage, the individual engages in intensive study of Avatara Adi Da's Wisdom-Teaching and adapts to the functional, practical, relational, and cultural disciplines of the Way of the Heart.

subtle (level of existence) (*See* **gross, subtle, causal**.)

Sukra Kendra The Sukra Kendras are small Temples used only by Avatara Adi Da as principal Places of His Divine Work.

Swami A title traditionally given to an individual who has demonstrated significant self-mastery in the context of a lifetime dedicated to Spiritual renunciation.

In the Way of the Heart, the title "Daswami" is given to members of the Free Renunciate Order who are acknowledged to be practicing in the second stage of the "Perfect Practice".

Swami Muktananda (*See* **Avatara Adi Da's Lineage of Blessing**.)

Swami Nityananda (*See* **Avatara Adi Da's Lineage of Blessing**.)

Swami Rudrananda (*See* **Avatara Adi Da's Lineage of Blessing**.)

tamas, rajas, sattva Avatara Adi Da Confirms the correctness of the Hindu teaching that manifested existence is a complex variable of three qualities, or gunas. These are tamas, rajas, and sattva. Tamas, or the tamasic quality, is the principle, or power, of inertia. Rajas, or the rajasic quality, is the principle, or power, of action or motivation. Sattva, or the sattvic quality, is the principle, or power, of balance or equanimity.

tapas "Tapas" is Sanskrit for "heat". The fire of self-frustrating discipline, rightly engaged, generates a heat that purifies the body-mind, transforms loveless habits, and liberates the practitioner from the consolations of ordinary egoic existence.

Tcha "Tcha" is the sacred sound that Avatara Adi Da characteristically makes as a form of Blessing in Acknowledgement of a devotee's response to Him.

technical forms of practice in the Way of the Heart Avatara Adi Da has provided a number of different approaches to the progressive process of Most Perfectly self-transcending God-Realization in the Way of the Heart. In this manner, He accounts for the differences in individuals' inclination toward and capability to develop the more intensive and more renunciate form of practice, as well as the technical details of practice.

Hridaya-Samartha Sat-Guru Da refers to the most detailed development of the practice of the Way of the Heart as the "technically 'fully elaborated'" form. In each successive stage of this practice, progressively more detailed responsibilities, disciplines, and practices are assumed in order to take responsibility for the signs of growing maturity in the process of Divine Awakening.

Uniquely exemplary practitioners, for whom a more intensive approach and a more technically detailed discipline of attention and energy are effective as self-transcending practice, may apply for formal acceptance into the Lay Renunciate Order, and thus into the technically "fully elaborated" form of practice (after a period of "testing and proving" in the student-beginner stage of practice).

All those who practice in this fashion are Called to demonstrate exemplary self-renunciation via an increasingly economized discipline of body, mind, and speech, and to maximize their growth in meditative self-surrender, self-forgetting, and self-transcendence through feeling-Contemplation of Avatara Adi Da's bodily (human) Form, His Spiritual (and Always Blessing) Presence, and His Very (and Inherently Perfect) State. Progress in the technically "fully elaborated" form of the Way of the Heart is monitored, measured, and evaluated through the devotee's direct accountability to the Free Renunciate Order, which is the senior practicing renunciate order in the Way of the Heart, and through his or her participatory submission to the sacred culture of either the Lay Renunciate Order (which is the second formal practicing renunciate order in the Way of the Heart) or, for the most exemplary practitioners in the ultimate, or sixth and seventh, stages of life, the Free Renunciate Order.

Yet most individuals will find, in the course of the student-beginner experiment in practice, that they are qualified for a less intensive approach and are served by a less technical form of the "conscious process" than is exercised in the technically "fully elaborated" form of practice and by a less intensive and renunciate approach to practice altogether. Thus, most individuals will take up the technically "simpler" (or even "simplest") form of practice of the Way of the Heart, as members of the Lay Congregationist Order, or "lay congregationists".

The technically "simpler" practice involves the use of either pondering, maturing as self-Enquiry and non-verbal Re-cognition, or Sat-Guru-Naama Japa—which is Name-Invocation of Avatara Adi Da via one (and only one) of the forms of the Sat-Guru-Naama Mantra that He has Given—as a supportive aid to feeling-Contemplation of Him.

The technically "simplest" form of the Way of the Heart is the practice of feeling-Contemplation of Avatara Adi Da's bodily (human) Form, His Spiritual (and Always Blessing) Presence, and His Very (and Inherently Perfect) State, which practice may be accompanied by the random use of His Principal Name, "Da" (or one, and only one, of the other Names Which He has Given to be engaged in the practice of simple Name-Invocation of Him)—a practice that He has Given for use by practitioners in every form and developmental stage of the Way of the Heart.

Whereas the technically "simpler" (or even "simplest") form of practice of the Way of the Heart evolves through the same developmental stages as the technically "fully elaborated" practice, the progress may not be as technically detailed in its demonstration or its description. No matter what elaborate signs of maturity may arise in the course of the technically "simpler" (or even "simplest") form of the Way of the Heart, the individual simply maintains the foundation practice of feeling-Contemplation of Avatara Adi Da by using either self-Enquiry or the Sat-Guru-Naama Mantra (in the technically "simpler" form of practice), or perhaps random Invocation of Avatara Adi Da via His Principal Name, "Da", or via any other of His Names that He has Given for the practice of simple Name-Invocation of Him (in the technically "simplest" form of practice), and he or she does not look to adopt technically more "elaborate" practices of the "conscious process" in response to these developmental signs.

Avatara Adi Da also uses the term "'simple' practice" (as distinct from "simpler" and "simplest") to describe the practice of feeling-Contemplation that is the foundation of all practice in the Way of the Heart, whatever the form of an individual's approach.

See pp. 246-47 for a descriptions of the Lay Renunciate Order, the Lay Congregationist Order, and the Free Renunciate Order.

ten Great Questions Sri Avatara Adi Da has created ten Great Questions for the use of His devotees in their formal listening to His Word of Instruction, and as aids to their feeling-Contemplation of Him as their Hridaya-Samartha Sat-Guru. All listening devotees in the Way of the Heart who have chosen to practice the Devotional Way of Insight, as well as student-beginners experimenting with the Devotional Way of Insight, may use any or all of these ten Great Questions when engaged in the practice of feeling-Contemplation of Avatara Adi Da's bodily (human) Form, His Spiritual (and Always Blessing) Presence, and His Very (and Inherently Perfect) State.

The self-Enquiry "Avoiding relationship?" is the primary question among the ten Great Questions.

For a full discussion of the ten Great Questions and their use, see chapter nineteen of *The Dawn Horse Testament Of Adi Da*.

thangka A symbolic painting, in the Tibetan Buddhist tradition, typically depicting deities, various Buddhas, and/or historical Buddhist figures.

three (possible) contexts of the fourth stage of life in the Way of the Heart Avatara Adi Da has Revealed that, in the Way of the Heart, the fourth stage of life is comprised of three "contexts", two of which are necessarily part of each maturing devotee's practice, and the third of which will be part of maturing practice only in the case of certain (relatively rare) individuals.

The "original", or beginner's, devotional context of the fourth stage of life involves the initial cultivation of devotional Heart-response to Avatara Adi Da (as Divine Self-Realizer and as Adept Heart-Teacher), and, thus and thereby, to the Divine Person, through consistent application to the practices of self-surrendering, self-forgetting, and self-transcending devotion, service, self-discipline, and meditation. In the Way of the Heart, this devotional course of discipline begins in the student-beginner stage of formally acknowledged practice (and even in the student-novice stage, of formal approach to the Way of the Heart), and it remains as the fundamental devotional context of every form and developmental stage of practice in the Way of the Heart.

The essential religious "considerations" and devotional practices Given to listening devotees and hearing devotees of Avatara Adi Da awaken the open-hearted love-feeling, gratitude, and self-surrender that characterize the fourth stage of life. They thus grant a fourth stage context to dimensions of practice that otherwise focus on developing responsibility for functions of the body-mind associated with the first three stages of life.

The "basic" context of the fourth stage of life is the true Spiritual Awakening enjoyed by devotees in the first actually seeing stage (and Initiated at the would-be-seeing, or progressively seeing, stage) of the Way of the Heart. Such devotees demonstrate seeing, or emotional conversion to actively radiant love, God-Communion, and receptivity to Avatara Adi Da's Spirit-Baptism, and then progressive responsibility for conducting that Spirit-Blessing in the context of the entire gross or frontal personality.

The "advanced" context of the fourth stage of life is characterized by the process of ascent of the Spirit-Current and attention toward the brain core. In the Way of the Heart, this process is a sign of readiness for entrance into practicing stage four of the technically "fully elaborated" form of practice, or its corresponding developmental stage in the technically "simpler", or even "simplest", form of practice. Most practitioners of the Way of the Heart will bypass practice in the ascending stages (the "advanced" context of the fourth stage of life, and the fifth stage of life) by entering the sixth stage of life directly from maturity in the first actually seeing stage (the fully established "basic" context of the fourth stage of life).

For more discussion of the early transition to the sixth stage of life, see chapter forty-three of *The Dawn Horse Testament Of Adi Da*, and also *The Adi Da Upanishad*.

transcendence Commonly used to convey the quality or state of surpassing, exceeding, or moving beyond a condition or limitation. Kantian metaphysics extends the term to refer to a state of being beyond the limits of all possible experience and knowledge.

Avatara Adi Da uses the term "transcendence" to mean "the action or process of transcending" in connection with the presumed limits of body, emotion, and mind, or even any and all of the conditional states of experience within the first six stages of human life—all of which must be transcended in order to Realize the Free, Unqualified, and Absolute Condition of Inherent Happiness, Consciousness Itself, or Love-Bliss Itself.

Transfigured, Transfiguration (*See* **Divine Transfiguration**.)

Transformed, Transformation (*See* **Divine Transformation**.)

True Heart-Master Avatara Adi Da is honored by the Title "True Heart-Master" (or "Heart-Master"), because He has Perfectly Realized, and He Perfectly Reveals, the Heart, or the Divine Self of all beings, and because, by virtue of His Divine Self-Realization, He Transmits Heart-Awakening to others and Calls His devotees to Liberating Conformity with Him and to submission to His Mastery as the Means of their true Salvation and Liberation.

"true intimacy" "True intimacy" is Avatara Adi Da's technical phrase for the sadhana (or Spiritual and Yogic discipline) of devotion to Him in the context of emotional-sexual intimacy, whether or not the intimates are sexually active. "True intimacy" is a discipline to which all intimately related devotees of Bhagavan Adi Da adapt, even from the beginning of their practice of the Way of the Heart. However, because "true intimacy" is, in its fullest sense, a Spiritual discipline, it is fully established and formally acknowledged only in the case of Beloved Adi Da's devotees who are in the first actually seeing stage and beyond.

For a full description of the discipline of "true intimacy", see chapter twenty-one of *The Dawn Horse Testament Of Adi Da* and "The ego-'I' is the Illusion of Relatedness", in *The Adi Da Upanishad*.

True Prayer The practice of prayerful Remembrance of Avatara Adi Da in the would-be-seeing stages and beyond in the Devotional Way of Faith in the Way of the Heart. The practice of True Prayer progresses from the "Easy Prayer" of Surrender to Avatara Adi Da (the devotional exercise of Divine Invocation combined with bodily relaxation into and reception of the Spirit-Current) to the Prayer of Remembrance (the process of Invoking, receiving, and surrendering body and mind into the Divine by means of the Name "Da") to Mahamantra Meditation (the process of devotional Invocation, reception, and submission via ascending meditation). See *The Dawn Horse Testament Of Adi Da* or *The (Shorter) Testament Of Secrets Of Adi Da* for Avatara Adi Da's Instructions on True Prayer.

Tui Fijian for "Great Sovereign". Avatara Adi Da is known as "Tui Naitauba".

Tumomama Sanctuary (*See* **Retreat Sanctuaries**.)

Turaga Pronounced "tu-rahng-ah", "Turaga" is Fijian for "Lord". This Title was given to Avatara Adi Da in 1994 by a native Fijian leader.

ultimate (*See* **advanced and ultimate**.)

Vedanta (*See* **Advaita Vedanta**.)

"vital" (*See* **"solid", "peculiar", and "vital"**.)

vital shock Avatara Adi Da uses the term "vital shock" to describe the primal recoil of every individual from the experience of being born—and, throughout the course of egoic life, from the vulnerable condition of bodily existence and of relationship itself.

Vunirarama "Vunirarama", Fijian for "the Source of 'Brightness'" ("Vu" means "source" or "origin", "ni" means "of", and "rarama" means "brightness"), can be used as an extension of Avatara Adi Da's Fijian Name, "Dau Loloma". This Name was given to Beloved in 1991 by members of the Fijian staff at Naitauba.

Witness, Witness-Position When Consciousness is free from identification with the body-mind, it takes up its natural "position" as the Conscious Witness of all that arises to and in and as the body-mind.

In the Way of the Heart, the stable Realization of the Witness-Position is associated with, or demonstrated via, the effortless surrender or relaxation of all the forms of seeking and all the motives of attention that characterize the first five stages of life. However, identification with the Witness-Position is not final (or Most Perfect) Realization of the Divine Self. Rather, it is the first stage of the "Perfect Practice" in the Way of the Heart, which Practice Realizes, by Avatara Adi Da's Liberating Grace, complete and irreversible Identification with Consciousness Itself.

Yajna Sanskrit for "sacrifice". Avatara Adi Da's entire Life may be rightly characterized as a Sacrifice, or Yajna, for the sake of bringing His Divine Gifts to all. However, the term is specifically used to refer to Avatara Adi Da's occasional travels during which He Blesses the world and all beings through His contact with many people and places.

yamas and niyamas Sanskrit for "restraints and observances". Yamas are restraints, or the things one must control or not do. Niyamas are disciplines, or the things one must do. The practice of yamas and niyamas is the foundation stage of traditional Yoga. In the Way of the Heart, various yamas and niyamas are taken on to support the practice of feeling-Contemplation of Avatara Adi Da.

yantra Sanskrit for "device". A yantra is a sacred diagram or esoteric geometric symbol of the cosmos in right alignment to its Divine Source-Condition. Yantras are therefore traditionally used to focus attention in meditation or contemplation.

yellow-red In the progression of lights seen in the Cosmic Mandala, the red and yellow, or gross physical, realms form the outer circles.

yin and yang   "Yin and yang" refer to the dynam-
ic mutual interrelatedness of natural processes,
which show an alternation between generally active,
heated, expansive, masculine, or yang qualities, and
generally passive, cooling, contractive, feminine, or
yin qualities. In traditional Chinese medicine and
philosophy, health and well-being are considered to
result from an appropriate balance of these opposing
forces.

The Divine Spirit-Baptism Which Avatara Adi Da
Transmits is Prior to these qualities, which are simply
various states of the etheric energy that pervades the
physical body. His Spiritual, Transcendental, and
Divine Grace is Reality Itself, Prior to Its stepped-
down modification that becomes yin and yang or
any other particularized state of the body-mind.

Yoga   "Yoga", in Sanskrit, is literally "yoking", or
"union", usually referring to any discipline or process
whereby an aspirant attempts to reunite with God.
Avatara Adi Da acknowledges this conventional and
traditional use of the term, but also, in reference to
the Great Yoga of the Way of the Heart, employs it
in a "radical" sense, free of the usual implication of
egoic separation and seeking.

Yoga of "Consideration"   Avatara Adi Da characterizes the stages of life and practice previous to
Divine Self-Realization in the seventh stage of life as
the Yoga of "Consideration". This Yoga involves the
progressive "consideration" and outgrowing of conditional existence (or all the forms of manifested
experience and knowledge with which the egoic
consciousness tends to be associated) from the
"Point of View" and Understanding of Divine
Enlightenment.

Yogic sexual sadhana   In *The Dawn Horse
Testament Of Adi Da*, Avatara Adi Da States that all
sexually active practitioners in the Way of the Heart
must eventually become qualified for a Yogic sexual
sadhana, in which ego-reinforcing involvement in
sexuality is profoundly conserved and converted into
true self-transcending and other-transcending Yoga,
and sexual activity becomes a profound exercise of
"conductivity", in devotional Communion with
Avatara Adi Da. For the qualifications for the Yogic
sexual sadhana, see *The Dawn Horse Testament Of
Adi Da*, chapter twenty-one.

INDEX

NOTE: Page references indicated by boldface type refer to entries within the Scriptural Text of *The Santosha Avatara Gita*.

and transcendence of self-contraction, **127**, **193**
two Devotional Ways and, 228-29
and <u>waiting</u> for devotion to happen <u>to</u> you, **143**
when to practice, **129**, **143**, **147**, **153**
Yield to the <u>feeling</u> of the Inherent "Bright"
   Attractiveness, **139**, **141**
You become whatever you Contemplate, or Meditate on, **139**
See also bodily (human) Form; Darshan;
   Ishta-Guru-Bhakti Yoga; meditation; Spiritual
   (and Always Blessing) Presence; Very (and Inherently
   Perfect) State,
Feeling-Enquiry, 301
Feeling of Being, 298
feeling of relatedness, 298
feeling-Remembrance
   of Avatara Adi Da, 7
   See also feeling-Contemplation; meditation
fifth stage conditional Nirvikalpa Samadhi, 260, 311
fifth stage of life, 259-60, 265
Fiji, regional center, 251
financial responsibilities, 234-35
First Person, The Feast of the, 298
first stage of life, 254, 255, 264
food disciplines, 236-37
forgetting
   separate self via feeling-Contemplation, 100, **135-37**
   Way of the Heart as self-forgetting Remembrance, **133**
fourth stage of life, 257-59, 264
   three (possible) contexts of, 318
Free Daism, 70, 87
   See also Way of the Heart
Free Daist Avataric Communion
   becoming a full member of, 225
   becoming a student-novice in, 224-25
   correspondence department, 251
   regional centers of, 222, 225, 251
Free Daist Radiant Life Clinic, 236, 243
Free Renunciate Order, **163-65**, 212-13, 246-47, 298-99
Free Transmission of Love-Bliss, **135**
Friend of Da Avatara International, 223
frontal line, 299
frontal personality, 299
frontal Yoga, 299
full devotional gesture, 299
full feeling-prostration, 299
"fully elaborated" form of practice, 317
   See also "elaborate" form of the Way of the Heart
functional disciplines, **145-47**, **173**, **181**, **183**, 210,
   234-39
   defined, 299
   See also disciplines

"Garbage and the Goddess", 44-46
Gautama Sakyamuni, 91, 299
Gavdevi, 299
Germany, regional center, 251

Gifts
   Divine Self-Realization as Adi Da's Gift, **121**
   <u>Only</u> I Am the Gift, the Object, the State, and the
      Realization, **193**
   self-understanding as, **111**, **135**
   of service, **157**
   Seven Gifts, **137**
God-Realization. *See* Divine Self-Realization
Grace
   Adi Da as the Person and Means of, **111**
   Guru as the means of, 6-7
   necessity of, 13
   Seven Gifts of, **137**, 209
   That Is My Good Company, **141**
   understanding and, **111**
   Way of the Heart as the Way of, **135**
"great path of return", 2, 16, 299
Great Questions
   defined, 318
   practice of pondering, 228
Great Tradition, 78, 93, 299
gross body, 254
gross dimension, 299
gross knot, 300
gross personality, 77, 300
Guru, as the means of Grace, 6-7
guru-bhakti, defined, 300
Guru-devotee relationship, 64-68
"Guru Enters Devotee", 43
Gurukula, 247, 249
Guru Mantra, 300
Guru Puja, 49
Guru-Shakti, 315
Guru Yoga, 64-68, 314

hamsadanda, 300
"Handle business", 71
Happy with the <u>Finding</u> of Me, **143**
Hatha Yoga, 300
Hawaii, regional center, 251
healing arts, 243
hearing, **171**, **191**, 215
   defined, 300
   and progression of practice, 233
heart
   esoteric structure of, 254-55
   right side of, 10, 17
   the Heart, defined, 301
Heart-"Bright" bodily (human) Form, **135**
heart chakra, 301
Heart-Word. *See* Teaching Word
Hermitage Ashram, **149**, 210
   search for, 55-56
Hero of Giving, The Feast of the, 298
higher spiritual development stage, 259-60, 265
horizontal plane of existence, 254-55

For information about forms of involvement
in the Way of the Heart Revealed by
Adi Da (The Da Avatar),
see "An Invitation" on pages 221-50,
or see page 251 for details on
how to contact the regional center
of the Free Daist Avataric Communion
nearest to you.